Taste of Home

CHURCH SUPPERS

TASTE OF HOME BOOKS • RDA ENTHUSIAST BRANDS, LLC • MILWAUKEE, WI

Taste *of* Home

EDITORIAL

Editor-in-Chief: Catherine Cassidy
Vice President, Content Operations: Kerri Balliet
Creative Director: Howard Greenberg

Managing Editor, Print & Digital Books: Mark Hagen
Associate Creative Director: Edwin Robles Jr.

Editor: Hazel Wheaton
Associate Editor: Molly Jasinski
Art Director: Raeann Thompson
Graphic Designer: Courtney Lovetere
Layout Designer: Sophie Beck
Editorial Production Manager: Dena Ahlers
Editorial Production Coordinator: Jill Banks
Copy Chief: Deb Warlaumont Mulvey
Copy Editors: Dulcie Shoener (senior), Ronald Kovach, Chris McLaughlin, Ellie Piper
Contributing Copy Editor: Michael Juley
Editorial Services Administrator: Marie Brannon

Content Director: Julie Blume Benedict
Food Editors: Gina Nistico; James Schend; Peggy Woodward, RDN
Recipe Editors: Sue Ryon (lead), Irene Yeh

Culinary Director: Sarah Thompson
Test Cooks: Nicholas Iverson (lead), Matthew Hass
Food Stylists: Kathryn Conrad (lead), Lauren Knoelke, Shannon Roum
Prep Cooks: Bethany Van Jacobson (lead), Melissa Hansen, Aria C. Thornton
Culinary Team Assistant: Maria Petrella

Photography Director: Stephanie Marchese
Photographers: Dan Roberts, Jim Wieland
Photographer/Set Stylist: Grace Natoli Sheldon
Set Stylists: Melissa Franco (lead), Stacey Genaw, Dee Dee Schaefer
Set Stylist Assistant: Stephanie Chojnacki

Business Architect, Publishing Technologies: Amanda Harmatys
Business Analyst, Publishing Technologies: Kate Unger
Junior Business Analyst, Publishing Technologies: Shannon Stroud

Editorial Business Manager: Kristy Martin
Rights & Permissions Associate: Samantha Lea Stoeger
Editorial Business Associate: Andrea Meiers

BUSINESS

Publisher: Donna Lindskog
Business Development Director, Taste of Home Live: Laurel Osman
Strategic Partnerships Manager, Taste of Home Live: Jamie Piette Andrzejewski

TRUSTED MEDIA BRANDS, INC.

President & Chief Executive Officer: Bonnie Kintzer
Chief Financial Officer: Dean Durbin
Chief Marketing Officer: C. Alec Casey
Chief Revenue Officer: Richard Sutton
Chief Digital Officer: Vince Errico
Senior Vice President, Global HR & Communications: Phyllis E. Gebhardt, SPHR; SHRM-SCP
General Counsel: Mark Sirota
Vice President, Product Marketing: Brian Kennedy
Vice President, Operations: Michael Garzone
Vice President, Consumer Marketing Planning: Jim Woods
Vice President, Digital Product & Technology: Nick Contardo
Vice President, Digital Content & Audience Development: Kari Hodes
Vice President, Financial Planning & Analysis: William Houston

For other *Taste of Home* books and products, visit us at tasteofhome.com.

International Standard Book Number: 978-1-61765-652-1
Library of Congress Control Number: 2017930995

Cover Photographer: Jim Wieland
Set Stylist: Dee Dee Schaefer
Food Stylist: Kathryn Conrad

Pictured on front cover:
Carmelized Ham & Swiss Buns , page 91; Strawberry Pretzel Dessert, page 183
Pictured on back cover (from left):
Argentine Lasagna, page 156; Strawberry Mascarpone Cake, page 178; Potluck Spareribs, page 123
Pictured on title page (from left):
Sweet 'n' Sour Beans, page 146; Ham & Swiss Egg Casserole, page 167; Ricotta Cheesecake, page 197

Printed in China.
3 5 7 9 10 8 6 4 2

GET SOCIAL WITH US

To find a recipe tasteofhome.com
To submit a recipe tasteofhome.com/submit
To find out about other *Taste of Home* products shoptasteofhome.com

LIKE US
facebook.com/tasteofhome

PIN US
pinterest.com/taste_of_home

FOLLOW US
@tasteofhome

TWEET US
twitter.com/tasteofhome

SPINACH BEEF
MACARONI BAKE, 113

CONTEST-WINNING MOIST
CHOCOLATE CAKE, 191

SPICY CHICKEN
WINGS, 218

ITALIAN BRUNCH
TORTE, 20

CONTENTS

OVER 300 RECIPES PERFECT FOR A POTLUCK!

FOOD BRINGS COMFORT AND FELLOWSHIP WHENEVER WE GATHER AROUND THE TABLE. THE BEST FOOD IS MADE TO SHARE, SO SHARE SOMETHING DELICIOUS!

With the all-new *Taste of Home* **Church Suppers,** you'll always have just the right dish when it's time to pass the platter. Whether you're planning for a church supper, a school potluck, a wedding shower or a neighborhood block party, you're sure to impress with the **308 crowd-pleasing recipes** in this book.

> *"Do not neglect to show hospitality to strangers, for by this some have entertained angels without knowing it."*
> **HEBREWS 13:2**

Every recipe found here serves 12 or more people, so they're all great for a gathering. Classic traditional dishes for **community dinners,** piping-hot casseroles for **charity meals,** scrumptious sweets perfect for **bake sales** and new interpretations of old favorites for **picnics and family reunions**—they're all here. Slow-cooked classics, delectable main courses, irresistible appetizers, salads, soups, side dishes and desserts—whatever the occasion, you'll always have a great dish to contribute to the feast.

CHICKEN & CHEDDAR BISCUIT CASSEROLE, 121

LAYERED SALAD
FOR A CROWD, 59

**Look for the handy
At-a-Glance icons scattered
throughout the book:**

MAKE AHEAD — recipes that you prepare
the night before or keep in the freezer to be
ready at a moment's notice!

FAST FIX — recipes that take 30 minutes
or less from basic prep to finished dish

SLOW COOKER — classics that take
advantage of the convenience and portability
of your slow cooker. Make it, carry it and keep
it hot—all in the same pot!

Two bonus chapters make contributing to a
church supper even easier. See the section
of **"Seasonal Delights"** for recipes that will
steer you through the year in food. Whatever
the holiday, create a dish that celebrates the
flavors and ingredients of the season. And
if you're looking for a recipe that will serve
more than the usual gathering, check out
the **"Feeding a Crowd"** chapter for dishes
that **serve 30 or more people!**

BACON CHEESEBURGER
SLIDER BAKE, 82

Every recipe in this all-new collection
is a favorite of a home cook like you,
and each has been approved by the
Taste of Home Test Kitchen and
includes step-by-step instructions,
so your contributions always turn
out perfect. Full-color photos,
how-to tips and inspirational
Bible quotes throughout make
the new **Church Suppers**
cookbook a keepsake you'll
turn to for years to come.

SAUSAGE QUICHE
SQUARES, PAGE 19

BREAKFAST & BRUNCH

"The whole earth is filled with awe at your wonders; where morning dawns, where evening fades, you call forth songs of joy."

PSALM 65:8

**BREAKFAST
SAUSAGE BREAD**

BREAKFAST SAUSAGE BREAD

Any time we take this savory, satisfying bread to a potluck, we never bring any home. My husband usually makes it. He prides himself on the beautiful golden loaves.

—**SHIRLEY CALDWELL** NORTHWOOD, OH

PREP: 25 MIN. + RISING • **BAKE:** 25 MIN.
MAKES: 2 LOAVES (16 SLICES EACH)

- 2 loaves (1 pound each) frozen white bread dough, thawed
- ½ pound mild pork sausage
- ½ pound bulk spicy pork sausage
- 1½ cups diced fresh mushrooms
- ½ cup chopped onion
- 3 large eggs, divided use
- 2½ cups shredded mozzarella cheese
- 1 teaspoon dried basil
- 1 teaspoon dried parsley flakes
- 1 teaspoon dried rosemary, crushed
- 1 teaspoon garlic powder

1. Cover dough and let it rise in a warm place until doubled. Preheat oven to 350°. In a large skillet, cook sausage, mushrooms and onion over medium-high heat for 6-8 minutes or until the sausage is no longer pink, breaking up sausage into crumbles. Drain. Transfer to a bowl; cool.
2. Stir in two eggs, cheese and seasonings. Roll each loaf of dough into a 16x12-in. rectangle. Spread half of the sausage mixture over each rectangle to within 1 in. of edges. Roll up jelly-roll style, starting with a short side; pinch seams to seal. Place rolls on a greased baking sheet.
3. In a small bowl, whisk the remaining egg. Brush over the tops of the rolls. Bake 25-30 minutes or until golden brown. Serve warm.
FREEZE OPTION *Securely wrap and freeze cooled loaves in foil and place in resealable plastic freezer bags. To use, place foil-wrapped loaf on a baking sheet and reheat in a 450° oven for 10-15 minutes or until heated through. Carefully remove foil; return to oven a few minutes longer until the crust is crisp.*

HASH BROWN NESTS WITH PORTOBELLOS AND EGGS

Hash browns make a fabulous crust for individual egg quiches. They look fancy but are actually easy to make. The little nests have been a hit at holiday brunches and other special occasions.

—**KATE MEYER** BRENTWOOD, TN

PREP: 30 MIN. • **BAKE:** 15 MIN.
MAKES: 12 SERVINGS

- 3 cups frozen shredded hash brown potatoes, thawed
- 3 cups chopped fresh portobello mushrooms
- ¼ cup chopped shallots
- 2 tablespoons butter
- 1 garlic clove, minced
- ½ teaspoon salt
- ¼ teaspoon pepper
- 2 tablespoons sour cream
- 1 tablespoon minced fresh basil
   Dash cayenne pepper
- 7 large eggs, beaten
- ¼ cup shredded Swiss cheese
- 2 bacon strips, cooked and crumbled
   Additional minced fresh basil, optional

1. Preheat the oven to 400°. Press ¼ cup hash browns onto the bottom and up the sides of each of 12 greased muffin cups; set aside.
2. In a large skillet, saute mushrooms and shallots in butter until tender. Add garlic, salt and pepper; cook 1 minute longer. Remove from heat; stir in sour cream, basil and cayenne.
3. Divide the eggs among the potato-lined muffin cups. Top with the mushroom mixture. Sprinkle with cheese and bacon.
4. Bake 15-18 minutes or until the eggs are completely set. Garnish with additional basil if desired. Serve warm.

SWEET POTATO-CRANBERRY DOUGHNUTS

I grew up near Idaho where they're famous for spudnuts, a doughnut made from mashed potatoes. These use sweet potatoes and tart cranberries!
—JONI HILTON ROCKLIN, CA

PREP: 25 MIN. + RISING • **COOK:** 5 MIN./BATCH
MAKES: 2 DOZEN

- ¼ cup sugar
- 1½ teaspoons active dry yeast
- 1 teaspoon ground cinnamon
- ½ teaspoon salt
- 4 to 4½ cups all-purpose flour, divided
- 1 cup 2% milk
- ¼ cup shortening
- 2 tablespoons water
- 2 large eggs
- ½ cup mashed sweet potatoes
- ½ cup finely chopped dried cranberries
  Oil for deep-fat frying
- 1 cup confectioners' sugar
- 2 to 3 tablespoons apple cider or juice

1. In a large bowl, combine the sugar, yeast, cinnamon, salt and 1½ cups flour. In a small saucepan, heat the milk, shortening and water to 120-130°; add to dry ingredients. Beat on medium speed for 2 minutes. Add the eggs, mashed potatoes and cranberries; beat 2 minutes longer. Stir in enough remaining flour to form a firm dough.

2. Do not knead. Place dough in a greased bowl, turning once to grease the top. Cover and let rise in a warm place until doubled, about 1 hour.

3. Punch dough down. Turn onto a lightly floured surface; roll out to ½-in. thickness. Cut with a floured 2½-in. doughnut cutter; reroll scraps. Place 1 in. apart on greased baking sheets. Cover and let rise until doubled, about 30 minutes.

4. In an electric skillet or deep fryer, heat oil to 375°. Fry doughnuts, a few at a time, until golden brown on both sides. Drain on paper towels. Combine the confectioners' sugar and apple cider; dip the warm doughnuts in the glaze.

FAST FIX

MAPLE-BACON OVEN PANCAKE

For years, my mother has served this tasty baked pancake for dinner. But it's so quick and easy I like to make it for breakfast, too.
—KARI KELLEY PLAINS, MT

START TO FINISH: 25 MIN.
MAKES: 12 SERVINGS

- 1½ cups biscuit/baking mix
- 1 tablespoon sugar
- ¾ cup 2% milk
- 2 large eggs
- ¼ cup maple syrup
- 1½ cups shredded cheddar cheese, divided
- ½ pound sliced bacon, cooked and crumbled
  Additional syrup, optional

1. In a large bowl, combine the biscuit mix and sugar. In a small bowl, combine the milk, eggs, syrup and ½ cup of the cheese. Stir into dry ingredients just until moistened. Pour into a greased 13x9-in. baking dish.

2. Bake, uncovered, at 425° for 10-15 minutes or until a toothpick inserted near the center comes out clean. Sprinkle with bacon and remaining cheese. Bake 3-5 minutes longer or until cheese is melted. Serve with syrup if desired.

RHUBARB SCONES

My grandfather grows rhubarb and gives us a great supply. The tartness is similar to a cranberry, making it perfect for tossing into a scone.
—**DANIELLE ULAM** HOOKSTOWN, PA

PREP: 30 MIN. • **BAKE:** 20 MIN.
MAKES: 16 SCONES

- 1¼ cups whole wheat pastry flour
- 1¼ cups all-purpose flour
- ½ cup sugar
- 1 tablespoon baking powder
- 1 teaspoon ground cardamom
- ½ teaspoon salt
- ½ cup cold unsalted butter, cubed
- 1½ cups finely chopped fresh or frozen rhubarb, thawed (3-4 stalks)
- ½ cup heavy whipping cream
- ¼ cup fat-free milk
- 1 teaspoon vanilla extract
  Coarse sugar

1. Preheat oven to 400°. In a large bowl, whisk the first six ingredients. Cut in butter until the mixture resembles coarse crumbs. Add rhubarb; toss to coat.

2. In another bowl, whisk cream, milk and vanilla; stir into the crumb mixture just until moistened.

3. Turn dough out onto a floured surface; knead gently 4-5 times. Divide dough in half; pat into two 6-in. circles. Cut each circle into eight wedges. Place wedges on parchment paper-lined baking sheets; sprinkle with coarse sugar. Bake for 18-22 minutes or until golden brown. Serve warm.

NOTE *If you're using frozen rhubarb, measure it while still frozen, then thaw completely. Drain in a colander, but do not press liquid out.*

TEST KITCHEN TIP
If you don't have the mini muffin tins called for in the Mini Spinach Frittatas recipe on this page, try using foil miniature muffin cup liners. Fill the cup liners with the appetizer mixture, then place them on a baking sheet and bake as usual.

FAST FIX

MINI SPINACH FRITTATAS

These mini frittatas are a cinch to make and just delicious. The recipe doubles easily for a crowd; they even freeze well for added convenience.
—**NANCY STATKEVICUS** TUCSON, AZ

START TO FINISH: 30 MIN.
MAKES: 2 DOZEN

- 1 cup whole-milk ricotta cheese
- ¾ cup grated Parmesan cheese
- ⅔ cup chopped fresh mushrooms
- 1 package (10 ounces) frozen chopped spinach, thawed and squeezed dry
- 1 large egg
- ½ teaspoon dried oregano
- ¼ teaspoon salt
- ¼ teaspoon pepper
- 24 slices pepperoni

1. Preheat oven to 375°. In a small bowl, combine the first eight ingredients. Place a pepperoni slice in each of 24 greased mini-muffin cups; fill three-fourths full with cheese mixture.

2. Bake 20-25 minutes or until completely set. Carefully run a knife around the sides of the muffin cups to loosen the frittatas. Serve warm.

ASPARAGUS PHYLLO BAKE

I'm Greek and grew up wrapping everything in phyllo. When asparagus is in season, I bring out the phyllo and start baking.
—**BONNIE GEAVARAS-BOOTZ** SCOTTSDALE, AZ

PREP: 25 MIN. • **BAKE:** 50 MIN.
MAKES: 12 SERVINGS

- 2 pounds fresh asparagus, trimmed and cut into 1-inch pieces
- 5 large eggs, lightly beaten
- 1 carton (15 ounces) ricotta cheese
- 1 cup shredded Swiss cheese
- 2 tablespoons grated Parmesan cheese
- 2 garlic cloves, minced
- ½ teaspoon salt
- ½ teaspoon grated lemon peel
- ½ teaspoon pepper
- ½ cup slivered almonds, toasted
- ¾ cup butter, melted
- 16 sheets phyllo dough (14x9 inches)

1. In a large saucepan, bring 8 cups water to a boil. Add asparagus; cook, uncovered, 30 seconds or just until the asparagus turns bright green. Remove asparagus and immediately drop into ice water. Drain and pat dry. In a large bowl, mix eggs, cheeses and seasonings; stir in the almonds and asparagus.
2. Preheat oven to 375°. Brush a 13x9-in. baking dish with some of the butter. Unroll the phyllo dough and layer eight sheets in the prepared dish, brushing each sheet with butter. Keep the remaining phyllo covered with plastic wrap and a damp towel to prevent it from drying out.
3. Spread the ricotta mixture over the phyllo layers. Top with the remaining phyllo sheets, brushing each with butter. Cut into 12 rectangles. Bake for 50-55 minutes or until golden brown.
NOTE *To toast nuts, bake in a shallow pan in a 350° oven for 5-10 minutes or cook in a skillet over low heat until lightly browned, stirring occasionally.*

MAKE AHEAD
BAKED FRENCH TOAST WITH STRAWBERRIES

French toast is a crowd-pleaser, but can be hard to make for a big group. This overnight recipe with a pecan topping and fresh strawberries will please the cook and the guests alike.
—**DAVID STELZL** WAXHAW, NC

PREP: 20 MIN. + CHILLING • **BAKE:** 40 MIN. + STANDING
MAKES: 12 SERVINGS

- 12 slices day-old French bread (1 inch thick)
- 6 large eggs
- 1½ cups 2% milk
- 1 cup half-and-half cream
- 2 tablespoons maple syrup
- 1 teaspoon vanilla extract
- ½ teaspoon ground cinnamon
- ¼ teaspoon ground nutmeg

TOPPING

- 1 cup packed brown sugar
- ½ cup butter, melted
- 2 tablespoons maple syrup
- 1 cup chopped pecans
- 4 cups chopped fresh strawberries
  Additional maple syrup

1. Place bread slices in a single layer in a greased 13x9-in. baking dish. In a large bowl, whisk eggs, milk, cream, syrup, vanilla, cinnamon and nutmeg; pour over bread. For topping, in a small bowl, mix brown sugar, butter and syrup; stir in pecans. Spread over bread. Refrigerate, covered, overnight.
2. Preheat oven to 350°. Remove French toast from the refrigerator while the oven heats. Bake, uncovered, 40-50 minutes or until a knife inserted in the center comes out clean. Let stand 10 minutes before serving. Serve with fresh strawberries and additional syrup.

**BAKED FRENCH
TOAST WITH
STRAWBERRIES**
David Stelzl
Waxhaw, NC

MAKE AHEAD

SPINACH FETA STRATA

This is a fairly new recipe for me, but my family loved it the first time I made it, so it'll be a regular. A friend shared it with me.

—PAT LANE PULLMAN, WA

PREP: 10 MIN. + CHILLING • **BAKE:** 40 MIN.
MAKES: 12 SERVINGS

- 10 slices French bread (1 inch thick) or 6 croissants, split
- 6 large eggs, lightly beaten
- 1½ cups 2% milk
- 1 package (10 ounces) frozen chopped spinach, thawed and squeezed dry
- ½ teaspoon salt
- ¼ teaspoon ground nutmeg
- ¼ teaspoon pepper
- 1½ cups shredded Monterey Jack cheese
- 1 cup crumbled feta cheese

1. In a greased 13x9-in. baking dish, arrange the bread slices or croissant halves with sides overlapping.
2. In a large bowl, combine the eggs, milk, spinach, salt, nutmeg and pepper; pour over bread. Sprinkle with cheeses. Cover and refrigerate for 8 hours or overnight.

3. Remove from the refrigerator 30 minutes before baking. Bake, uncovered, at 350° for 40-45 minutes or until a knife inserted near the center comes out clean. Let stand for 5 minutes before cutting. Serve strata warm.

PARADISE GRANOLA

Even my friends who aren't usually big fans of dried fruit can't get enough of this tropical island-inspired granola. It's low in fat and just plain delicious.

—ROBYN LARABEE LUCKNOW, ON

PREP: 20 MIN. • **BAKE:** 20 MIN. + COOLING
MAKES: 7 CUPS

- 2 cups old-fashioned oats
- ½ cup flaked coconut
- ½ cup toasted wheat germ
- ¼ cup oat bran
- ¼ cup sunflower kernels
- ¼ cup slivered almonds
- ¼ cup chopped pecans
- 2 tablespoons sesame seeds
- ¼ cup honey
- 2 tablespoons canola oil
- 2 tablespoons grated orange peel
- 1 teaspoon vanilla extract
- ½ teaspoon salt
- 1 cup dried cranberries
- ¾ cup chopped dates
- ½ cup chopped dried figs
- ½ cup chopped dried apricots
- 3 tablespoons raisins

1. In a large bowl, combine the first eight ingredients. In a small bowl, whisk the honey, oil, orange peel, vanilla and salt; pour over the oat mixture and mix well. Spread evenly into an ungreased 15x10x1-in. baking pan.
2. Bake at 350° for 20-25 minutes or until golden brown, stirring once. Cool completely on a wire rack. Stir in dried fruits. Store in an airtight container.

CREAMY
CRANBERRY
COFFEE CAKE

CREAMY CRANBERRY COFFEE CAKE

Chopped cranberries and orange peel give this coffee cake bursts of tart flavor, but a cream cheese layer on top sweetens it nicely. It's so lovely, you'll want to serve it when company comes.

—**NANCY ROPER** ETOBICOKE, ON

PREP: 15 MIN. • **BAKE:** 70 MIN. + COOLING
MAKES: 12 SERVINGS

- 2 cups all-purpose flour
- 1 cup sugar
- 1½ teaspoons baking powder
- ½ teaspoon baking soda
- 1 large egg
- 1 tablespoon grated orange peel
- ¾ cup orange juice
- ¼ cup butter, melted
- 1 teaspoon vanilla extract
- 2 cups coarsely chopped fresh or frozen cranberries

CREAM CHEESE LAYER
- 1 package (8 ounces) cream cheese, softened
- ⅓ cup sugar
- 1 large egg
- 1 teaspoon vanilla extract

TOPPING
- ¾ cup all-purpose flour
- ½ cup sugar
- ½ cup cold butter. cubed

1. Preheat oven to 350°. In a large bowl, whisk the first four ingredients. In another bowl, whisk egg, orange peel, orange juice, melted butter and vanilla until blended. Add to flour mixture; stir just until moistened. Fold in the cranberries. Transfer to a greased 9-in. springform pan.

2. For the cream cheese layer, in a small bowl, beat cream cheese and sugar until smooth. Add egg and vanilla; beat on low speed just until blended. Spread over batter.

3. For the topping, mix flour and sugar in a small bowl; cut in butter until crumbly. Sprinkle over the cream cheese layer. Place pan on a baking sheet. Bake for 70-75 minutes or until golden brown.

4. Cool in the pan for 15 minutes. Run a knife around the inside of the pan, and remove the sides of the springform pan. Refrigerate leftovers.

**PETITE SAUSAGE
QUICHES**

PETITE SAUSAGE QUICHES

You won't be able to eat just one of these cute mini quiches. Filled with savory sausage, Swiss cheese and a dash of cayenne, the mouthwatering morsels will disappear fast from the breakfast or buffet table.
—**DAWN STITT** HESPERIA, MI

PREP: 25 MIN. • **BAKE:** 30 MIN.
MAKES: 3 DOZEN

- 1 cup butter, softened
- 6 ounces cream cheese, softened
- 2 cups all-purpose flour

FILLING

- 6 ounces bulk Italian sausage
- 1 cup shredded Swiss cheese
- 1 tablespoon minced chives
- 1 large egg
- ½ cup half-and-half cream
- ¼ teaspoon salt
  Dash cayenne pepper

1. Preheat oven to 375°. Beat butter, cream cheese and flour until smooth. Shape tablespoonfuls of dough into balls; press onto the bottom and up the sides of greased miniature muffin cups.
2. In a large skillet, cook sausage over medium heat until no longer pink; drain and crumble. Sprinkle the sausage, Swiss cheese and chives into the muffin cups. Beat egg, cream, salt and pepper until blended; pour into the shells.
3. Bake until browned, 28-30 minutes (for a browner bottom crust, bake on a lower rack). Serve warm.

★ ★ ★ ★ ★ **READER REVIEW**

"I was skeptical of the cottage cheese and yogurt but these cinnamon rolls were fabulous! Tender and scrumptious—my whole family loved them!"

SEMINOLES TASTEOFHOME.COM

BRUNCH CINNAMON ROLLS

A sweet maple and vanilla glaze accentuates the cinnamon flavor in these friendly breakfast buns.
—**RITA VOGEL** MALCOM, IA

PREP: 30 MIN. • **BAKE:** 20 MIN.
MAKES: 1 DOZEN

- ¾ cup 4% small-curd cottage cheese
- ⅓ cup reduced-fat plain yogurt
- ¼ cup sugar
- ¼ cup butter, melted
- 1 teaspoon vanilla extract
- 2 cups all-purpose flour
- 2 teaspoons baking powder
- ¼ teaspoon baking soda
- ½ teaspoon salt

FILLING

- 2 tablespoons butter, melted
- 1 cup chopped pecans
- ⅔ cup packed brown sugar
- 1½ teaspoons ground cinnamon

MAPLE GLAZE

- ⅔ cup confectioners' sugar
- 3 tablespoons maple syrup
- 1 teaspoon vanilla extract

1. In a food processor, combine the first five ingredients; cover and process until smooth. Add flour, baking powder, baking soda and salt; cover and pulse until the mixture forms a soft dough.
2. Transfer to a lightly floured surface; knead 4-5 times. Roll dough into a 15x12-in. rectangle. Brush melted butter to within ½ in. of edges. Combine pecans, brown sugar and cinnamon; sprinkle over the dough. Roll up jelly-roll style, starting with a long side; pinch seam to seal. Cut into 12 slices. Place slices cut-side down in a greased 9-in. round baking pan.
3. Bake at 400° for 20-25 minutes or until golden brown. Cool for 5 minutes before inverting onto a serving plate. Combine the glaze ingredients; drizzle over the rolls. Serve warm.

DELICIOUS ALMOND BRAIDS

Similar to an almond crescent, this coffee cake is light and flaky, with a rich almond center. It's so versatile you can serve it for dessert, breakfast or brunch. It tastes like it came from a high-end bakery, but puff pastry dough makes it easy.

—**GINA IDONE** STATEN ISLAND, NY

PREP: 25 MIN. • **BAKE:** 30 MIN. + COOLING
MAKES: 2 BRAIDS (6 SLICES EACH)

- 1 package (7 ounces) almond paste
- ½ cup butter
- ½ cup sugar
- 1 large egg
- 2 tablespoons all-purpose flour
- 1 package (17.3 ounces) frozen puff pastry, thawed

GLAZE

- ¾ cup plus 1 tablespoon confectioners' sugar
- 2 tablespoons 2% milk
- ½ teaspoon almond extract
- ¼ cup sliced almonds, toasted

1. Place the almond paste, butter and sugar in a food processor; cover and pulse until chopped. Add the egg and flour; process until smooth.

2. Unfold puff pastry sheets onto a greased baking sheet. Spread half of the filling mixture down the center third of one pastry sheet. On each side, cut eight strips about 3½ in. into the center. Starting at one end, fold alternating strips at an angle across filling. Pinch the ends of the strips to seal. Repeat with remaining pastry and filling. Bake at 375° for 30-35 minutes or until golden brown. Remove to a wire rack to cool.

3. Combine the confectioners' sugar, milk and almond extract. Drizzle over the braids; sprinkle with almonds. Cut into slices.

MAKE AHEAD

HAM AND CHEESE PUFF

For brunch, lunch or anytime, people really seem to go for the big chunks of ham combined with the flavors of mustard and cheese. Assembled the night before, it's a great make-ahead potluck dish.

—**NINA CLARK** WAREHAM, MA

PREP: 15 MIN. + CHILLING • **BAKE:** 55 MIN.
MAKES: 24-30 SERVINGS

- 2 loaves (1 pound each) Italian bread, cut into 1-inch cubes
- 6 cups cubed fully cooked ham
- 1½ pounds Monterey Jack or Muenster cheese, cubed
- 1 medium onion, chopped
- ¼ cup butter
- 16 large eggs
- 7 cups milk
- ½ cup prepared mustard

1. Toss bread, ham and cheese; divide between two greased 13x9-in. baking dishes. In a skillet, saute onion in butter until tender; transfer to a bowl. Add eggs, milk and mustard; mix well. Pour over the bread mixture. Cover and refrigerate overnight.

2. Remove from the refrigerator 30 minutes before baking. Bake, uncovered, at 350° for 55-65 minutes or until a knife inserted near the center comes out clean. Serve immediately.

BERRY CHEESECAKE MUFFINS

I've adapted this recipe over the years to suit my family, and they think it's wonderful. As well as being delicious, the muffins are bursting with color.

—JEANNE BILHIMER MIDLAND, MI

PREP: 30 MIN. • **BAKE:** 30 MIN.
MAKES: 1½ DOZEN

- ⅓ cup butter, softened
- ¾ cup sugar
- 2 large eggs
- ⅓ cup 2% milk
- 1½ cups all-purpose flour
- 1½ teaspoons baking powder
- 1 teaspoon ground cinnamon

CREAM CHEESE FILLING

- 6 ounces cream cheese, softened
- ⅓ cup sugar
- 1 large egg
- ¾ cup fresh raspberries
- ¾ cup fresh blueberries

STREUSEL TOPPING

- ¼ cup all-purpose flour
- 2 tablespoons brown sugar
- ½ teaspoon ground cinnamon
- 1 tablespoon cold butter

1. Preheat oven to 375°. In a large bowl, cream the butter and sugar until light and fluffy. Add eggs, one at a time, beating well after each addition. Beat in milk. In another bowl, whisk flour, baking powder and cinnamon; add to creamed mixture just until moistened. Fill greased or paper-lined muffin cups one-quarter full.

2. For filling, in a small bowl, beat cream cheese, sugar and egg until smooth. Fold in the berries. Drop a rounded tablespoonful into the center of each muffin.

3. For topping, in a small bowl, mix flour, brown sugar and cinnamon; cut in butter until crumbly. Sprinkle over batter.

4. Bake for 27-32 minutes or until a toothpick inserted near the center comes out clean. Cool in pan for 5 minutes, then remove from pans to wire racks. Serve warm. Refrigerate leftovers.

SAUSAGE QUICHE SQUARES

Having done some catering, I especially appreciate interesting, appetizing finger foods. I'm constantly asked to make these squares to serve at parties and potlucks. They're like zippy crustless quiche.

—LINDA WHEELER MIDDLEBURG, FL

PREP: 15 MIN. • **BAKE:** 20 MIN. + COOLING
MAKES: ABOUT 8 DOZEN

- 1 pound bulk pork sausage
- 1 cup shredded cheddar cheese
- 1 cup shredded Monterey Jack cheese
- ½ cup finely chopped onion
- 1 can (4 ounces) chopped green chilies
- 1 tablespoon minced jalapeno pepper, optional
- 10 large eggs
- 1 teaspoon chili powder
- 1 teaspoon ground cumin
- 1 teaspoon salt
- ½ teaspoon garlic powder
- ½ teaspoon pepper

1. In a large skillet, cook sausage until no longer pink; drain. Place in a greased 13x9-in. baking dish. Layer with cheeses, onion, chilies and jalapeno if desired. In a bowl, beat the eggs and seasonings. Pour over cheese.

2. Bake, uncovered, at 375° for 18-22 minutes or until a knife inserted near the center comes out clean. Cool for 10 minutes; cut into 1-in. squares.

NOTE *Wear disposable gloves when cutting hot peppers; the oils can burn skin. Avoid touching your face.*

★ ★ ★ ★ ★ **READER REVIEW**

"I took the muffins to a bridal shower and some people thought they were professionally made. I will be making these often!."

STUBUS TASTEOFHOME.COM

BREAKFAST BURRITOS

I discovered this recipe at a workshop of holiday breakfasts our church offered. It was a big hit! Burritos work really well when you're cooking for a crowd. I like to serve salsa or hot sauce alongside.

—CATHERINE ALLAN TWIN FALLS, ID

PREP: 20 MIN. • **BAKE:** 15 MIN.
MAKES: 12 SERVINGS

- 1 package (16 ounces) frozen cubed hash brown potatoes
- 12 large eggs
- 1 large onion, chopped
- 1 medium green pepper, chopped
- ½ pound bulk pork sausage, browned and drained
- 12 flour tortillas (10 inches), warmed
- 3 cups shredded cheddar cheese
  Salsa, optional

1. In a large skillet, fry the hash browns according to the package directions; remove and set aside.
2. In a large bowl, beat eggs; add the onions and green pepper. Pour into the same skillet; cook and stir until the eggs are set. Remove from heat. Add the hash browns and sausage; mix gently.
3. Place about ¾ cup filling on each tortilla and top with about ¼ cup cheese. Roll up tortillas and place on a greased baking sheet. Bake at 350° for 15-20 minutes or until heated through. Serve with salsa or hot sauce if desired.

ITALIAN BRUNCH TORTE

We always pair this impressive layered breakfast bake with a salad of mixed greens and tomato wedges. Served warm or cold, it's one of our most requested dishes.

—DANNY DIAMOND FARMINGTON HILLS, MI

PREP: 50 MIN. • **BAKE:** 1 HOUR + STANDING
MAKES: 12 SERVINGS

- 2 tubes (8 ounces each) refrigerated crescent rolls, divided
- 1 teaspoon olive oil
- 1 package (6 ounces) fresh baby spinach
- 1 cup sliced fresh mushrooms
- 7 large eggs
- 1 cup grated Parmesan cheese
- 2 teaspoons Italian seasoning
- ⅛ teaspoon pepper
- ½ pound thinly sliced deli ham
- ½ pound thinly sliced hard salami
- ½ pound sliced provolone cheese
- 2 jars (12 ounces each) roasted sweet red peppers, drained, sliced and patted dry

1. Preheat oven to 350°. Place a greased 9-in. springform pan on a double thickness of heavy-duty foil (about 18 in. square). Securely wrap the foil around the pan. Unroll one tube of crescent dough and separate into triangles. Press onto bottom of prepared pan to form a crust, sealing seams well. Bake for 10-15 minutes or until set.
2. Meanwhile, in a large skillet, heat the oil over medium-high heat. Add spinach and mushrooms; cook and stir until the mushrooms are tender. Drain on several layers of paper towels, blotting well. In a large bowl, whisk six eggs, Parmesan cheese, Italian seasoning and pepper.
3. Layer crust with half of each of the following: ham, salami, provolone cheese, red peppers and spinach mixture. Pour half of the egg mixture over top. Repeat layers; top with remaining egg mixture.
4. On a work surface, unroll and separate the remaining crescent dough into triangles. Press together to form a circle and seal seams; place over filling. Whisk remaining egg; brush over dough.
5. Bake, uncovered, for 1-1¼ hours or until a thermometer reads 160°. Cover loosely with foil if needed to prevent overbrowning. Carefully loosen sides from pan with a knife; remove rim from pan. Let stand 20 minutes.

TEST KITCHEN TIP
It's not unusual for springform pans to spring a leak around the bottom seam. It might be because of too much butter in a crust—or a savory dish releasing liquid during cooking. You can wrap the bottom of the pan in a layer of foil, or just place the pan on a baking sheet with a lip to catch and contain any lost liquid.

ITALIAN BRUNCH TORTE

1. In a large bowl, dissolve the yeast in warm water. In another large bowl, combine the buttermilk, egg, oil, sugar, salt, baking soda, yeast mixture and 2 cups flour; beat on medium until smooth. Stir in enough of the remaining flour to form a stiff dough.

2. Turn dough onto a floured surface; knead until smooth and elastic, about 6-8 minutes. Place in a greased bowl, turning once to grease the top. Cover with plastic wrap and let rise in a warm place until doubled, about 1 hour.

3. Punch dough down, then turn it onto a lightly floured surface and roll it into a 16x8-in. rectangle. Cut into 24 rectangles. Cover with a clean kitchen towel and let rest for 1 hour.

4. In an electric skillet or deep fryer, heat oil to 375°. Fry scones, a few at a time, until golden brown on both sides. Drain on paper towels.

5. For the honey butter, in a large bowl, combine the butter, honey, confectioners' sugar and vanilla; beat until smooth. Serve with the scones.

UTAH BUTTERMILK SCONES

These scones are deep-fried, and buttermilk makes them so moist and tender you'll most likely eat too many. The texture is light and airy, and the flavor is delightful. Don't forget the honey butter—the perfect addition to the perfect scone.

—NICHOLE JONES IDAHO FALLS, ID

PREP: 30 MIN. + RISING • **COOK:** 5 MIN./BATCH
MAKES: 2 DOZEN

  1 tablespoon active dry yeast
½ cup warm water (110° to 115°)
  1 cup warm buttermilk (110° to 115°)
  1 large egg
  3 tablespoons canola oil
1½ teaspoons sugar
½ teaspoon salt
¼ teaspoon baking soda
  4 to 4½ cups all-purpose flour
     Oil for deep-fat frying

HONEY BUTTER

½ cup butter, softened
¼ cup honey
¼ cup confectioners' sugar
¼ teaspoon vanilla extract

MAKE AHEAD

SAUSAGE BACON BITES

These tasty morsels are perfect with almost any egg dish or as finger foods that party guests can just pop into their mouths.

—PAT WAYMIRE YELLOW SPRINGS, OH

PREP: 20 MIN. + CHILLING • **BAKE:** 35 MIN.
MAKES: ABOUT 3½ DOZEN

¾ pound sliced bacon
  2 packages (8 ounces each) frozen fully cooked breakfast sausage links, thawed
½ cup plus 2 tablespoons packed brown sugar, divided

1. Preheat oven to 350°. Cut the bacon strips widthwise in half; cut sausage links in half. Wrap a piece of bacon around each piece of sausage. Place ½ cup brown sugar in a shallow bowl; roll the wrapped sausages in sugar. Secure each with a toothpick. Place in a foil-lined 15x10x1-in. baking pan. Cover and refrigerate 4 hours or overnight.

2. Sprinkle with 1 tablespoon brown sugar. Bake for 35-40 minutes or until the bacon is crisp, turning once. Sprinkle with the remaining brown sugar.

MAKE-AHEAD BLINTZ CASSEROLE
Ann Hillmeyer
Sandia Park, NM

MAKE AHEAD

MAKE-AHEAD BLINTZ CASSEROLE

Blintzes are thin pancakes filled with cheese or fruits. For my casserole version, I created a souffle with cheese filling and topped it with apples.

—**ANN HILLMEYER** SANDIA PARK, NM

PREP: 30 MIN. + CHILLING • **BAKE:** 45 MIN. + STANDING
MAKES: 12 SERVINGS

- 2 cups 2% cottage cheese
- 1 carton (8 ounces) mascarpone cheese
- 3 large egg yolks
- 2 tablespoons sugar
- 1 teaspoon rum or vanilla extract
- ¼ teaspoon ground cinnamon

BATTER
- 1½ cups sour cream
- 6 large eggs
- ½ cup butter, softened
- ½ cup frozen apple juice concentrate, thawed
- 1¼ cups all-purpose flour
- ¼ cup sugar
- 2 teaspoons baking powder
- 1 teaspoon grated lemon peel

TOPPING
- ¼ cup butter, cubed
- 3 medium apples, peeled and chopped
- 1 tablespoon lemon juice
- ¾ cup packed brown sugar
- ¼ teaspoon salt
- 1 teaspoon rum or vanilla extract

1. For the filling, place the first six ingredients in a food processor; process until smooth. Transfer to a small bowl.

2. Place the batter ingredients in food processor; process until smooth. Pour half of the batter into a greased 13x9-in. baking dish. Drop tablespoonfuls of filling over the batter; cover with the remaining batter. Refrigerate several hours or overnight.

3. Preheat oven to 350°. Remove the casserole from the refrigerator while the oven heats. Bake for 45-50 minutes or until a knife inserted near the center comes out clean. Let stand 10 minutes.

4. Meanwhile, in a large skillet, melt butter over medium heat. Add apples and lemon juice. Cook and stir for 5-7 minutes or until the apples are tender. Add brown sugar and salt; cook 1 minute longer or until thickened. Stir in extract; cool slightly. Serve with casserole.

OVERNIGHT PUMPKIN
FRENCH TOAST
CASSEROLE

OVERNIGHT PUMPKIN FRENCH TOAST CASSEROLE

Recipes that don't tie me to the kitchen—I'm all about those! I make this luscious dish the night before breakfast or brunch with guests.

—PATRICIA HARMON BADEN, PA

PREP: 20 MIN. + CHILLING • **BAKE:** 65 MIN.
MAKES: 12 SERVINGS

- 1 loaf (1 pound) cinnamon-raisin bread
- 1 package (8 ounces) reduced-fat cream cheese, cut into ¾-inch cubes
- 8 large eggs
- 1 can (12 ounces) evaporated milk
- 1 cup canned pumpkin
- ⅔ cup packed brown sugar
- ½ cup fat-free milk
- 2 teaspoons ground cinnamon
- ¼ teaspoon ground nutmeg
- ¼ teaspoon ground ginger
- ⅛ teaspoon ground cloves
- ½ teaspoon salt
- ½ cup chopped pecans
  Confectioners' sugar, optional
  Maple syrup, warmed, optional

1. Cut each slice of bread into quarters. Arrange half of the bread quarters in a greased 13x9-in. baking dish; layer with cubed cream cheese and remaining bread, pressing down slightly.

2. In a large bowl, whisk eggs, evaporated milk, pumpkin, brown sugar, fat-free milk, spices and salt. Pour over top. Refrigerate, covered, overnight.

3. Preheat oven to 350°. Remove casserole from refrigerator while oven heats. Bake, covered, for 40 minutes. Uncover; sprinkle with pecans. Bake, uncovered, 25-30 minutes or until lightly browned and a knife inserted in center comes out clean.

4. Let stand 5-10 minutes before serving. If desired, dust casserole with confectioners' sugar and serve with maple syrup.

NUT-TOPPED STRAWBERRY RHUBARB MUFFINS

If the muffin top is your favorite part of the muffin, these tasty treats should get your attention. Pecans, cinnamon and brown sugar give a sweet crunch to every bite.

—AUDREY STALLSMITH HADLEY, PA

PREP: 25 MIN. • **BAKE:** 20 MIN. + COOLING
MAKES: 1½ DOZEN

- 2¾ cups all-purpose flour
- 1⅓ cups packed brown sugar
- 2½ teaspoons baking powder
- ½ teaspoon baking soda
- ½ teaspoon ground cinnamon
- ¼ teaspoon salt
- 1 large egg
- 1 cup buttermilk
- ½ cup canola oil
- 2 teaspoons vanilla extract
- 1 cup chopped fresh strawberries
- ¾ cup diced fresh or frozen rhubarb

TOPPING
- ½ cup chopped pecans
- ⅓ cup packed brown sugar
- ½ teaspoon ground cinnamon
- 1 tablespoon cold butter

1. In a large bowl, combine the first six ingredients. In another bowl, whisk the egg, buttermilk, oil and vanilla. Stir into dry ingredients just until moistened. Fold in the strawberries and rhubarb. Fill greased or paper-lined muffin cups two-thirds full.

2. In a small bowl, combine the pecans, brown sugar and cinnamon. Cut in butter until the mixture resembles coarse crumbs. Sprinkle over the batter.

3. Bake at 400° for 20-25 minutes or until a toothpick inserted in the center comes out clean. Cool in pans for 5 minutes before removing from pans to wire racks. Serve warm.

NOTE *If using frozen rhubarb, measure rhubarb while still frozen, then thaw completely. Drain in a colander, but do not press out the liquid.*

APPLE PULL-APART BREAD

Drizzled with icing, each finger-licking piece of this bread has a yummy filling of apples and pecans. The recipe is well worth the bit of extra effort.
—**CAROLYN GREGORY** HENDERSONVILLE, TN

PREP: 40 MIN. + RISING • **BAKE:** 35 MIN. + COOLING
MAKES: 1 LOAF

- 1 package (¼ ounce) active dry yeast
- 1 cup warm milk
- ½ cup butter, melted, divided
- 1 large egg
- ⅔ cup plus 2 tablespoons sugar, divided
- 1 teaspoon salt
- 3 to 3½ cups all-purpose flour
- 1 medium tart apple, peeled and chopped
- ½ cup finely chopped pecans
- ½ teaspoon ground cinnamon

ICING

- 1 cup confectioners' sugar
- 3 to 4½ teaspoons hot water
- ½ teaspoon vanilla extract

1. In a large bowl, dissolve the yeast in milk. Add 2 tablespoons butter, egg, 2 tablespoons sugar, salt and 3 cups flour; beat until smooth. Add enough of the remaining flour to form a stiff dough. Turn dough onto a floured surface; knead until smooth and elastic, 6-8 minutes. Place in a greased bowl, turning once to grease top. Cover and let rise in a warm place until doubled, about 1 hour.

2. Combine the apple, pecans, cinnamon and remaining sugar; set aside. Punch dough down; divide in half. Cut each half into 16 pieces. On a lightly floured surface, pat or roll out each piece into a 2½-in. circle. Place 1 teaspoon apple mixture in center of circle; pinch edges together and seal, forming a ball. Dip in remaining butter.

3. Place 16 balls seam-side down in a greased 10-in. tube pan; sprinkle with ¼ cup apple mixture. Layer the remaining balls; sprinkle with the remaining apple mixture. Cover and let rise until nearly doubled, about 45 minutes.

4. Bake at 350° for 35-40 minutes or until golden brown. Cool for 10 minutes; remove from pan to a wire rack. Combine icing ingredients; drizzle over warm bread.

FAST FIX ▶

DUTCH HONEY SYRUP

I grew up on a farm where a big breakfast was an everyday occurrence. Still, it was a special treat when Mom served this scrumptious syrup with our pancakes.
—**KATHY SCOTT** LINGLE, WY

START TO FINISH: 15 MIN.
MAKES: 2 CUPS

- 1 cup sugar
- 1 cup corn syrup
- 1 cup heavy whipping cream
- 1 teaspoon vanilla extract

In a saucepan, combine sugar, corn syrup and cream. Bring to a boil over medium heat; boil for 5 minutes or until slightly thickened, stirring occasionally. Stir in the vanilla. Serve warm over pancakes, waffles or French toast.

BLUEBERRY OATMEAL PANCAKES

Wonderful blueberry flavor abounds in these thick and moist pancakes. My kids love them, and they are nutritious, easy and inexpensive!

—**AMY SPAINHOWARD** BOWLING GREEN, KY

PREP: 20 MIN. • **COOK:** 5 MIN./BATCH
MAKES: 14 PANCAKES (1¼ CUPS SYRUP)

- 2 cups all-purpose flour
- 2 packets (1.51 ounces each) instant maple and brown sugar oatmeal mix
- 2 tablespoons sugar
- 2 teaspoons baking powder
- ⅛ teaspoon salt
- 2 large egg whites
- 1 large egg
- 1½ cups fat-free milk
- ½ cup reduced-fat sour cream
- 2 cups fresh or frozen blueberries

BLUEBERRY SYRUP

- 1½ cups fresh or frozen blueberries
- ½ cup sugar

1. In a large bowl, combine the first five ingredients. In another bowl, whisk the egg whites, egg, milk and sour cream. Stir into dry ingredients just until moistened. Fold in blueberries.

2. Spoon batter by ¼ cupfuls onto a hot griddle coated with cooking spray. Turn pancakes when bubbles form in the tops; cook until the second side is golden brown.

3. In a microwave-safe bowl, combine the syrup ingredients. Microwave, uncovered, on high for 1 minute; stir. Microwave 1-2 minutes longer or until hot and bubbly. Serve warm with pancakes.

NOTE *If using frozen blueberries in the pancakes, do not thaw them before adding to the batter. This recipe was tested in a 1,100-watt microwave.*

TEST KITCHEN TIP
For a special treat, make whipped butter to go with pancakes. Let your butter soften at room temperature, then beat with a mixer until light and fluffy. Mix in a little honey, confectioners' sugar or orange peel for added flavor.

FAST FIX
APPLE SAUSAGE PUFFS

I keep my recipe for sausage puffs close at hand for entertaining. Just about everyone loves them, and I need only four ingredients.

—**VERONICA JOHNSON** JEFFERSON CITY, MO

START TO FINISH: 25 MIN.
MAKES: 2 DOZEN

- 1 pound bulk pork sausage
- 1 medium apple, finely chopped
- 3 ounces cream cheese, softened
- 3 tubes (8 ounces each) refrigerated crescent rolls

1. Preheat oven to 375°. In a large skillet, cook sausage and apple over medium heat until the meat is no longer pink; drain. Stir in cream cheese.

2. Unroll one tube of crescent dough; separate into eight triangles. Place 1 tablespoon filling on the long side of each triangle. Roll up each triangle, starting with the long side; pinch the seams to seal.

3. Place rolls point side down 2 in. apart on a greased baking sheet. Bake 10-12 minutes or until golden brown. Serve warm.

GINGERBREAD PANCAKES WITH BANANA CREAM

To save some time during the holidays, I make and refrigerate the batter two hours before cooking. This way I don't have to bother with measuring ingredients while my guests mill about the kitchen anxiously awaiting brunch.

—**BARBARA BRITTAIN** SANTEE, CA

PREP: 25 MIN. • **COOK:** 5 MIN./BATCH
MAKES: 42 PANCAKES (4⅔ CUPS TOPPING)

- 2 cups heavy whipping cream
- ⅓ cup confectioners' sugar
- 2 medium bananas, chopped
- ¾ cup butter, softened
- 1½ cups packed brown sugar
- 6 large eggs
- 1½ cups molasses
- 6 cups all-purpose flour
- 4½ teaspoons baking powder
- 1 tablespoon ground ginger
- 1 tablespoon ground cinnamon
- 2¼ teaspoons salt
- ¾ teaspoon ground allspice
- 4 cups 2% milk

1. In a large bowl, beat cream until it begins to thicken. Add the confectioners' sugar; beat until soft peaks form. Fold in bananas. Cover and chill until serving.

2. In a very large bowl, cream butter and brown sugar until light and fluffy. Add the eggs, one at a time, beating well after each addition. Beat in the molasses. Combine the flour, baking powder, ginger, cinnamon, salt and allspice; add to the creamed mixture alternately with milk, beating well after each addition.

3. Pour batter by ¼ cupfuls onto a greased hot griddle; turn when bubbles form on top. Cook until the second side is golden brown. Serve with banana cream.

CRAB-SPINACH EGG CASSEROLE

I've developed a strong interest in cooking over the years, and so I came up with this casserole as a special breakfast treat for our daughter when she was home for a visit.

—**STEVE HEATON** DELTONA, FL

PREP: 10 MIN. • **BAKE:** 30 MIN. + STANDING
MAKES: 12-16 SERVINGS

- 8 large eggs
- 2 cups half-and-half cream
- 2 cans (6 ounces each) crabmeat, drained
- 1 package (10 ounces) frozen chopped spinach, thawed and squeezed dry
- 1 cup dry bread crumbs
- 1 cup shredded Swiss cheese
- ½ teaspoon salt
- ¼ teaspoon pepper
- ¼ teaspoon ground nutmeg
- 2 celery ribs, chopped
- ½ cup chopped onion
- ½ cup chopped sweet red pepper
- 3 medium fresh mushrooms, chopped
- 2 tablespoons butter

1. In a large bowl, beat eggs and cream. Stir in the crab, spinach, bread crumbs, cheese, salt, pepper and nutmeg; set aside. In a skillet, saute the celery, onion, red pepper and mushrooms in butter until tender. Add to the spinach mixture.

2. Transfer to a greased shallow 2½-qt. baking dish. Bake, uncovered, at 375° for 30-35 minutes or until a thermometer reads 160°. Let stand for 10 minutes before serving.

★ ★ ★ ★ ★ **READER REVIEW**

"We made this for a brunch and it was a huge hit! Easy to throw together and great as leftovers, too!"

MORNINGORANGE TASTEOFHOME.COM

CRAB-SPINACH EGG
CASEROLE

**HOT SAUSAGE
& BEAN DIP, PAGE 48**

APPETIZERS & SNACKS

"*Every day they continued to meet together in the temple courts. They broke bread in their homes and ate together with glad and sincere hearts.*"

ACTS 2:46

MUFFULETTA CHEESECAKE

After searching for the perfect party appetizer, I created my own. This savory spread boasts the flavors of a classic Italian muffuletta sandwich.

—HELEN FLAMM DAYTON, OH

PREP: 25 MIN. + CHILLING • **BAKE:** 35 MIN. + CHILLING
MAKES: 24 SERVINGS

- 1½ cups crushed butter-flavored crackers (40-45 crackers)
- ⅓ cup butter, melted
- 2 packages (8 ounces each) cream cheese, softened
- 1½ cups sour cream
- ½ teaspoon Italian seasoning
- 1 large egg, lightly beaten
- 1 large egg yolk
- 2 cups shredded provolone cheese
- 1 cup chopped salami

OLIVE SALAD

- ½ cup pimiento-stuffed olives
- ¼ cup pitted Greek olives
- 4 pickled onions
- 2 tablespoons capers, drained
- 2 tablespoons olive oil
- 1 pepperoncini, stem removed
- 2 teaspoons lemon juice
- 1 teaspoon Italian seasoning
- 1 garlic clove

SERVING

Assorted crackers or baguette slices

1. Preheat oven to 375°. In a small bowl, mix cracker crumbs and butter. Press onto the bottom and 1 in. up the sides of a greased 9-in. springform pan. Place the pan on a baking sheet.

2. In a large bowl, beat cream cheese until smooth. Gradually beat in sour cream and Italian seasoning. Add egg and egg yolk; beat on low just until blended. Fold in provolone and salami. Pour into the crust. Bake 35-45 minutes or until the center is almost set.

3. Meanwhile, place the olive salad ingredients in a food processor; process until coarsely chopped. Refrigerate, covered, overnight.

4. Cool cheesecake on a wire rack 10 minutes.

Loosen sides from pan with a knife, and cool for 1 hour longer. Refrigerate overnight, covering when completely cooled.

5. Remove the rim from the pan. Top cheesecake with olive salad; serve with crackers.

BACON-WRAPPED SHRIMP

I tweaked this recipe to please my family, and now it's a hit! If you want to deliver less heat, you can skip the jalapenos.

—DEBBIE CHEEK STATE ROAD, NC

PREP: 25 MIN. + MARINATING • **BROIL:** 5 MIN.
MAKES: 2½ DOZEN

- 30 uncooked shrimp (31-40 per pound), peeled and deveined
- 6 tablespoons creamy Caesar salad dressing, divided
- 15 bacon strips, halved crosswise
- 2 jalapeno peppers, seeded and thinly sliced

1. Preheat broiler. In a large bowl, toss shrimp with 4 tablespoons dressing; let stand for 15 minutes.

2. Meanwhile, in a large skillet, cook bacon over medium heat until partially cooked but not crisp. Remove to paper towels to drain; keep warm.

3. Remove shrimp from the marinade; discard the marinade. Top each shrimp with a jalapeno slice and wrap with a bacon strip; secure with a toothpick. Place on a greased rack of a broiler pan.

4. Broil 4 in. from heat 2-3 minutes on each side or until shrimp turn pink, basting frequently with the remaining dressing after turning.

NOTE *Wear disposable gloves when cutting hot peppers; the oils can burn skin. Avoid touching your face.*

TEST KITCHEN TIP
If you want to cut down on grease splatter (and cleanup time!), try cooking your bacon in the oven instead of in a skillet. Use a foil-lined baking sheet with sides and bake at 350° for 30 minutes to get crispy bacon; cut the baking time for the Bacon-Wrapped Shrimp, above.

BACON-WRAPPED
SHRIMP

POPPY SEED CHEESE BREAD

This easy-to-make bread goes well with a salad luncheon or a casserole dinner. I especially like to serve it with spaghetti and pasta dishes. Cheese topping is its crowning glory!

—**ELAINE MUNDT** DETROIT, MI

PREP: 20 MIN. + RISING • **BAKE:** 15 MIN.
MAKES: 15 SERVINGS

- 1 package (¼ ounce) active dry yeast
- 2 teaspoons sugar
- ¼ cup warm water (110° to 115°)
- ¾ cup warm milk (110° to 115°)
- 2 tablespoons shortening
- 1 teaspoon salt
- 2¼ to 2½ cups all-purpose flour

TOPPING

- 2 cups shredded cheddar cheese
- 1 large egg
- ⅓ cup whole milk
- 1 teaspoon finely chopped onion
  Poppy seeds

1. Dissolve yeast and sugar in water. Combine the milk, shortening and salt; stir into the yeast mixture. Add enough flour to form a soft dough. Turn dough onto a floured surface; knead until smooth and elastic, about 3 minutes. Place in a greased bowl, turning once to grease top. Cover and let rise in a warm place until doubled, about 1½ hours.
2. Punch down the dough and press it into a greased 13x9-in. baking pan. Cover and let rise in a warm place until doubled, about 45 minutes.
3. Preheat oven to 425°. Combine the cheese, egg, milk and onion; spread over the dough. Sprinkle with poppy seeds. Bake 15-20 minutes. Cut into squares; serve warm.

BBQ CHICKEN PIZZA ROLL-UP

These appetizer slices make for fab, filling small bites with loads of sweet and tangy flavor.

—**TRACEY BIRCH** QUEEN CREEK, AZ

PREP: 15 MIN. • **BAKE:** 15 MIN. + COOLING
MAKES: 2 DOZEN

- 1 tube (13.8 ounces) refrigerated pizza crust
- ¼ cup honey barbecue sauce
- 1½ cups shredded part-skim mozzarella cheese
- 1½ cups shredded cooked chicken breast
- 1 small red onion, finely chopped
- ¼ cup minced fresh cilantro
- 1 teaspoon Italian seasoning, optional
- 1 large egg white
- 1 tablespoon water
- ¼ teaspoon garlic powder

1. On a lightly floured surface, roll the crust into a 12x9-in. rectangle; brush with barbecue sauce. Layer with cheese, chicken, onion, cilantro and if desired, Italian seasoning.
2. Roll up crust jelly-roll style, starting with a long side; pinch the seams to seal. Place roll seam side down on a baking sheet coated with cooking spray.
3. Beat egg white and water; brush over the top of the roll. Sprinkle with garlic powder. Bake at 400° for 15-20 minutes or until lightly browned. Cool for 10 minutes before slicing.

GREEK BREADSTICKS

Get ready for rave reviews with these crispy Greek-inspired appetizers. They're best served warm with your favorite tzatziki sauce.

—JANE WHITTAKER PENSACOLA, FL

PREP: 20 MIN. • **BAKE:** 15 MIN.
MAKES: 32 BREADSTICKS

- ¼ cup marinated quartered artichoke hearts, drained
- 2 tablespoons pitted Greek olives
- 1 package (17.3 ounces) frozen puff pastry, thawed
- 1 carton (6½ ounces) spreadable spinach and artichoke cream cheese
- 2 tablespoons grated Parmesan cheese
- 1 large egg
- 1 tablespoon water
- 2 teaspoons sesame seeds
  Refrigerated tzatziki sauce, optional

1. Place artichokes and olives in a food processor; cover and pulse until finely chopped. Unfold one pastry sheet on a lightly floured surface; spread half of the cream cheese over half of the pastry. Top with half of the artichoke mixture. Sprinkle with half of the Parmesan cheese. Fold the plain half of the pastry over the filling; press gently to seal.
2. Repeat with the remaining pastry, cream cheese, artichoke mixture and Parmesan cheese. Whisk egg and water; brush over tops. Sprinkle with sesame seeds. Cut each rectangle into sixteen ¾-in.-wide strips. Twist each strip several times; place strips 2 in. apart on greased baking sheets.
3. Bake at 400° for 12-14 minutes or until golden brown. Serve warm with tzatziki sauce if desired.

ROASTED RED PEPPER TAPENADE

When entertaining, I often rely on my pepper tapenade recipe because it takes only 15 minutes to whip up and pop in the fridge. You can use walnuts or pecans instead of almonds.

—DONNA MAGLIARO DENVILLE, NJ

PREP: 15 MIN. + CHILLING
MAKES: 2 CUPS

- 3 garlic cloves, peeled
- 2 cups roasted sweet red peppers, drained
- ½ cup blanched almonds
- ⅓ cup tomato paste
- 2 tablespoons olive oil
- ¼ teaspoon salt
- ¼ teaspoon pepper
  Minced fresh basil
  Toasted French bread baguette slices or water crackers

1. In a small saucepan, bring 2 cups water to a boil. Add garlic; cook, uncovered, for 6-8 minutes or just until tender. Drain and pat dry. Place red peppers, almonds, tomato paste, oil, garlic, salt and pepper in a small food processor; process until blended. Transfer to a small bowl. Refrigerate at least 4 hours to allow flavors to blend.
2. Sprinkle with basil. Serve with baguette slices.

MINI CORN MUFFINS WITH SPICY CHEDDAR FILLING

MINI CORN MUFFINS WITH SPICY CHEDDAR FILLING

I'm an Iowa gardener who likes to feature sweet corn in my recipes. These cute, easy-to-eat bites are a fun change from the usual chip appetizers, and they're a hit at card parties.

—**MARGARET BLAIR** LORIMOR, IA

PREP: 30 MIN. • **BAKE:** 25 MIN.
MAKES: 4 DOZEN

- 1½ cups all-purpose flour
- 1 cup cornmeal
- 2 teaspoons sugar
- ¾ teaspoon baking powder
- ½ teaspoon salt
- 1 large egg
- ¾ cup milk
- ¼ cup canola oil
- 1 can (14¾ ounces) cream-style corn

FILLING

- 2 cups shredded cheddar cheese
- 1 can (4 ounces) chopped green chilies
- ¼ cup diced pimientos
- 1 teaspoon chili powder
- ¼ teaspoon hot pepper sauce

1. Preheat oven to 400°. In a large bowl, whisk the first five ingredients. In another bowl, whisk egg, milk and oil until blended. Add to flour mixture; stir just until moistened. Fold in corn.

2. Fill greased mini-muffin cups three-fourths full. Bake 15-18 minutes or until a toothpick inserted in center comes out clean. Cool 5 minutes before removing from pans to wire racks. Reduce oven setting to 350°.

3. Meanwhile, in a large bowl, combine filling ingredients. Using a small melon baller, scoop out the center of each muffin; spoon in a rounded teaspoonful of filling into the center. Bake 10-12 minutes or until cheese is melted.

BAKED BABY POTATOES WITH OLIVE PESTO

These little cuties pack all the appeal of a dinner baked potato into the perfect bite-sized appetizer. I top off each one with a dollop of sour cream and coarsely ground pepper.

—**SARAH SHAIKH** MUMBAI, INDIA

PREP: 35 MIN. • **BAKE:** 30 MIN.
MAKES: ABOUT 3 DOZEN

- 3 pounds baby red potatoes (1¾-inch wide, about 36)
- 6 tablespoons olive oil, divided
- 2 teaspoons salt
- 1½ cups pimiento-stuffed olives
- ½ cup chopped onion
- ¼ cup pine nuts, toasted
- 2 garlic cloves, minced
- ½ cup sour cream
- Coarsely ground pepper, optional

1. Preheat oven to 400°. Place potatoes in a large bowl. Add 2 tablespoons oil and salt; toss to coat. Transfer to a greased 15x10x1-in. baking pan. Bake 30-35 minutes or until tender.

2. Meanwhile, place olives, onion, pine nuts and garlic in a food processor; pulse until chopped. Gradually add remaining oil; process to reach desired pesto consistency.

3. When the potatoes are cool enough to handle, cut thin slices off bottoms to allow potatoes to sit upright. Cut an "X" in the top of each potato; squeeze sides to open tops slightly. Place on a serving platter.

4. Spoon olive pesto onto potatoes; top with sour cream. If desired, sprinkle with pepper. Serve warm.

TEST KITCHEN TIP
To toast nuts, bake in a shallow pan in a 350° oven for 5-10 minutes or cook in a skillet over low heat until lightly browned, stirring occasionally.

CHIVE MASCARPONE DIP WITH HERBED PITA CHIPS

With a large herb garden I usually can count on an abundance of chives, but you can find fresh herbs at the grocery store. This dip, with mascarpone and bacon, has the best flavor if made 2 to 3 days ahead.

—**SARAH VASQUES** MILFORD, NH

PREP: 25 MIN. + CHILLING • **BAKE:** 10 MIN.
MAKES: 2 CUPS (48 CHIPS)

- 1 carton (8 ounces) Mascarpone cheese
- ¾ cup minced fresh chives
- ¾ cup sour cream
- 4 bacon strips, cooked and crumbled
- ¼ teaspoon salt
- ¼ teaspoon pepper

PITA CHIPS
- 8 whole wheat pita breads (6 inches)
- ¼ cup minced fresh oregano
- ¼ cup olive oil
- ½ teaspoon salt
- ½ teaspoon pepper
  Assorted fresh vegetables

1. In a small bowl, combine the first six ingredients. Chill until serving.

2. Cut each pita bread into six wedges; arrange in a single layer on ungreased baking sheets. In a small bowl, combine the oregano, oil, salt and pepper; brush on the pita wedges. Bake pitas at 400° for 8-10 minutes or until crisp, turning once. Serve dip with chips and your choice of vegetables.

ZESTY SNACK MIX

Friends and family hint, year after year, that they're looking forward to this well-seasoned snack mix. The sesame snack sticks and shoestring potatoes are fun surprise additions.

—**BLANCHE SWALWELL** THUNDER BAY, ON

PREP: 15 MIN. • **BAKE:** 1 HOUR
MAKES: 12 QUARTS

- 11 cups Cheerios
- 8 cups Crispix
- 8 cups Corn Chex
- 6 cups bite-size Shredded Wheat
- 1 package (10 ounces) corn chips
- 1 jar (8 ounces) salted peanuts
- 1 package (8 ounces) pretzel sticks
- 1 package (7 ounces) sesame snack sticks
- 1 package (7 ounces) shoestring potato sticks
- 1 pound butter, cubed
- 3 tablespoons garlic powder
- 3 tablespoons onion powder
- 2 tablespoons hot pepper sauce
- 2 tablespoons lemon juice
- 2 tablespoons Worcestershire sauce
- 2 teaspoons garlic salt

1. In a large bowl, combine the first nine ingredients. In a large saucepan over low heat, melt the butter. Add the seasonings; stir until dissolved. Pour the butter mixture over the cereal mixture; stir to coat.

2. Spread in large greased roasting pans. Bake, uncovered, at 250° for 1 hour, stirring every 15 minutes. Store in airtight containers.

AUSSIE SAUSAGE ROLLS

AUSSIE SAUSAGE ROLLS

I was born and raised in Australia but moved to the U.S. when I married my husband. When I long for a taste of my homeland, I bake up a batch of these cute little sausage rolls and share them with my neighbors or co-workers.

—**MELISSA LANDON** PORT CHARLOTTE, FL

PREP: 30 MIN. • **BAKE:** 20 MIN.
MAKES: 3 DOZEN

- 1 **medium onion, finely chopped**
- 2 **tablespoons minced fresh chives or
  2 teaspoons dried chives**
- 2 **teaspoons minced fresh basil or
  ½ teaspoon dried basil**
- 2 **garlic cloves, minced**
- ½ **teaspoon salt**
- ¼ **teaspoon pepper**
- 1 **teaspoon paprika, divided**
- 1¼ **pounds bulk pork sausage**
- 1 **package (17.3 ounces) frozen puff pastry, thawed**

1. Preheat oven to 350°. Combine the first six ingredients and ¾ teaspoon paprika. Add sausage; mix lightly but thoroughly.

2. On a lightly floured surface, roll each pastry sheet into an 11x10½-in. rectangle. Cut lengthwise into three strips. Spread ½ cup sausage mixture lengthwise down the center of each strip. Fold over the sides to form a log, pinching the edges to seal. Cut each log into six pieces.

3. Place the rolls seam side down on a rack in a 15x10x1-in. pan. Sprinkle with the remaining paprika. Bake until golden brown and the sausage is no longer pink, 20-25 minutes.

PASTRAMI ROLL-UPS

For a book club event, I created pastrami roll-ups with cream cheese and a pickle. Those tasty appetizers quickly pulled a disappearing act.
—MERRITT HEINRICH OSWEGO, IL

START TO FINISH: 15 MIN.
MAKES: 4 DOZEN

- ¾ cup spreadable cream cheese
- ½ cup crumbled blue cheese
- 12 slices lean deli pastrami
- 12 dill pickle spears

1. In a small bowl, mix cream cheese and blue cheese until blended. If necessary, pat pastrami and pickles dry with paper towels.
2. Spread about 1 tablespoon of the cheese mixture over each pastrami slice; top with a pickle spear. Roll up tightly. Cut each roll into four slices. Refrigerate leftovers.

CHUNKY BLUE CHEESE DIP

Every time I make this quick dip, someone asks for the recipe. It only requires a few items, so it's a snap to put together. I often prepare the thick spread with Gorgonzola cheese and serve it with toasted pecans.
—SANDY SCHNEIDER NAPERVILLE, IL

START TO FINISH: 15 MIN.
MAKES: 12 SERVINGS (2 TABLESPOONS EACH)

- 1 package (8 ounces) cream cheese, softened
- ⅓ cup sour cream
- ½ teaspoon white pepper
- ¼ to ½ teaspoon salt
- 1 cup crumbled blue cheese
- ⅓ cup minced fresh chives
  Toasted chopped pecans, optional
  Apple and pear slices

Beat the first four ingredients until blended; gently stir in blue cheese and chives. Transfer to a serving bowl. If desired, sprinkle with pecans. Serve with apple and pear slices.

CRANBERRY HOT WINGS

Cranberry wings remind me of all the wonderful celebrations and parties we've had through the years. My daughter's friends can't get enough of them.
—NOREEN MCCORMICK DANEK CROMWELL, CT

PREP: 45 MIN. • **COOK:** 3 HOURS
MAKES: ABOUT 4 DOZEN

- 1 can (14 ounces) jellied cranberry sauce
- ½ cup orange juice
- ¼ cup hot pepper sauce
- 2 tablespoons soy sauce
- 2 tablespoons honey
- 1 tablespoon packed brown sugar
- 1 tablespoon Dijon mustard
- 2 teaspoons garlic powder
- 1 teaspoon dried minced onion
- 1 garlic clove, minced
- 5 pounds chicken wings (about 24 wings)
- 1 teaspoon salt
- 4 teaspoons cornstarch
- 2 tablespoons cold water

1. Whisk together the first 10 ingredients. To prepare the chicken, use a sharp knife to cut through two wing joints; discard the wing tips. Place wings in a 6-qt. slow cooker; sprinkle with salt. Pour cranberry mixture over top. Cook, covered, on low until tender, 3-4 hours.
2. To serve, remove wings to a 15x10x1-in. pan; arrange in a single layer. Preheat broiler.
3. Transfer the cooking juices to a skillet; skim fat. Bring juices to a boil; cook until mixture is reduced by half, about 15-20 minutes, stirring occasionally. Mix cornstarch and water until smooth; stir into the juices. Return to a boil, stirring constantly; cook and stir until thickened, 1-2 minutes.
4. Meanwhile, broil wings 3-4 in. from heat until lightly browned, 2-3 minutes. Brush with glaze before serving. Serve with the remaining glaze.

**CRANBERRY
HOT WINGS**
Noreen McCormick
Danek
Cromwell, CT

ROASTED RED PEPPER TRIANGLES

Full-flavored meats, cheeses and sweet peppers top a golden crust in this sensational treat. I recommend marinara sauce for dipping.

—AMY BELL ARLINGTON, TN

PREP: 35 MIN. • **BAKE:** 50 MIN.
MAKES: 2 DOZEN

- 2   tubes (8 ounces each) refrigerated crescent rolls
- 1½ cups finely diced fully cooked ham
- 1   cup shredded Swiss cheese
- 1   package (3 ounces) sliced pepperoni, chopped
- 8   slices provolone cheese
- 1   jar (12 ounces) roasted sweet red peppers, well drained and cut into strips
- 4   large eggs
- ¼   cup grated Parmesan cheese
- 3   teaspoons Italian salad dressing mix

1. Unroll one tube of crescent dough into a long rectangle; press onto the bottom and ¾ in. up the sides of a greased 13x9-in. baking dish. Seal seams and perforations. Top with half of the ham; layer with Swiss cheese, pepperoni, provolone cheese and remaining ham. Top with red peppers.

2. In a small bowl, whisk the eggs, Parmesan cheese and salad dressing mix. Set aside ¼ cup of the egg mixture and pour the rest over the peppers.

3. On a lightly floured surface, roll out the remaining crescent dough into a 13x9-in. rectangle; seal the seams and perforations. Place over filling; pinch edges to seal.

4. Cover and bake at 350° for 30 minutes. Uncover; brush with reserved egg mixture. Bake 20-25 minutes longer or until crust is golden brown. Cool on a wire rack for 5 minutes. Cut into triangles. Serve warm with marinara sauce if desired.

HOT COLLARDS AND ARTICHOKE DIP

You've probably had spinach and artichoke dip lots of times, but now it's time to swap in collard greens for the spinach to try a Southern twist. Serve this dish with warm garlic naan or tortilla chips.

—BILLIE WILLIAMS-HENDERSON BOWIE, MD

PREP: 20 MIN. • **BAKE:** 25 MIN.
MAKES: 24 SERVINGS (¼ CUP EACH)

- 12 ounces frozen chopped collard greens (about 4 cups), thawed and squeezed dry
- 2   jars (7½ ounces each) marinated quartered artichoke hearts, drained and chopped
- 1   cup sour cream
- 1   package (6½ ounces) garlic-herb spreadable cheese
- 1   cup grated Parmesan cheese
- 10 thick-sliced peppered bacon strips, cooked and crumbled
- ¾   cup mayonnaise
- 1½ cups shredded part-skim mozzarella cheese, divided
     Garlic naan flatbreads, warmed and cut into wedges

1. In a large bowl, mix the first seven ingredients and 1 cup mozzarella cheese until blended. Transfer to a greased 11x7-in. baking dish. Sprinkle with the remaining mozzarella cheese.

2. Bake, uncovered, at 350° for 20-25 minutes or until heated through and cheese is melted. Serve with naan.

FAST FIX ▶

SPICED NUT MIX

When we were newlyweds, our first Christmas was pretty lean. I usually made presents, but that year I had no idea what I could afford to put together. A good friend gave me a special gift—this recipe and a sack of ingredients. I think of her every time I stir up this mix.

—PATTI HOLLAND PARKER, CO

START TO FINISH: 30 MIN.
MAKES: ABOUT 10 CUPS

  3 large egg whites
  2 teaspoons water
  2 cans (12 ounces each) salted peanuts
  1 cup whole blanched almonds
  1 cup walnut halves
1¾ cups sugar
  3 tablespoons pumpkin pie spice
  ¾ teaspoon salt
  1 cup raisins

1. In a bowl, beat egg whites and water until frothy. Add nuts; stir gently to coat. Combine sugar, pie spice and salt; add to nut mixture and stir gently to coat. Fold in raisins. Spread into two greased 15x10x1-in. baking pans.
2. Bake, uncovered, at 300° for 20-25 minutes or until lightly browned, stirring every 10 minutes. Cool. Store in an airtight container.

★ ★ ★ ★ ★ **READER REVIEW**

"I made this recipe twice this Christmas season and gave the nuts to friends in pretty jars with a ribbon attached. I also added pecan halves and dried cranberries. This recipe is definitely a keeper."

CACTUSPAT TASTEOFHOME.COM

BLUE CHEESE-STUFFED SHRIMP

Shrimp look beautiful when stuffed with blue cheese and parsley. We serve them on their own, or sometimes pass the cocktail sauce.

—AMY DOLLIMOUNT GLACE BAY, NS

PREP: 20 MIN. + CHILLING
MAKES: 2 DOZEN

  3 ounces cream cheese, softened
  ⅔ cup minced fresh parsley, divided
  ¼ cup crumbled blue cheese
  1 teaspoon chopped shallot
  ½ teaspoon Creole mustard
 24 cooked jumbo shrimp, peeled and deveined

1. In a small bowl, beat the cream cheese until smooth. Beat in ⅓ cup parsley, blue cheese, shallot and mustard. Refrigerate for at least 1 hour.
2. Starting with the tail end of each shrimp, make a deep slit along the deveining line to within ¼ to ½ in. of the bottom. Stuff with cream cheese mixture; press remaining parsley onto cream cheese mixture.

CORN BREAD
PIZZA WHEELS

CORN BREAD PIZZA WHEELS

Sweet corn bread and chili ingredients make up this impressive—and impressively easy—appetizer.

—**PATRICK LUCAS** COCHRAN, GA

PREP: 25 MIN. • **BAKE:** 15 MIN.
MAKES: 2 PIZZAS (8 SERVINGS EACH)

- 1 pound ground beef
- 1 can (16 ounces) kidney beans, rinsed and drained
- 1 can (8 ounces) tomato sauce
- 4 teaspoons chili powder
- 1 jar (4 ounces) diced pimientos, drained
- 1 can (4 ounces) chopped green chilies, drained
- 1 cup shredded cheddar cheese
- 2 tablespoons cornmeal
- 2 tubes (11½ ounces each) refrigerated corn bread twists
  Shredded lettuce, sliced tomatoes and sour cream

1. In a large skillet, cook the beef over medium heat until no longer pink; drain. Add beans, tomato sauce and chili powder. Simmer, uncovered, until liquid has evaporated. Remove from the heat; cool. Stir in the pimientos, chilies and cheese; set aside.
2. Sprinkle two greased 14-in. pizza pans with cornmeal. Pat the corn bread dough into a 14-in. circle on each pan. With a sharp knife, cut a 7-in. "X" in the center of the dough. Cut another 7-in. "X" to form eight pie-shaped wedges in the center.
3. Spoon filling around the uncut edge of the dough. Fold the points of the dough wedges over the filling and tuck them under the outer edge of the ring; pinch to seal (the filling will be visible).
4. Bake at 400° for 15-20 minutes or until golden brown. Fill the center with lettuce, tomatoes and sour cream.

TEST KITCHEN TIP
For longer storage, sweet onions can be frozen. Chop and place in a 15x10x1-in. pan in the freezer. When they're frozen, place in freezer bags or containers and freeze for up to 1 year.

BAKED ONION DIP

I've found that some people like this cheesy dip so much, they can't tear themselves away from the appetizer table to eat dinner!

—**MONA ZIGNEGO** HARTFORD, WI

PREP: 5 MIN. • **BAKE:** 40 MIN.
MAKES: 2 CUPS

- 1 cup mayonnaise
- 1 cup chopped sweet onion
- 1 tablespoon grated Parmesan cheese
- ¼ teaspoon garlic salt
- 1 cup shredded Swiss cheese
  Minced fresh parsley, optional
  Assorted crackers

1. In a large bowl, combine mayonnaise, onion, Parmesan cheese and garlic salt; stir in Swiss cheese. Spoon into a 1-qt. baking dish.
2. Bake, uncovered, at 325° for 40 minutes or until golden brown. If desired sprinkle with parsley. Serve with crackers.

FAST FIX

SMOKED SALMON PINWHEELS

Inexpensive and impressive, this must-have recipe will let you wow your guests without spending all day in the kitchen!

—**CRISSY MATHERS** SAN MIGUEL, CA

START TO FINISH: 20 MIN.
MAKES: 32 APPETIZERS

- 1 package (8 ounces) cream cheese, softened
- 1 tablespoon snipped fresh dill
- 1 tablespoon capers, drained
- ½ teaspoon garlic powder
- ½ teaspoon lemon juice
- 4 spinach tortillas (8 inches), room temperature
- ½ pound smoked salmon fillets, flaked

1. In a small bowl, combine the cream cheese, dill, capers, garlic powder and lemon juice. Spread over tortillas; top with salmon. Roll up tightly.
2. Cut roll into 1-in. pieces; secure with toothpicks. Chill. Discard toothpicks before serving.

APPETIZER TOMATO CHEESE BREAD

I found this recipe a few years ago in a dairy cookbook, and it has become a family favorite. We milk 180 cows and have a large garden, so we welcome dishes that use both dairy and fresh vegetables. My husband and our two children are mostly meat-and-potato eaters...but I don't hear any complaints when I make this bread!

—**PENNEY KESTER** SPRINGVILLE, NY

PREP: 20 MIN. • **BAKE:** 25 MIN. + STANDING
MAKES: 12 SERVINGS

- 2 **tablespoons butter**
- 1 **medium onion, minced**
- 1 **cup shredded cheddar cheese**
- ½ **cup sour cream**
- ¼ **cup mayonnaise**
- ¾ **teaspoon salt**
- ¼ **teaspoon pepper**
- ¼ **teaspoon dried oregano**
  Pinch rubbed sage
- 2 **cups biscuit/baking mix**
- ⅔ **cup milk**
- 3 **medium tomatoes, cut into ¼-inch slices**
  Paprika

1. In a small skillet, heat butter over medium heat. Add the onion and cook until tender. Remove from the heat. Stir in the cheese, sour cream, mayonnaise and seasonings; set aside.

2. In a bowl, combine the baking mix and milk to form a soft dough. Turn the dough onto a well-floured surface; knead lightly 10-12 times. Pat into a greased 13x9-in. baking dish, pushing dough up the sides of the dish to form a shallow rim. Arrange tomato slices over the dough. Spread with topping; sprinkle with paprika.

3. Bake at 400° for 25 minutes. Let stand for 10 minutes before cutting.

WHITE CHOCOLATE PARTY MIX

I get rave reviews every time I prepare this crispy combo of cereal, popcorn, pretzels, nuts and candies. Coated in white chocolate, this mix is great for meetings, parties, potlucks and gifts.

—**ROSE WENTZEL** ST. LOUIS, MO

PREP: 10 MIN. + STANDING • **COOK:** 5 MIN.
MAKES: 9½ QUARTS

- 16 **cups popped popcorn**
- 3 **cups Frosted Cheerios**
- 1 **package (10 ounces) fat-free pretzel sticks**
- 2 **cups milk chocolate M&M's**
- 1½ **cups pecan halves**
- 1 **package (8 ounces) milk chocolate English toffee bits or brickle toffee bits**
- 2 **packages (10 to 12 ounces each) white baking chips**
- 2 **tablespoons canola oil**

1. In a large bowl, combine the first six ingredients. In a microwave or heavy saucepan over low heat, melt the baking chips with oil; stir until smooth.

2. Pour over the popcorn mixture and toss to coat. Immediately spread the mix onto two baking sheets; let stand until set, about 2 hours. Store in airtight containers.

PORK MEATBALLS WITH
CHIMICHURRI SAUCE

PORK MEATBALLS WITH CHIMICHURRI SAUCE

If you've never had chimichurri sauce with meatballs, it's time to give it a try!

—**AMY CHASE** VANDERHOOF, BC

PREP: 20 MIN. • **BAKE:** 15 MIN.
MAKES: 5 DOZEN (⅔ CUP SAUCE)

- ½ cup dry bread crumbs
- ½ cup 2% milk
- 2 tablespoons grated onion
- 1 tablespoon ground cumin
- 1 tablespoon dried oregano
- 1 tablespoon lemon juice
- 2 teaspoons salt
- ¼ teaspoon coarsely ground pepper
- 2 pounds ground pork

CHIMICHURRI SAUCE

- 3 garlic cloves, peeled
- 1 cup packed Italian flat leaf parsley
- ¼ cup packed fresh cilantro leaves
- 1 teaspoon salt
- ¼ teaspoon coarsely ground pepper
- 2 tablespoons red wine vinegar
- ½ cup extra virgin olive oil

1. Preheat oven to 450°. In a large bowl, combine the first eight ingredients. Add the pork; mix lightly but thoroughly. Shape into 1-in. balls. Place on a greased rack in a 15x10x1-in. baking pan. Bake 15-20 minutes or until the meatballs are cooked through. Let stand 5 minutes.

2. Meanwhile, place the garlic in a small food processor; pulse until chopped. Add the parsley, cilantro, salt and pepper; pulse until finely chopped. Add vinegar. While processing, gradually add oil in a steady stream.

3. In a large bowl, toss the meatballs with half of the chimichurri sauce. Transfer to a platter. Serve with the remaining sauce for dipping.

PARMESAN SESAME CRACKERS

These rustic-looking crackers are crispy, crunchy and topped with cheese and plenty of seeds. Perfect for parties, they have none of the preservatives and additives of store-bought alternatives!

—ELENA IORGA HELENA, MT

PREP: 25 MIN. • **BAKE:** 15 MIN. + COOLING
MAKES: 4 DOZEN

- 2 cups all-purpose flour
- ⅓ cup sesame seeds
- ⅓ cup shredded Parmesan cheese
- 2 tablespoons poppy seeds
- 1 teaspoon baking powder
- ½ teaspoon salt
- ⅔ cup plus 2 tablespoons warm water, divided
- ⅓ cup canola oil
- 1 large egg white

TOPPING

- 2 tablespoons shredded Parmesan cheese
- 1 tablespoon sesame seeds
- 1 tablespoon poppy seeds

1. In a small bowl, combine the first six ingredients. Gradually add ⅔ cup water and oil, tossing with a fork until the dough forms a ball. Turn onto a lightly floured surface; knead 8-10 times.

2. Divide the dough in half. Working directly on a baking sheet coated with cooking spray, roll each ball into a 12x9-in. rectangle. Pierce the dough with a fork.

3. Whisk together the egg white and remaining water; brush over the dough. Combine topping ingredients; sprinkle over the dough.

4. Score dough in each pan into 24 pieces. Bake at 400° for 15-18 minutes or until golden brown. Immediately cut along the scored lines; cool in pans on wire racks. Store in an airtight container.

HOT SAUSAGE & BEAN DIP

This is a spin-off of a Mexican dip I once had. The original was wicked good, but I was going through an I'm-so-over-Mexican-dip phase and decided to switch it up. If you take this one to a party you can be sure no one else will bring anything like it!

—MANDY RIVERS LEXINGTON, SC

PREP: 25 MIN. • **BAKE:** 20 MIN.
MAKES: 16 SERVINGS (¼ CUP EACH)

- 1 pound bulk hot Italian sausage
- 1 medium onion, finely chopped
- 4 garlic cloves, minced
- ½ cup dry white wine or chicken broth
- ½ teaspoon dried oregano
- ¼ teaspoon salt
- ¼ teaspoon dried thyme
- 1 package (8 ounces) cream cheese, softened
- 1 package (6 ounces) fresh baby spinach, coarsely chopped
- 1 can (15 ounces) cannellini beans, rinsed and drained
- 1 cup chopped seeded tomatoes
- 1 cup shredded part-skim mozzarella cheese
- ½ cup shredded Parmesan cheese
  Assorted crackers or toasted French bread baguette slices

1. Preheat oven to 375°. In a large skillet, cook sausage, onion and garlic over medium heat until the sausage is no longer pink, breaking up the meat into crumbles; drain. Stir in wine, oregano, salt and thyme. Bring to a boil; cook until the liquid is almost evaporated.

2. Add cream cheese; stir until melted. Stir in spinach, beans and tomatoes; cook and stir until the spinach is wilted. Transfer to a greased 8-in. square or 1½-qt. baking dish. Sprinkle with cheeses.

3. Bake until bubbly, 20-25 minutes. Serve with crackers.

**HOT SAUSAGE
& BEAN DIP**
Mandy Rivers
Lexington, SC

RISOTTO BALLS (ARANCINI)

My Italian Grandma made these for me. I still ask for them when I visit her, and so do my children. They freeze well, so I make my own ahead of time.

—**GRETCHEN WHELAN** SAN FRANCISCO, CA

PREP: 35 MIN. • **BAKE:** 25 MIN.
MAKES: ABOUT 3 DOZEN

- 1½ cups water
- 1 cup uncooked arborio rice
- 1 teaspoon salt
- 2 large eggs, lightly beaten
- ⅔ cup sun-dried tomato pesto
- 2 cups panko (Japanese) bread crumbs, divided
  Marinara sauce, warmed

1. Preheat oven to 375°. In a large saucepan, combine water, rice and salt; bring to a boil. Reduce heat; simmer, covered, 18-20 minutes or until liquid is absorbed and rice is tender. Let stand, covered, 10 minutes. Transfer to a large bowl; cool slightly. Add eggs and pesto; stir in 1 cup bread crumbs.
2. Place the remaining bread crumbs in a shallow bowl. Shape rice mixture into 1¼-in. balls. Roll balls in bread crumbs, patting to help coating adhere. Place on greased 15x10x1-in. baking pans. Bake 25-30 minutes or until golden brown. Serve with marinara sauce.

SMOKED SALMON DEVILED EGGS

Flaky salmon and creamy sauce go so well over hard-boiled eggs. Drizzle the sauce or serve it on the side—it's fantastic either way.

—**MARINELA DRAGAN** PORTLAND, OR

PREP: 30 MIN. • **COOK:** 20 MIN.
MAKES: 32 APPETIZERS

- 16 hard-cooked large eggs
- 4 ounces cream cheese, softened
- ⅓ cup mayonnaise
- 2 tablespoons snipped fresh dill
- 1 tablespoon capers, drained and finely chopped
- 1 tablespoon lemon juice
- 1 teaspoon horseradish sauce
- 1 teaspoon prepared mustard
- ½ teaspoon freshly ground pepper
- ¾ cup flaked smoked salmon fillet

SAUCE

- 1 cup mayonnaise
- ¼ cup plus 2 tablespoons ketchup
- 1 tablespoon horseradish sauce
- 1 tablespoon prepared mustard
- ¼ cup diced smoked salmon fillets, optional

1. Cut eggs lengthwise in half. Remove the yolks, reserving the whites. In a small bowl, mash yolks. Mix in the cream cheese, mayonnaise, dill, capers, lemon juice, horseradish sauce, mustard and pepper. Fold in salmon. Spoon into the egg whites. Refrigerate, covered, until serving.
2. For the sauce, in a small bowl, mix mayonnaise, ketchup, horseradish sauce and mustard. If desired, top eggs with salmon; serve with sauce.

TEST KITCHEN TIP
The easiest way to transport deviled eggs is in an egg plate—they're widely available in stores. If you don't have one, you can use mini cupcake papers (paper or foil) to hold the eggs in place when you're transporting and serving them.

MAKE AHEAD
TOMATO-HERB FOCACCIA

With its medley of herbs and tomatoes, this rustic bread will enliven any occasion, whether it's a family dinner or a gathering of friends. It never lasts long!
—JANET MILLER INDIANAPOLIS, IN

PREP: 30 MIN. + RISING • **BAKE:** 20 MIN.
MAKES: 1 LOAF (12 PIECES)

- 1 package (¼ ounce) active dry yeast
- 1 cup warm water (110° to 115°)
- 2 tablespoons olive oil, divided
- 1½ teaspoons salt
- 1 teaspoon sugar
- 1 teaspoon garlic powder
- 1 teaspoon each dried oregano, thyme and rosemary, crushed
- ½ teaspoon dried basil
  Dash pepper
- 2 to 2½ cups all-purpose flour, divided
- 2 plum tomatoes, thinly sliced
- ¼ cup shredded part-skim mozzarella cheese
- 1 tablespoon grated Parmesan cheese

1. In a large bowl, dissolve yeast in warm water. Add 1 tablespoon oil, salt, sugar, garlic powder, herbs, pepper and 1½ cups flour. Beat until smooth. Stir in enough of the remaining flour to form a soft dough (dough will be sticky).
2. Turn dough onto a floured surface; knead until smooth and elastic, 6-8 minutes. Place in a greased bowl, turning once to grease the top. Cover and let rise in a warm place until doubled, about 1 hour.
3. Punch dough down. Cover and let rest for 10 minutes. Shape into a 13x9-in. rectangle; place on a greased baking sheet. Cover and let rise until doubled, about 30 minutes. With fingertips, make several dimples in the top of the dough.
4. Brush dough with the remaining oil; arrange tomatoes over the top. Sprinkle with cheeses. Bake at 400° for 20-25 minutes or until golden brown. Remove to a wire rack.
FREEZE OPTION *Freeze cooled focaccia squares in freezer containers, separating layers with waxed paper. To use, reheat squares on a baking sheet in a preheated 400° oven until heated through.*

MEATBALL SLIDERS

You can make the patties ahead of time and keep them warm in the slow cooker or on the stovetop.
—HILARY BREINHOLT GLENWOOD, UT

PREP: 15 MIN. • **BAKE:** 25 MIN.
MAKES: 16 SERVINGS

- 1½ pounds bulk Italian sausage
- 16 cubes part-skim mozzarella cheese (1-inch; about 8 ounces total)
- 1 jar (24 ounces) spaghetti sauce
- 1 jar (8.1 ounces) prepared pesto
- 16 dinner rolls, split and toasted

1. Divide sausage into 16 portions. Shape each portion around a cube of cheese. Place on a greased rack in a shallow baking pan. Bake at 350° for 25-30 minutes or until the meat is no longer pink. Remove to paper towels to drain.
2. In a large saucepan, combine spaghetti sauce and pesto; bring just to a boil over medium heat, stirring occasionally. Add the meatballs; heat through, stirring gently. Serve on rolls.

**POLENTA
MUSHROOM
APPETIZERS**

POLENTA MUSHROOM APPETIZERS

You probably have most of the simple ingredients on hand already for this fantastic appetizer.

—META WEST ABILENE, KS

PREP: 40 MIN. + COOLING • **BAKE:** 15 MIN.
MAKES: 32 APPETIZERS

- 2 cups chicken broth
- 2 cups 2% milk
- ½ teaspoon salt
- 1 cup cornmeal
- ¼ cup grated Parmesan cheese

MUSHROOM TOPPING

- ½ pound thinly sliced fresh mushrooms
- 3 tablespoons olive oil
- 1 tablespoon butter
- 6 garlic cloves, minced
- 1 teaspoon minced fresh thyme or
  ¼ teaspoon dried thyme
- ½ teaspoon salt
- ¼ teaspoon pepper
- 2 tablespoons white wine or
  additional chicken broth
- 1 tablespoon lemon juice
- ¼ cup grated Parmesan cheese

1. In a large heavy saucepan, bring the broth, milk and salt to a boil. Reduce heat to a gentle boil; slowly whisk in the cornmeal. Cook and stir with a wooden spoon for 15-20 minutes or until the polenta is thickened and pulls away cleanly from the sides of the pan. Stir in cheese.
2. Spread into a greased 11x7-in. baking dish. Cool to room temperature, about 30 minutes. Cut the polenta into 16 pieces, then cut each diagonally in half to make 32 triangles; place on a greased baking sheet. Bake at 350° for 12-15 minutes or until light golden brown.
3. Saute mushrooms in oil and butter until tender. Add garlic, thyme, salt and pepper; cook 1 minute longer. Add wine and lemon juice; cook and stir until the liquid is almost absorbed.
4. Top each polenta triangle with 1½ teaspoons of the mushrooms; sprinkle with cheese. Serve warm.

FAST FIX ▶

SMOKED SALMON CHEESE SPREAD

Pretzels, chips and veggies would all make delicious dippers for this creamy salmon dip. It's wonderful during the holidays with crackers and wine.

—JILL CAMPBELL HUNTSVILLE, TX

START TO FINISH: 15 MIN.
MAKES: 2½ CUPS

- 2 packages (8 ounces each) cream cheese, softened
- 1 package (4 ounces) smoked salmon or lox
- 3 tablespoons horseradish sauce
- 1 tablespoon lemon juice
- 1 tablespoon Worcestershire sauce
- ¼ teaspoon Creole seasoning
- ¼ teaspoon coarsely ground pepper
  Chopped walnuts and snipped fresh dill
  Assorted crackers

Place the first seven ingredients in a food processor; process until blended. Transfer to a serving dish; sprinkle with walnuts and dill. Refrigerate, covered, until serving. Serve with crackers.
NOTE *The following spice mix may be substituted for 1 teaspoon Creole seasoning: ¼ teaspoon each salt, garlic powder and paprika; and a pinch each of dried thyme, ground cumin and cayenne pepper.*

TEST KITCHEN TIP

If you decide to buy a chunk of Parmesan cheese and grate your own, be sure to use the finest section on your grating tool. You can also use a blender or food processor. Simply cut the cheese into 1-inch cubes and process 1 cup of cubes at a time on high until finely grated.

SUMMER ORZO,
PAGE 66

SIDES & SALADS

"He has shown kindness by giving you rain from heaven and crops in their seasons; he provides you with plenty of food and fills your hearts with joy."

ACTS 14:17

MINTY WATERMELON-CUCUMBER SALAD
Roblynn Hunnisett
Guelph, ON

MINTY WATERMELON-CUCUMBER SALAD

Capturing fantastic flavors of summer, this refreshing, beautiful salad will be the talk of any picnic or potluck.

—ROBLYNN HUNNISETT GUELPH, ON

START TO FINISH: 20 MIN.
MAKES: 16 SERVINGS

- 8 cups cubed seedless watermelon
- 2 English cucumbers, halved lengthwise and sliced
- 6 green onions, chopped
- ¼ cup minced fresh mint
- ¼ cup balsamic vinegar
- ¼ cup olive oil
- ½ teaspoon salt
- ½ teaspoon pepper

In a large bowl, combine watermelon, cucumbers, green onions and mint. In a small bowl, whisk the remaining ingredients. Pour over the salad and toss to coat. Serve immediately or refrigerate, covered, up to 2 hours before serving.

CATALINA TACO SALAD

The teen campers at the youth camp my husband directs love this quick and easy taco salad. Our daughter has requested it two years in a row for her birthday dinner.

—KAY CURTIS GUTHRIE, OK

START TO FINISH: 25 MIN.
MAKES: 12 SERVINGS

- 1½ pounds lean ground beef (90% lean)
- 3 cups shredded cheddar cheese
- 1 can (15 ounces) pinto beans, rinsed and drained
- 2 medium tomatoes, seeded and chopped
- 1 large onion, chopped
- 1 bunch romaine, torn
- 1 package (12 ounces) corn chips
- 1 bottle (24 ounces) Catalina salad dressing

1. In a large skillet, cook the beef over medium heat until no longer pink; drain. Transfer to a large serving bowl.
2. Add the cheese, beans, tomatoes, onion, romaine and corn chips. Drizzle with dressing; gently toss to coat.

HASH BROWN BROCCOLI BAKE

Here's a perfect dish for a potluck or buffet. It goes well with fish, poultry, pork or beef. Cheddar cheese can be substituted for Swiss. I'll often double the recipe to serve a crowd.

—JEANETTE VOLKER WALTON, NE

PREP: 25 MIN. • **BAKE:** 50 MIN.
MAKES: 14 SERVINGS

- 4 tablespoons butter, divided
- 2 tablespoons all-purpose flour
- 1 teaspoon salt
- ⅛ teaspoon ground nutmeg
- ⅛ teaspoon pepper
- 2 cups 2% milk
- 1 package (8 ounces) cream cheese, cubed
- 2 cups shredded Swiss cheese
- 6 cups frozen shredded hash brown potatoes (about 20 ounces), thawed
- 1 package (16 ounces) frozen chopped broccoli, thawed
- ½ cup dry bread crumbs

1. Preheat oven to 350°. In a large saucepan, melt 2 tablespoons of the butter. Stir in the flour, salt, nutmeg and pepper until smooth; gradually add milk. Bring to a boil; cook and stir until thickened, about 2 minutes. Remove from heat. Add cheeses; stir until melted. Stir in the potatoes.
2. Spoon half the potato mixture into a greased 2-qt. baking dish. Top with the broccoli and the remaining potato mixture. Bake, covered, for 35 minutes.
3. Melt the remaining butter; toss with bread crumbs. Sprinkle over casserole. Bake, covered, until heated through and topping is golden, 15-20 minutes.

TRIPLE MASH WITH HORSERADISH BREAD CRUMBS

Rutabagas have a subtle sweetness we love to pair with Yukon Gold potatoes and parsnips. Add a zip of horseradish, and you've got a creamy treat.

—LILY JULOW LAWRENCEVILLE, GA

START TO FINISH: 30 MIN.
MAKES: 12 SERVINGS

- 1¾ pounds Yukon Gold potatoes, peeled and cubed
- 4 medium parsnips (about 1¼ pounds), peeled and cubed
- 2½ cups cubed peeled rutabaga
- 2 teaspoons salt
- ½ cup butter, divided
- 1 cup soft bread crumbs
- 2 tablespoons prepared horseradish
- 1 cup whole milk
- ¼ teaspoon pepper

1. Place the potatoes, parsnips, rutabaga and salt in a 6-qt. stockpot; add water to cover. Bring to a boil. Reduce heat; cook, uncovered, 15-20 minutes or until tender.

2. Meanwhile, in a skillet, heat ¼ cup butter over medium heat. Add bread crumbs; cook and stir 3-5 minutes or until toasted. Stir in horseradish; remove from heat.

3. Drain the vegetables; return to pot and mash over low heat, gradually adding milk, pepper and remaining butter. Transfer to a serving dish; sprinkle with bread crumbs.

LEMON RICE SALAD

This refreshing salad is wonderful year-round. The people I serve it to like the combination of flavors—I like that it can be prepared ahead!

—MARGERY RICHMOND LACOMBE, AB

PREP: 25 MIN. + CHILLING
MAKES: 16 SERVINGS

- 1 cup olive oil
- ⅓ cup white wine vinegar
- 1 garlic clove, minced
- 1 to 2 teaspoons grated lemon peel
- 2 teaspoons sugar
- 1 teaspoon Dijon mustard
- ½ teaspoon salt
- 6 cups cooked long grain rice
- 2 cup cooked wild rice
- 2 cups diced seeded cucumbers
- ⅔ cup thinly sliced green onions
- ¼ cup minced fresh parsley
- ¼ cup minced fresh basil or 1 tablespoon dried basil
- ½ teaspoon pepper
- ½ cup chopped pecans, toasted

1. For dressing, place the first seven ingredients in a jar with a tight-fitting lid; shake well. In a large bowl, toss long grain rice and wild rice with the dressing. Refrigerate, covered, overnight.

2. Stir cucumbers, green onions, parsley, basil and pepper into the rice mixture. Refrigerate, covered, for 2 hours. Stir in pecans just before serving.

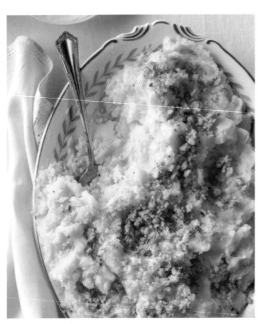

SLOW COOKER
WILD RICE WITH DRIED BLUEBERRIES

I love the combination of rice and fruit, so this is a go-to Thanksgiving side dish at my house. I toss in mushrooms and toasted almonds; you can also include dried cherries or cranberries if you like.

—JANIE COLLE HUTCHINSON, KS

PREP: 15 MIN. • **COOK:** 3¼ HOURS
MAKES: 16 SERVINGS

- 2   tablespoons butter
- 8   ounces sliced fresh mushrooms
- 3   cups uncooked wild rice
- 8   green onions, sliced
- 1   teaspoon salt
- ½   teaspoon pepper
- 4   cans (14½ ounces each) vegetable broth
- 1   cup chopped pecans, toasted
- 1   cup dried blueberries

In a large skillet, heat butter over medium heat. Add mushrooms; cook and stir for 4-5 minutes or until tender. In a 5-qt. slow cooker, combine rice, mushrooms, onions, salt and pepper. Pour broth over the rice mixture. Cook, covered, on low for 3-4 hours or until rice is tender. Stir in pecans and blueberries. Cook, covered, 15 minutes longer or until heated through.

NOTE *To toast nuts, bake in a shallow pan in a 350° oven for 5-10 minutes or cook in a skillet over low heat until lightly browned, stirring occasionally.*

TEST KITCHEN TIP
You can store white and wild rice in airtight containers indefinitely. Always rinse wild rice before cooking.

FAST FIX
LAYERED SALAD FOR A CROWD

This salad is a favorite with my three sons. I took it to a luncheon honoring our school district's food service manager, and she asked for the recipe! I like to make the dressing the day before so the flavors blend together.

—LINDA ASHLEY LEESBURG, GA

START TO FINISH: 20 MIN.
MAKES: 20 SERVINGS

- 1   cup mayonnaise
- ¼   cup whole milk
- 2   teaspoons dill weed
- ½   teaspoon seasoning blend
- 1   bunch romaine, torn
- 2   medium carrots, grated
- 1   cup chopped red onion
- 1   medium cucumber, sliced
- 1   package (10 ounces) frozen peas, thawed
- 1½ cups shredded cheddar cheese
- 8   bacon strips, cooked and crumbled

1. For the dressing, in a small bowl, whisk the mayonnaise, milk, dill and seasoning blend.
2. In a 4-qt. clear glass serving bowl, layer the romaine, carrots, onion and cucumber (do not toss). Pour the dressing over the top; sprinkle with peas, cheese and bacon. Cover and refrigerate until serving.

FAST FIX
BRUSSELS SPROUTS & KALE SAUTE

This colorful side dish is filled with healthy greens. It pairs well with turkey, potatoes and other potluck staples. The crispy salami—my kid's favorite ingredient—makes it over-the-top delicious.
—**JENNIFER MCNABB** BRENTWOOD, TN

START TO FINISH: 30 MIN.
MAKES: 12 SERVINGS

- ¼ pound thinly sliced hard salami, cut into ¼-inch strips
- 1½ teaspoons olive oil
- 2 tablespoons butter
- 2 pounds fresh Brussels sprouts, thinly sliced
- 2 cups shredded fresh kale
- 1 large onion, finely chopped
- ½ teaspoon kosher salt
- ⅛ teaspoon cayenne pepper
- ¼ teaspoon coarsely ground pepper
- 1 garlic clove, minced
- ½ cup chicken broth
- ½ cup chopped walnuts
- 1 tablespoon balsamic vinegar

1. In a Dutch oven, cook and stir salami in oil over medium-high heat for 3-5 minutes or until crisp. Remove to paper towels with a slotted spoon; reserve the drippings in the pan.
2. Add butter to the drippings; heat over medium-high heat. Add Brussels sprouts, kale, onion, salt, cayenne and black pepper; cook and stir until vegetables are crisp-tender. Add garlic; cook for 1 minute longer.
3. Stir in the broth; bring to a boil. Reduce heat; cover and cook for 4-5 minutes or until Brussels sprouts are tender. Stir in walnuts and vinegar. Serve with salami strips.

CORN BREAD PUDDING

Ready for the oven in just 5 minutes, this comforting side dish pairs perfectly with every thing from eggs to seafood. I adapted it from my mom's recipe. It never fails to please a crowd.
—**BOB GEBHARDT** WAUSAU, WI

PREP: 5 MIN. • **BAKE:** 40 MIN.
MAKES: 12 SERVINGS

- 2 large eggs
- 1 cup sour cream
- 1 can (15¼ ounces) whole kernel corn, drained
- 1 can (14¾ ounces) cream-style corn
- ½ cup butter, melted
- 1 package (8½ ounces) corn bread/muffin mix
- ¼ teaspoon paprika

1. In a large bowl, combine the first five ingredients. Stir in corn bread mix just until blended. Pour into a greased 3-qt. baking dish. Sprinkle with paprika.
2. Bake, uncovered, at 350° for 40-45 minutes or until a knife inserted in the center comes out clean. Serve warm.

FAST FIX
EASY PEASY SLAW

I get tons of compliments when I bring out this slaw. Brightened up with peas, peanuts and poppy seed dressing, it's fresh and colorful and has a nice, satisfying crunch.
—**SUE ORT** DES MOINES, IA

START TO FINISH: 5 MIN.
MAKES: 12 SERVINGS

- 4 cups frozen peas (about 16 ounces), thawed
- 1 package (14 ounces) coleslaw mix
- 4 green onions, chopped
- 1 cup poppy seed salad dressing
- 1 cup sweet and crunchy peanuts or honey-roasted peanuts

Place peas, coleslaw mix and green onions in a large bowl. Pour dressing over the salad and toss to coat. Stir in the peanuts just before serving.

CORN BREAD
PUDDING

TANGY POTATO SALAD WITH RADISHES

Summer's approach makes my family think of potato salad. This tangy side is also great in the winter—serve it hot with cubed ham.

—**PEGGY GWILLIM** STRASBOURG, SK

PREP: 40 MIN. + CHILLING
MAKES: 13 SERVINGS

- 4 pounds red potatoes, cubed
- 3 tablespoons plus ⅔ cup white wine vinegar, divided
- 8 hard-cooked large eggs, sliced
- 6 radishes, thinly sliced
- ½ cup minced chives
- 1 cup buttermilk
- ½ cup mayonnaise
- 2 tablespoons prepared mustard
- 1 tablespoon dried minced onion
- 1 tablespoon dill weed
- ¼ teaspoon salt
- ¼ teaspoon pepper

1. Place potatoes in a Dutch oven; cover with water. Bring to a boil. Reduce heat; cover and cook for 10-15 minutes or until tender. Drain. Immediately sprinkle with 3 tablespoons white wine vinegar; cool.

2. Place the potatoes in a large bowl. Add the eggs, radishes and chives. In a small bowl, combine the buttermilk, mayonnaise, mustard, onion, dill, salt, pepper and remaining vinegar. Pour over the potato mixture and gently stir to coat. Refrigerate until chilled.

FAST FIX
SHRIMP ORZO SALAD

A half-hour is all you need to mix up this colorful crowd-pleaser. With plenty of shrimp, artichoke hearts, olives, peppers and a host of herbs, it's a tasty change of pace from the usual pasta salad. The dish completes any buffet.

—**GINGER JOHNSON** POTTSTOWN, PA

START TO FINISH: 30 MIN.
MAKES: 16 SERVINGS

- 1 package (16 ounces) orzo pasta
- ¾ pound cooked medium shrimp, peeled, deveined and cut into thirds
- 1 cup finely chopped green pepper
- 1 cup finely chopped sweet red pepper
- 1 can (14 ounces) water-packed artichoke hearts, rinsed, drained and quartered
- ¾ cup finely chopped red onion
- ½ cup minced fresh parsley
- ⅓ cup chopped fresh dill
- ⅓ cup chopped pimiento-stuffed olives
- ½ cup white wine vinegar
- 3 garlic cloves, minced
- 1 teaspoon salt
- ½ teaspoon dried basil
- ½ teaspoon dried oregano
- ½ teaspoon pepper
- ¼ cup olive oil

1. Cook pasta according to package directions; drain and rinse in cold water. Place in a large bowl; add the shrimp, peppers, artichokes, onion, parsley, dill and olives.

2. In a small bowl, combine the vinegar, garlic, salt, basil, oregano and pepper. Slowly whisk in oil. Pour over the pasta mixture and toss to coat. Refrigerate until serving.

**GARDEN BOUNTY
PANZANELLA SALAD**
Jannine Fisk
Malden, MA

GARDEN BOUNTY
PANZANELLA SALAD

*When my sister gave me fresh tomatoes and basil,
I made this traditional bread salad. The longer it sits,
the more the bread soaks up the seasonings.*
—**JANNINE FISK** MALDEN, MA

PREP: 15 MIN. • **COOK:** 20 MIN.
MAKES: 16 SERVINGS

- ¼ cup olive oil
- 12 ounces French or ciabatta bread, cut into
    1-inch cubes (about 12 cups)
- 4 large tomatoes, coarsely chopped
- 1 English cucumber, coarsely chopped
- 1 medium green pepper, cut into 1-inch pieces
- 1 medium sweet yellow pepper, cut into
    1-inch pieces
- 1 small red onion, halved and thinly sliced
- ½ cup coarsely chopped fresh basil
- ¼ cup grated Parmesan cheese
- ¾ teaspoon kosher salt
- ¼ teaspoon coarsely ground pepper
- ½ cup Italian salad dressing

1. In a large skillet, heat 2 tablespoons oil over medium heat. Add half of the bread cubes; cook and stir until toasted, about 8 minutes. Remove from the pan. Repeat with the remaining oil and bread cubes.

2. Combine the bread cubes, tomatoes, cucumber, peppers, onion, basil, cheese, salt and pepper. Toss with dressing.

BALSAMIC
THREE-BEAN
SALAD

BALSAMIC THREE-BEAN SALAD

Here's my little girl's favorite salad. She eats it just about as fast as I can make it. Make it ahead so the flavors have plenty of time to get to know one another.

—STACEY FEATHER JAY, OK

PREP: 25 MIN. + CHILLING
MAKES: 12 SERVINGS

- 2 pounds fresh green beans, trimmed and cut into 2-inch pieces
- ½ cup balsamic vinaigrette
- ¼ cup sugar
- 1 garlic clove, minced
- ¾ teaspoon salt
- 2 cans (16 ounces each) kidney beans, rinsed and drained
- 2 cans (15 ounces each) cannellini beans, rinsed and drained
- 4 fresh basil leaves, torn

1. Fill a Dutch oven three-fourths full with water; bring to a boil. Add green beans; cook, uncovered, for 3-6 minutes or until crisp-tender. Drain and immediately drop into ice water. Drain and pat dry.

2. In a large bowl, whisk vinaigrette, sugar, garlic and salt until sugar is dissolved. Add canned beans and green beans; toss to coat. Refrigerate, covered, at least 4 hours. Stir in basil just before serving.

★ ★ ★ ★ ★ **READER REVIEW**

"These carrots had such a wonderful caramelized flavor. My daughter had thirds and would have had more if there'd been any left!"

PDARWIN TASTEOFHOME.COM

FAST FIX
CREAMY GRAPE SALAD

Everyone raves when I bring this refreshing, creamy salad to potlucks. It's a special finishing touch to sprinkle it with brown sugar and pecans.

—MARGE ELLING JENISON, MI

START TO FINISH: 20 MIN.
MAKES: 21-24 SERVINGS

- 1 package (8 ounces) cream cheese, softened
- 1 cup sour cream
- ⅓ cup sugar
- 2 teaspoons vanilla extract
- 2 pounds seedless red grapes
- 2 pounds seedless green grapes
- 3 tablespoons brown sugar
- 3 tablespoons chopped pecans

1. In a large bowl, beat the cream cheese, sour cream, sugar and vanilla until blended. Add grapes and toss to coat.

2. Transfer to a serving bowl. Cover and refrigerate until serving. Sprinkle with brown sugar and pecans just before serving.

FAST FIX
THYME-ROASTED CARROTS

Cutting carrots lengthwise gives a simple side dish a special look. If you like, garnish with sprigs of fresh thyme or parsley.

—DEIRDRE COX KANSAS CITY, MO

START TO FINISH: 30 MIN.
MAKES: 10-12 SERVINGS

- 3 pounds medium carrots, halved lengthwise
- 2 tablespoons minced fresh thyme or 2 teaspoons dried thyme
- 2 tablespoons canola oil
- 1 tablespoon honey
- 1 teaspoon salt

Preheat oven to 400°. Divide carrots between two greased 15x10x1-in. baking pans. In a small bowl, mix thyme, oil, honey and salt; brush over the carrots. Roast 20-25 minutes or until tender.

SUMMER ORZO

I'm always looking for fun ways to use the fresh veggies that come in my Community Supported Agriculture box, and this salad is one of my favorite creations. I like to improvise with whatever I have on hand—feel free to do the same!

—SHAYNA MARMAR PHILADELPHIA, PA

PREP: 30 MIN. + CHILLING
MAKES: 16 SERVINGS

- 1 package (16 ounces) orzo pasta
- ¼ cup water
- 1½ cups fresh or frozen corn
- 24 cherry tomatoes, halved
- 2 cups crumbled feta cheese
- 1 medium cucumber, seeded and chopped
- 1 small red onion, finely chopped
- ¼ cup minced fresh mint
- 2 tablespoons capers, drained and chopped, optional
- ½ cup olive oil
- ¼ cup lemon juice
- 1 tablespoon grated lemon peel
- 1½ teaspoons salt
- 1 teaspoon pepper
- 1 cup sliced almonds, toasted

1. Cook orzo according to package directions for al dente. Drain the orzo; rinse with cold water and drain well. Transfer to a large bowl.
2. In a large nonstick skillet, heat water over medium heat. Add corn; cook and stir 3-4 minutes or until crisp-tender. Add to orzo; stir in tomatoes, feta cheese, cucumber, onion, mint and, if desired, capers. In a small bowl, whisk oil, lemon juice, lemon peel, salt and pepper until blended. Pour over the orzo mixture; toss to coat. Refrigerate 30 minutes.
3. Just before serving, stir in almonds.

BEET SALAD WITH ORANGE-WALNUT DRESSING

Light and refreshing, this salad goes nicely with the heavier dishes of the season. Your family and friends will also appreciate the tasty homemade dressing.

—MARIAN PLATT SEQUIM, WA

PREP: 20 MIN. • **BAKE:** 40 MIN. + COOLING
MAKES: 12 SERVINGS (ABOUT 1 CUP DRESSING)

- 1 pound fresh beets
- 6 cups torn Bibb or Boston lettuce
- 3 medium navel oranges, peeled and sectioned
- 2 cups torn curly endive
- 2 cups watercress
- ⅔ cup chopped walnuts, toasted

DRESSING

- ½ cup canola oil
- ⅓ cup orange juice
- 3 tablespoons white wine vinegar
- 1 green onion, finely chopped
- 1 tablespoon lemon juice
- 1 tablespoon Dijon mustard
- ½ teaspoon salt
- ⅛ teaspoon white pepper

1. Place beets in a 13x9-in. baking dish; add 1 in. of water. Cover and bake at 400° for 40-45 minutes or until tender. Cool; peel and julienne.
2. In a serving bowl, combine the lettuce, oranges, endive and watercress. Add the beets and walnuts.
3. In a small bowl, whisk oil, orange juice, vinegar, onion, lemon juice, mustard, salt and pepper. Drizzle over the salad; toss gently to coat.

GREEK HERB RATATOUILLE

When I lived in Florida, I went to a dinner at a friend's home. His wife, who is Greek, served a beautiful side dish that she called an eggplant fan, and she shared the recipe with me. While I've made her version many times with great success, I was inspired by the movie Ratatouille *and created this version.*

—JOE SHERWOOD TRYON, NE

PREP: 30 MIN. + CHILLING • **BAKE:** 45 MIN.
MAKES: 13 SERVINGS

- 1 small eggplant
- 2 small zucchini
- 2 small yellow summer squash
- 4 plum tomatoes
- 1 large sweet onion
- ½ cup butter, melted
- ½ cup minced fresh parsley
- 3 garlic cloves, minced
- ½ teaspoon salt
- ½ teaspoon each dried thyme, oregano, tarragon and basil
- ½ teaspoon dried rosemary, crushed
- ½ teaspoon pepper
- 1 cup shredded part-skim mozzarella cheese

1. Cut vegetables into ¼-in. thick slices.
2. In a greased 13x9-in. baking dish, layer the eggplant, zucchini, squash, tomatoes and onion. In a small bowl, combine the butter, parsley, garlic and seasonings; pour over the vegetables. Cover and refrigerate overnight.
3. Remove from the refrigerator 30 minutes before baking. Bake, uncovered, at 375° for 35 minutes. Sprinkle with cheese, then bake 10-15 minutes longer or until the cheese is melted. Serve with a slotted spoon.

BALSAMIC HERB VINAIGRETTE

A variety of savory seasonings gives this dressing a tangy kick. It's the perfect complement to a bed of fresh greens.

—EDGAR WRIGHT SILVER SPRING, MD

START TO FINISH: 25 MIN.
MAKES: 2¼ CUPS

- ½ cup balsamic vinegar
- ½ cup honey
- 1 tablespoon minced fresh basil
- 1½ teaspoons onion powder
- 1½ teaspoons snipped fresh dill
- 1½ teaspoons minced fresh oregano
- 1½ teaspoons minced fresh thyme
- 1 garlic clove, peeled
- ½ teaspoon white pepper
- ½ teaspoon prepared mustard
- 1½ cups canola oil

In a blender, combine the first 10 ingredients; cover and process until blended. While processing, gradually add the oil in a steady stream. Cover and refrigerate until serving.

SUMMERTIME TOMATO SALAD

Here is the best of summer in one cool, refreshing salad. Cherry tomatoes make it pretty and colorful, and the blueberry surprise sweetens it up along with a hint of mint.

—THOMAS FAGLON SOMERSET, NJ

PREP: 25 MIN. + CHILLING
MAKES: 12 SERVINGS

- 4 medium ears sweet corn, husks removed
- 2 pounds cherry tomatoes (about 6 cups), halved
- 1 small yellow summer squash, halved lengthwise and sliced
- 1 cup fresh blueberries
- 1 small red onion, halved and thinly sliced
- ¼ cup olive oil
- 2 tablespoons lemon juice
- 1 tablespoon minced fresh mint
- ½ teaspoon salt
- ½ teaspoon freshly ground pepper

1. In a 6-qt. stockpot, bring 8 cups water to a boil. Add corn; cook, uncovered, 2-4 minutes or until crisp-tender. Remove corn and immediately drop into ice water to cool; drain well.
2. Cut corn from the cobs and place in a bowl. Add the remaining ingredients; toss to combine. Refrigerate, covered, until cold, about 30 minutes.

TEST KITCHEN TIP
Cutting sweet corn kernels off of a cob can be trying because the cobs are awkward to manipulate and can easily slip and roll. Try cutting the cob in half so that you have two flat ends, then place the flat end against your cutting surface and slice downward.

YOU'RE-BACON-ME-CRAZY POTATO SALAD

My kids and I always want potato salad when we grill or barbecue, but we don't like the store-bought versions. I toyed with many combinations until I developed this one. Now if I mention grilling to the family, this is their top side-dish request.

—PAUL COGSWELL LEAGUE CITY, TX

PREP: 10 MIN. • **COOK:** 25 MIN. + CHILLING
MAKES: 12 SERVINGS

- 2½ pounds small red potatoes, cut into 1-inch pieces
- 3 teaspoons salt
- 1 pound bacon strips, finely chopped
- 1 large onion, chopped
- 3 celery ribs, finely chopped
- 2 cups mayonnaise
- 2 tablespoons Dijon or yellow mustard
- ¾ teaspoon dill weed
- ½ teaspoon celery salt
- ¼ teaspoon celery seed

1. Place potatoes in a 6-qt. stockpot; add water to cover. Add salt; bring to a boil. Reduce heat; cook, uncovered, 12-15 minutes or until the potatoes are tender.
2. Meanwhile, in a large skillet, cook bacon over medium heat until crisp, stirring occasionally. Remove with a slotted spoon and drain on paper towels; reserve 4 tablespoons of the bacon drippings. Cook and stir onion in the reserved drippings for 6-8 minutes or until browned.
3. Reserve ¼ cup cooked bacon for topping. Add onion, drippings, celery and the remaining bacon to the potatoes.
4. In a small bowl, mix mayonnaise, mustard and seasonings. Pour over the potato mixture and toss to coat. Refrigerate, covered, 1 hour or until chilled. Just before serving, sprinkle with the reserved bacon.

**YOU'RE-BACON-ME-CRAZY
POTATO SALAD**

GARLIC-SESAME GREEN BEANS

Sauteed bits of garlic and shallot, plus a sprinkling of toasted sesame seeds, turn ordinary beans into something special. Keep the recipe in mind for your garden crop in summer, too.
—**DEIRDRE COX** KANSAS CITY, MO

PREP: 25 MIN. • **COOK:** 10 MIN.
MAKES: 12 SERVINGS

  3 pounds fresh green beans, trimmed
  1 tablespoon sesame oil
  1 tablespoon canola oil
  1 shallot, finely chopped
  6 garlic cloves, minced
1½ teaspoons salt
½ teaspoon pepper
  2 tablespoons sesame seeds, toasted

1. In a Dutch oven, bring 10 cups water to a boil. Add green beans; cook, uncovered, 6-8 minutes or until tender.
2. Meanwhile, in a small skillet, heat oils over medium heat. Add shallot, garlic, salt and pepper; cook and stir 2-3 minutes or until tender.
3. Drain the green beans and return them to the Dutch oven. Add the shallot mixture; toss to coat. Sprinkle with sesame seeds.

APRICOT GELATIN MOLD

After my husband and I got married, he asked me to get this special holiday recipe from my mother. Mom prepared it for every family celebration, and now I make it for family! You can substitute peach or orange gelatin if you prefer.
—**SUZANNE HOLCOMB** ST. JOHNSVILLE, NY

PREP: 25 MIN. + CHILLING
MAKES: 12 SERVINGS

  1 can (8 ounces) unsweetened crushed pineapple
  2 packages (3 ounces each) apricot or peach gelatin
  1 package (8 ounces) reduced-fat cream cheese
¾ cup grated carrots
  1 carton (8 ounces) frozen fat-free whipped topping, thawed

1. Drain pineapple, reserving the juice in a 2-cup measuring cup; add enough water to measure 2 cups. Set the pineapple aside. Pour the juice mixture into a small saucepan. Bring to a boil; remove from heat. Dissolve gelatin in the juice mixture. Cool for 10 minutes.
2. In a large bowl, beat cream cheese until creamy. Gradually add the gelatin mixture, beating until smooth. Refrigerate for 30-40 minutes or until slightly thickened.
3. Fold in the pineapple and carrots, then the whipped topping. Transfer to an 8-cup ring mold coated with cooking spray. Refrigerate until set. Unmold onto a serving platter.

★ ★ ★ ★ ★   **READER REVIEW**

"Light and tasty— a great recipe!."
DIGSCHULTZ TASTEOFHOME.COM

LEMON PARSLEY
POTATOES

FAST FIX ▶
LEMON PARSLEY POTATOES

For a simply delicious side dish, I often prepare these potatoes. I like the fact that there are so few ingredients and they take such little time to prepare.
—**DOROTHY PRITCHETT** WILLS POINT, TX

START TO FINISH: 20 MIN.
MAKES: 10-12 SERVINGS

3   pounds small red new potatoes, quartered
½   cup butter, melted
3   tablespoons lemon juice
3   tablespoons minced fresh parsley

Cook the potatoes in boiling salted water until tender, about 15 minutes; drain. Combine butter, lemon juice and parsley; pour over the potatoes and stir gently to coat.

PESTO BUTTERMILK DRESSING

A good dressing is hard to beat; a great one is brilliant. We love the tangy blend of buttermilk and Greek yogurt.
—**LIZ BELLVILLE** HAVELOCK, NC

PREP: 10 MIN. + CHILLING
MAKES: 1¾ CUPS

⅔   cup buttermilk
½   cup fat-free plain Greek yogurt
½   cup prepared pesto
¼   cup shredded Parmesan cheese
1   tablespoon white wine vinegar
1   tablespoon grated lemon peel
1   garlic clove, minced
½   teaspoon coarsely ground pepper
⅛   teaspoon salt

Place all the ingredients in a jar with a tight-fitting lid; shake well. Refrigerate for 1 hour. Just before serving, shake the dressing again.

CREOLE CORN BREAD

CREOLE CORN BREAD

Corn bread is a staple of Cajun and Creole cuisine. This is an old favorite that I found in the bottom of my recipe drawer, and it really tastes wonderful.

—ENID HEBERT LAFAYETTE, LA

PREP: 15 MIN. • **BAKE:** 45 MIN.
MAKES: 12 SERVINGS

- 2 cups cooked rice
- 1 cup yellow cornmeal
- ½ cup chopped onion
- 1 to 2 tablespoons seeded chopped jalapeno peppers
- 1 teaspoon salt
- ½ teaspoon baking soda
- 2 large eggs
- 1 cup whole milk
- ¼ cup canola oil
- 1 can (16½ ounces) cream-style corn
- 3 cups shredded cheddar cheese
  Additional cornmeal

1. In a large bowl, combine rice, cornmeal, onion, peppers, salt and baking soda.
2. In another bowl, beat eggs, milk and oil. Add the corn; mix well. Stir into the rice mixture until blended. Fold in cheese. Sprinkle a well-greased 10-in. ovenproof skillet with cornmeal. Pour batter into skillet.
3. Bake at 350° for 45-50 minutes or until bread tests done. Cut into wedges and serve warm.
NOTE *Wear disposable gloves when cutting hot peppers; the oils can burn skin. Avoid touching your face.*

★ ★ ★ ★ ★ **READER REVIEW**

"Wish there were more than 5 stars to rate this. This blueberry salad deserves at least 10!"

JOSCY TASTEOFHOME.COM

CREAMY BLUEBERRY GELATIN SALAD

Plump blueberries and a fluffy topping star in this pretty, refreshing salad. My mom's blueberry salad was served at every holiday and celebration. Now, my grandchildren look forward to sampling it at family gatherings.

—SHARON HOEFERT GREENDALE, WI

PREP: 30 MIN. + CHILLING
MAKES: 12-15 SERVINGS

- 2 packages (3 ounces each) grape gelatin
- 2 cups boiling water
- 1 can (21 ounces) blueberry pie filling
- 1 can (20 ounces) unsweetened crushed pineapple, undrained

TOPPING
- 1 package (8 ounces) cream cheese, softened
- 1 cup sour cream
- ½ cup sugar
- 1 teaspoon vanilla extract
- ½ cup chopped walnuts

1. In a large bowl, dissolve gelatin in boiling water. Cool for 10 minutes. Stir in pie filling and pineapple until blended. Transfer to a 13x9-in. dish. Cover and refrigerate until partially set, about 1 hour.
2. For topping, in a small bowl, combine the cream cheese, sour cream, sugar and vanilla. Carefully spread over the gelatin; sprinkle with walnuts. Cover and refrigerate until firm.
STRAWBERRY GELATIN SALAD *Prepare salad with strawberry gelatin and pie filling instead of grape and blueberry. Stir in 1¼ cups chilled lemon-lime soda instead of the pineapple. Use the topping above, if desired.*
CHERRY COLA SALAD *Prepare salad with cherry gelatin and pie filling instead of grape and blueberry. Substitute 20 ounces crushed pineapple (drained) for undrained pineapple and add ¾ cup chilled cola. Omit topping.*

MAKE AHEAD

MAKE-AHEAD CREAMY POTATOES

For the holidays, I usually serve the traditional foods plus a new spin or two on old family favorites. I put these creamy potatoes together the night before and bake the next day to save precious holiday time.

—**WENDY G. BALL** BATTLE CREEK, MI

PREP: 1 HOUR + CHILLING • **BAKE:** 55 MIN.
MAKES: 16 SERVINGS

- 5 pounds potatoes (about 6 large)
- ½ cup butter, divided
- ½ cup chopped fresh mushrooms
- 2 tablespoons all-purpose flour
- 1 cup 2% milk or half-and-half cream
- 1 teaspoon salt
- ½ teaspoon pepper
- ½ teaspoon dried thyme
- 2 cups shredded sharp cheddar cheese
- 2 cups sour cream
- 1 medium onion, chopped
- ½ cup dry bread crumbs
- ¼ cup grated Parmesan cheese

1. Place whole potatoes in a large stockpot; add enough water to cover. Bring to a boil. Reduce heat; cook, uncovered, 20-25 minutes or until tender. Drain.

2. Meanwhile, in a large saucepan, heat ¼ cup butter over medium-high heat. Add mushrooms; cook and stir for 2-4 minutes or until tender. Stir in flour until blended; gradually whisk in the milk, salt, pepper and thyme. Bring to a boil, stirring constantly; cook and stir 1-2 minutes or until thickened.

3. Peel and cube the potatoes when they are cool enough to handle. Press through a potato ricer or strainer into a large bowl; stir in cheddar, sour cream, mushroom mixture, onion and remaining butter. Transfer the potato mixture to a greased 13x9-in. baking dish. Refrigerate, covered, overnight.

4. Preheat oven to 375°. Remove potatoes from refrigerator; uncover and let stand while the oven heats. Sprinkle with bread crumbs and Parmesan cheese. Bake, uncovered, 55-65 minutes or until heated through.

FAST FIX

AVOCADO DRESSING

Buttermilk and fat-free yogurt create the base for a creamy and delicious dressing. The avocado, parsley and dill add freshness, flavor and a lovely color to this easy choice for summer pasta.

—**TASTE OF HOME** TEST KITCHEN

START TO FINISH: 10 MIN.
MAKES: 2 CUPS

- 1 cup buttermilk
- ½ cup fat-free plain yogurt
- 1 ripe avocado, peeled and sliced
- 2 green onions, chopped
- ¼ cup minced fresh parsley
- ½ teaspoon salt
- ½ teaspoon garlic powder
- ¼ teaspoon dill weed
- ⅛ teaspoon pepper

In a blender, combine all ingredients; cover and process until blended. Transfer to a jar with a tight-fitting lid or small bowl. Serve immediately or refrigerate.

SPINACH AND ARTICHOKE CASSEROLE

Fans of spinach and artichoke dip will be excited to see this recipe re-created for a side dish. This one gets a little kick from the cayenne; if you don't have heat lovers at the table, you can cut the amount in half.

—**JUDY ARMSTRONG** PRAIRIEVILLE, LA

PREP: 35 MIN. • **BAKE:** 30 MIN.
MAKES: 12 SERVINGS

- 5 celery ribs, finely chopped
- 2 medium sweet red peppers, chopped
- 2 medium onions, finely chopped
- 2 tablespoons butter
- 1 tablespoon canola oil
- 6 garlic cloves, minced
- 3 tablespoons all-purpose flour
- 1 cup half-and-half cream
- 1 cup fat-free milk
- 3 cups shredded reduced-fat Mexican cheese blend
- 4 packages (10 ounces each) frozen chopped spinach, thawed and squeezed dry
- 2 cans (14 ounces each) water-packed artichoke hearts, rinsed, drained and quartered
- 1 teaspoon salt
- 1 teaspoon cayenne pepper
- 1 teaspoon pepper
- ½ teaspoon crushed red pepper flakes
- 1 cup grated Parmesan cheese

1. Preheat oven to 350°. In a Dutch oven, saute the celery, red peppers and onions in butter and oil until tender. Add garlic; cook 1 minute longer. Stir in flour until blended; gradually add cream and milk. Bring to a boil; cook and stir 2 minutes or until thickened. Stir in the shredded cheese until melted.
2. Add the spinach, artichokes, salt, cayenne, pepper and pepper flakes. Transfer to a 13x9-in. baking dish coated with cooking spray. Sprinkle with Parmesan cheese.
3. Bake, uncovered, 30-35 minutes or until bubbly.

FAST FIX
FRUIT SALAD WITH APRICOT DRESSING

Whenever I serve this lovely, refreshing salad for picnics, potlucks and holidays, the bowl empties in a hurry!

—**CAROL LAMBERT** EL DORADO, AR

START TO FINISH: 30 MIN.
MAKES: 26 SERVINGS

- 1 cup sugar
- 1 tablespoon cornstarch
- 2 cans (5½ ounces each) apricot nectar
- 1 teaspoon vanilla extract
- 6 large red apples, coarsely chopped
- 8 medium firm bananas, sliced
- 1 medium fresh pineapple, peeled and cut into chunks (about 5 cups)
- 1 quart fresh strawberries, quartered
- 2 cups green grapes

1. In a microwave-safe bowl, stir the sugar, cornstarch and apricot nectar until smooth. Microwave, uncovered, on high for 4-6 minutes or until slightly thickened, stirring every 2 minutes. Stir in the vanilla. Refrigerate.
2. In a large bowl, combine all of the fruit. Drizzle with dressing; gently toss to coat. Cover and refrigerate until serving.
NOTE *This recipe was tested with a 1,100-watt microwave.*

FAST FIX ▶
PORTOBELLO GNOCCHI SALAD

Pan-sauteing the gnocchi eliminates the need to boil it and creates a wonderful, crispy coating. The baby bellas lend an earthiness to this Italian-influenced salad.
—**FRAN FEHLING** STATEN ISLAND, NY

START TO FINISH: 25 MIN.
MAKES: 14 SERVINGS

- 1 package (16 ounces) potato gnocchi
- 2 tablespoons plus ⅓ cup olive oil, divided
- ½ pound sliced baby portobello mushrooms
- 3 teaspoons lemon juice
- 3 large plum tomatoes, seeded and chopped
- 1 can (15 ounces) chickpeas, rinsed and drained
- 1 package (5 ounces) fresh baby arugula or fresh baby spinach, coarsely chopped
- ½ cup pitted Greek olives, cut in half
- ⅓ cup minced fresh parsley
- 2 tablespoons capers, drained and chopped
- 2 teaspoons grated lemon peel
- ½ teaspoon salt
- ¼ teaspoon coarsely ground pepper
- ½ cup crumbled feta cheese
- ¼ cup chopped walnuts, toasted

1. In large nonstick skillet over medium-high heat, cook gnocchi in 1 tablespoon oil for 6-8 minutes or until lightly browned, turning once. Remove from the skillet; cool slightly.
2. In the same skillet, saute the mushrooms in 1 tablespoon oil until tender. Place mushrooms and gnocchi in a serving bowl. Add lemon juice and remaining oil; gently toss to coat.
3. Add the tomatoes, chickpeas, arugula, olives, parsley, capers, lemon peel, salt and pepper; toss to combine. Garnish with cheese and walnuts.
NOTE *Look for potato gnocchi in the pasta or frozen foods section.*

CASHEW-CHICKEN ROTINI SALAD

Of all the many chicken salad recipes I've tried over the years, this is my favorite. It's fresh, fruity and refreshing, and the cashews add wonderful crunch.
—**KARA COOK** ELK RIDGE, UT

PREP: 30 MIN. + CHILLING
MAKES: 12 SERVINGS

- 1 package (16 ounces) spiral or rotini pasta
- 4 cups cubed cooked chicken
- 1 can (20 ounces) pineapple tidbits, drained
- 1½ cups sliced celery
- ¾ cup thinly sliced green onions
- 1 cup seedless red grapes
- 1 cup seedless green grapes
- 1 package (5 ounces) dried cranberries
- 1 cup ranch salad dressing
- ¾ cup mayonnaise
- 2 cups salted cashews

1. Cook pasta according to package directions. Meanwhile, in a large bowl, combine the chicken, pineapple, celery, onions, grapes and cranberries. Drain the pasta and rinse in cold water; stir into the chicken mixture.
2. In a small bowl, whisk the ranch dressing and mayonnaise. Pour over the salad and toss to coat. Cover and refrigerate for at least 1 hour. Just before serving, stir in cashews.

★ ★ ★ ★ ★ **READER REVIEW**

"I made this chicken salad for homecoming at our church and it got rave reviews! It's a wonderful combination of ingredients, flavors and textures."

MIKELSSWORD TASTEOFHOME.COM

CASHEW-CHICKEN ROTINI SALAD

CARAMELIZED HAM &
SWISS BUNS, PAGE 91

SOUPS & SANDWICHES

"Let them give thanks to the Lord for his unfailing love and his wonderful deeds for mankind, for he satisfies the thirsty and fills the hungry with good things."

PSALM 107:8-9

MAKE AHEAD | SLOW COOKER

CUBANO PORK SANDWICHES

When we're feeding a hungry crowd, we make our juicy pork sandwiches. I call the sauce Mojo because it's loaded with zingy flavors.

—THERESA YARDAS SHERIDAN, IN

PREP: 1¾ HOURS + MARINATING • **COOK:** 8 HOURS
MAKES: 24 SERVINGS

- ⅓ cup ground cumin
- ¼ cup sugar
- 2 tablespoons onion powder
- 1 tablespoon kosher salt
- ½ teaspoon pepper
- 1 boneless pork shoulder roast (6 to 7 pounds)
- 2 teaspoons olive oil
- 1 large onion, quartered
- 1 cup dry red wine or beef broth
- ⅔ cup lime juice
- ⅓ cup lemon juice
- ⅓ cup orange juice
- 1 bay leaf
- 1 teaspoon dried cilantro flakes
- 1 teaspoon dried oregano
- 1 teaspoon dried thyme
- 1 teaspoon ground allspice
- 4 teaspoons olive oil

SANDWICHES

- 2 loaves unsliced French bread (1 pound each)
- ¼ cup sweet pickle relish
- ¼ cup Dijon mustard
- 8 slices Swiss cheese

1. In a small bowl, mix the first five ingredients. Cut the roast into thirds and rub it with oil. Rub the spice mixture over meat; wrap in plastic wrap. Refrigerate, covered, for 24 hours.
2. In a large saucepan, combine the onion, wine, juices, bay leaf and seasonings. Bring to a boil. Reduce heat; simmer, covered, 45 minutes. Strain the sauce, discarding the onion and seasonings.
3. In a large skillet, heat oil over medium heat. Brown roast on all sides; drain. Transfer to a 6-qt. slow cooker. Pour the sauce over the meat. Cook, covered, on low 8-10 hours or until the meat is tender. Remove roast; cool slightly. Skim fat from the cooking juices. Shred pork with two forks. Return pork to the slow cooker; heat through.
4. Preheat oven to 325°. Split bread horizontally. Hollow out the bottoms of the loaves, leaving ¾-in. shells. Spread relish and mustard inside the shells. Layer with meat and cheese. Replace tops.
5. Wrap each sandwich tightly in heavy-duty foil. Place on baking sheets; bake for 20-25 minutes or until they are heated through. Cut each of them crosswise into 12 slices.

CHICKEN LIMA BEAN SOUP

When I was little, my father could be found in the kitchen during his free time. This soup is one of his most memorable dishes...and one of my most treasured recipes.

—CAROL ANN KAISER PENDLETON, OR

PREP: 15 MIN. • **COOK:** 2½ HOURS
MAKES: 12-14 SERVINGS (3½ QUARTS)

- 1 pound dried large lima beans
- 1 broiler/fryer chicken (3 to 3½ pounds)
- 3 quarts water
- 2 celery ribs with leaves, sliced
- 4 chicken bouillon cubes
- 2½ teaspoon salt
- ½ teaspoon pepper
- 3 medium carrots, chopped
- 4 cups chopped fresh spinach
- 2 tablespoons minced fresh parsley

1. In a Dutch oven, combine the beans, chicken, water, celery, bouillon, salt and pepper; bring to a boil. Reduce heat; cover and simmer for 2 hours or until the beans are tender.
2. Remove the chicken from the pot. When cool enough to handle, remove meat from the bones; discard bones. Cut meat into bite-size pieces and return them to the pot. Add carrots; simmer for 30 minutes or until carrots are tender. Stir in the spinach and parsley; heat through.

CUBANO PORK SANDWICHES

MAKE AHEAD

BACON CHEESEBURGER SLIDER BAKE

You can bring these to a party, but I love them at dinner (and sometimes breakfast). My wife claims she doesn't like them, but she always has one.

—NICK IVERSON MILWAUKEE, WI

PREP: 20 MIN. • **BAKE:** 25 MIN.
MAKES: 2 DOZEN

- 2 packages (18 ounces each) Hawaiian sweet rolls
- 4 cups shredded cheddar cheese, divided
- 2 pounds ground beef
- 1 cup chopped onion
- 1 can (14½ ounces) diced tomatoes with garlic and onion, drained
- 1 tablespoon Dijon mustard
- 1 tablespoon Worcestershire sauce
- ¾ teaspoon salt
- ¾ teaspoon pepper
- 24 bacon strips, cooked and crumbled

GLAZE

- 1 cup butter, cubed
- ¼ cup packed brown sugar
- 4 teaspoons Worcestershire sauce
- 2 tablespoons Dijon mustard
- 2 tablespoons sesame seeds

1. Preheat oven to 350°. Without separating rolls, cut each package horizontally in half; arrange the bottom halves in two greased 13x9-in. baking pans. Sprinkle each pan of rolls with 1 cup cheese. Bake 3-5 minutes or until cheese is melted.

2. In a large skillet, cook beef and onion over medium heat 6-8 minutes or until the beef is no longer pink and the onion is tender, breaking up the beef into crumbles; drain. Stir in tomatoes, mustard, Worcestershire sauce, salt and pepper. Cook and stir 1-2 minutes or until combined.

3. Spoon beef mixture over rolls; sprinkle with remaining cheese. Top with bacon. Replace tops.

4. For glaze, in a microwave-safe bowl combine butter, brown sugar, Worcestershire sauce and mustard. Microwave, covered, on high until butter is melted, stirring occasionally. Pour over the rolls; sprinkle with sesame seeds. Bake, uncovered, 20-25 minutes or until golden brown and heated through.

FREEZE OPTION *Cover and freeze unbaked sandwiches; prepare and freeze glaze. To use, partially thaw in refrigerator overnight. Remove from the refrigerator 30 minutes before baking. Preheat oven to 350°. Pour glaze over buns and sprinkle with sesame seeds. Bake sandwiches as directed, increasing time by 10-15 minutes or until cheese is melted and a thermometer inserted in center reads 165°.*

 **READER REVIEW**

"These are messy to eat, but worth every single drip of ooey gooey deliciousness! This is going into my regular rotation of party foods."

SHANNONDOBOS TASTEOFHOME.COM

BRAIDED PIZZA LOAF

You can take the frozen bread dough out in the morning and then finish the meat-filled loaf after work. It's important to let the filling cool completely before spreading it on the dough.

—DEBBIE MEDUNA PLAZA, ND

PREP: 50 MIN. + RISING • **BAKE:** 30 MIN.
MAKES: 1 LOAF

- 1 loaf (1 pound) frozen bread dough, thawed
- 1 pound ground beef
- 1 medium onion, finely chopped
- 1 can (8 ounces) tomato sauce
- 1 teaspoon salt
- 1 teaspoon dried oregano
- 1 teaspoon paprika
- 1 teaspoon pepper
- ½ teaspoon garlic salt
- 1 cup shredded cheddar cheese
- 1 cup shredded part-skim mozzarella cheese
    Melted butter

1. Place dough in a greased bowl, turning once to grease the top. Cover and let rise in a warm place until doubled, about 1 hour.

2. Meanwhile, in a large skillet, cook beef and onion over medium heat until the meat is no longer pink; drain. Stir in tomato sauce and seasonings. Bring to a boil. Reduce the heat; simmer, uncovered, for 30 minutes, stirring occasionally. Remove from heat and cool completely.

3. Punch dough down. Turn onto a lightly floured surface; roll into a 15x12-in. rectangle. Place on a greased baking sheet. Spread the filling lengthwise down the center third of the rectangle. Sprinkle cheeses over the filling.

4. On each long side, cut strips that are 1½ in. wide and extend about 2½ in. into center. Starting at one end, fold alternating strips at an angle across the filling. Brush with butter.

5. Bake at 350° for 30-35 minutes or until golden brown. Serve warm. Refrigerate leftovers.

HEARTY PASTA FAJIOLI

Here's a classic Italian favorite. Spaghetti sauce and canned broth form the flavorful base.

—CINDY GARLAND LIMESTONE, TN

PREP: 40 MIN. • **COOK:** 40 MIN.
MAKES: 24 SERVINGS (7½ QUARTS)

- 2 pounds ground beef
- 6 cans (14½ ounces each) beef broth
- 2 cans (28 ounces each) diced tomatoes, undrained
- 2 jars (26 ounces each) spaghetti sauce
- 3 large onions, chopped
- 8 celery ribs, diced
- 3 medium carrots, sliced
- 2 cups canned cannellini beans, rinsed and drained
- 2 cups canned kidney beans, rinsed and drained
- 3 teaspoons minced fresh oregano or
    1 teaspoon dried oregano
- 2½ teaspoons pepper
- 1½ teaspoons hot pepper sauce
- 8 ounces uncooked medium pasta shells
- 5 teaspoons minced fresh parsley

1. In a large stockpot, cook beef over medium heat until no longer pink; drain. Add the broth, tomatoes, spaghetti sauce, onions, celery, carrots, beans, oregano, pepper and pepper sauce.

2. Bring to a boil. Reduce heat; simmer, covered, for 30 minutes. Add the pasta and parsley; simmer, covered, for 10-14 minutes or until pasta is tender.

MUSHROOM BARLEY SOUP

MUSHROOM BARLEY SOUP

A friend at work shared the recipe for this wonderful soup. With beef, barley and vegetables, it's hearty enough to be a meal. A big bowl of it is so satisfying, in warm weather as well as cold.

—LYNN THOMAS LONDON, ON

PREP: 25 MIN. • **COOK:** 1¾ HOURS
MAKES: ABOUT 11 SERVINGS (2¾ QUARTS)

- 1½ pounds boneless beef chuck, cut into ¾-inch cubes
- 1 tablespoon canola oil
- 2 cups finely chopped onions
- 1 cup diced carrots
- ½ cup sliced celery
- 1 pound fresh mushrooms, sliced
- 2 garlic cloves, minced
- ½ teaspoon dried thyme
- 1 can (14½ ounces) beef broth
- 1 can (14½ ounces) chicken broth
- 2 cups water
- ½ cup medium pearl barley
- 1 teaspoon salt, optional
- ½ teaspoon pepper
- 3 tablespoons chopped fresh parsley

1. In a Dutch oven or stockpot, cook meat in oil over medium heat until no longer pink. Remove the meat with a slotted spoon; set aside and keep warm.

2. Saute onions, carrots and celery in the pan drippings over medium heat until tender, about 5 minutes. Add mushrooms, garlic and thyme; cook and stir for 3 minutes. Stir in broths, water, barley, salt (if desired) and pepper.

3. Return the meat to the pot; bring to a boil. Reduce heat; cover and simmer 1½ to 2 hours or until barley and meat are tender. Add parsley.

SLOW COOKER
CRANBERRY BBQ PULLED PORK

Cranberry sauce adds a yummy twist to traditional pulled pork my family can't get enough of! The pork cooks to tender perfection in the slow cooker, which also makes this dish conveniently portable.

—CARRIE WIEGAND MOUNT PLEASANT, IA

PREP: 20 MIN. • **COOK:** 9 HOURS
MAKES: 14 SERVINGS

- 1 boneless pork shoulder roast (4 to 6 pounds)
- ⅓ cup cranberry juice
- 1 teaspoon salt

SAUCE

- 1 can (14 ounces) whole-berry cranberry sauce
- 1 cup ketchup
- ⅓ cup cranberry juice
- 3 tablespoons brown sugar
- 4½ teaspoons chili powder
- 2 teaspoons garlic powder
- 1 teaspoon onion powder
- ½ teaspoon salt
- ¼ teaspoon ground chipotle pepper
- ½ teaspoon liquid smoke, optional
- 14 hamburger buns, split

1. Cut roast in half. Place in a 4-qt. slow cooker. Add cranberry juice and salt. Cover and cook on low for 8-10 hours or until meat is tender.

2. Remove the roast and set it aside. In a small saucepan, combine the cranberry sauce, ketchup, cranberry juice, brown sugar, seasonings and liquid smoke (if desired). Cook and stir over medium heat for 5 minutes or until slightly thickened.

3. Skim the fat from the cooking juices; set aside ½ cup of the juices and discard the rest. When cool enough to handle, shred the pork with two forks and return the meat to the slow cooker.

4. Stir in the sauce mixture and reserved cooking juices. Cover and cook on low for 1 hour or until heated through. Serve on buns.

SLOW COOKER

SPICY LENTIL SOUP

I've finally found a lentil soup my husband enjoys! Adjust the spice level to your taste, and present this yummy soup with warm pita bread.

—EVA BARKER LEBANON, NH

PREP: 25 MIN. • **COOK:** 9 HOURS
MAKES: 14 SERVINGS (3½ QUARTS)

1½ pounds potatoes, peeled and cubed (about 5 cups)
1 large onion, chopped
2 large carrots, chopped
2 celery ribs, chopped
¼ cup olive oil
4 teaspoons ground cumin
2 teaspoons chili powder
1 teaspoon salt
1 teaspoon ground coriander
1 teaspoon coarsely ground pepper
½ teaspoon ground turmeric
½ teaspoon cayenne pepper
5 garlic cloves, minced
2 cartons (32 ounces each) reduced-sodium chicken broth
2 cans (15 ounces each) tomato sauce
1 package (16 ounces) dried lentils, rinsed
¼ cup lemon juice

1. Place potatoes, onion, carrots and celery in a 6-qt. slow cooker. In a small skillet, heat oil over medium heat. Add seasonings; cook and stir for 2 minutes. Add garlic; cook 1-2 minutes longer. Transfer to slow cooker.
2. Stir in broth, tomato sauce and lentils. Cook, covered, on low for 9-11 hours or until the lentils are tender. Stir in lemon juice.

MINI CHICKEN SALAD CROISSANTS

My chicken salad is great for any get-together. It could also be served on lettuce or sliced melon. I substitute halved red seedless grapes for the peppers when I know there will be kids in the crowd.

—PATRICIA TJUGUM TOMAHAWK, WI

PREP: 20 MIN. + CHILLING
MAKES: 20 SANDWICHES

⅓ cup sour cream
⅓ cup mayonnaise
4 teaspoons lemon juice
1 teaspoon salt
¼ teaspoon pepper
3 cups cubed cooked chicken
4 celery ribs, thinly sliced
1 cup chopped fresh mushrooms
¼ cup chopped green pepper
¼ cup chopped sweet red pepper
4 bacon strips, cooked and crumbled
½ cup chopped pecans, toasted
20 lettuce leaves
20 miniature croissants, split

1. In a small bowl, combine the sour cream, mayonnaise, lemon juice, salt and pepper. In a large bowl, combine the chicken, celery, mushrooms and peppers; stir in the sour cream mixture until combined. Cover and refrigerate this for at least 4 hours.
2. Just before serving, stir in the bacon and pecans. Line each croissant with a lettuce leaf and fill with ¼ cup chicken salad.

SPEEDY HAM
SLIDERS

FAST FIX ▶
SPEEDY HAM SLIDERS

It's easy to make these delicious Cuban-style sliders by the panful, which is great because they go fast! Bake the pan until the rolls are lightly toasted and the cheese melts, then set them out and just watch them disappear.

—SERENE HERRERA DALLAS, TX

START TO FINISH: 30 MIN.
MAKES: 2 DOZEN

- 2 packages (12 ounces each) Hawaiian sweet rolls
- 1¼ pounds thinly sliced deli ham
- 9 slices Swiss cheese (about 6 ounces)
- 24 dill pickle slices

TOPPING
- ½ cup butter, cubed
- 2 tablespoons finely chopped onion
- 2 tablespoons Dijon mustard

1. Preheat oven to 350°. Without separating the rolls, cut each package of rolls in half horizontally; arrange the bottom halves in a greased 13x9-in. baking pan. Layer with ham, cheese and pickles; replace the top halves of rolls.
2. In a microwave, melt butter; stir in onion and mustard. Drizzle over the rolls. Bake, covered, for 10 minutes. Uncover; bake until golden brown and heated through, 5-10 minutes longer. Remove from pan; cut into sliders.

FAST FIX

FOCACCIA SANDWICHES

Slices of this pretty sandwich are great for any casual get-together. Add or change ingredients to your taste.

—PEGGY WOODWARD SHULLSBURG, WI

START TO FINISH: 15 MIN.
MAKES: 24 SERVINGS

- ⅓ cup mayonnaise
- 1 can (4¼ ounces) chopped ripe olives, drained
- 1 Focaccia bread (about 12 ounces), halved lengthwise
- 4 romaine leaves
- ¼ pound shaved deli ham
- 1 medium sweet red pepper, thinly sliced into rings
- ¼ pound shaved deli turkey
- 1 large tomato, thinly sliced
- ¼ pound thinly sliced hard salami
- 1 jar (7 ounces) roasted sweet red peppers, drained
- 4 to 6 slices provolone cheese

In a small bowl, combine mayonnaise and olives; spread over the bottom half of bread. Layer with remaining ingredients; replace bread top. Cut into wedges; secure with toothpicks.

A rectangular-shaped focaccia bread, measuring about 12x8 in., works best for this sandwich.

CHRISTINA'S ITALIAN WEDDING SOUP

I have an affinity for soup featuring tiny meatballs and pasta. When I make this recipe, I double the number of meatballs, poach them in the broth, remove half, and freeze them for another time.

—CHRISTINA HITCHCOCK MADISON TOWNSHIP, PA

PREP: 40 MIN. • **COOK:** 20 MIN.
MAKES: 12 SERVINGS (5 QUARTS)

- 2 large eggs, lightly beaten
- ⅓ cup grated Parmesan cheese
- ¼ cup dry bread crumbs
- 2 tablespoons minced fresh parsley
- 2 tablespoons 2% milk
- 4 garlic cloves, minced
- 4 teaspoons grated onion
- 1 teaspoon salt
- 1 teaspoon pepper
- ½ teaspoon grated lemon peel
- 1½ pounds ground chicken

SOUP

- 2 tablespoons olive oil
- 4 medium carrots, chopped
- 4 celery ribs, chopped
- 2 small onions, chopped
- 6 garlic cloves, minced
- 4 cartons (26 ounces each) chicken stock
- 1 teaspoon salt
- 1 teaspoon pepper
- 1½ cups acini di pepe pasta
- 2 packages (10 ounces each) fresh spinach
  Additional minced fresh parsley and grated Parmesan cheese

1. In a large bowl, combine the first 10 ingredients. Add chicken; mix lightly but thoroughly. Shape into 1-in. balls.

2. For soup, in a stockpot, heat oil over medium-high heat. Add carrots, celery and onions; cook and stir for 6-8 minutes or until the onions are tender. Add garlic; cook 1 minute longer.

3. Stir in stock, salt and pepper; bring to a boil. Drop the meatballs into soup; cook, uncovered, 10 minutes. Gently stir in pasta; cook 10-12 minutes longer or until the meatballs are cooked through and the pasta is tender.

4. Stir in the spinach. Top servings with parsley and cheese.

★ ★ ★ ★ ★ **READER REVIEW**

"I've been looking for the best meatball recipe out there and finally found it! Love this Italian soup, too!"

BMOORE1948 TASTEOFHOME.COM

CHRISTINA'S ITALIAN WEDDING SOUP
Christina Hitchcock
Madison Twp, PA

SLOW COOKER 🍲

SANTA FE CHILI

Fall and chili go together like summer and corn. I use black and pinto beans and heirloom shoepeg corn in my meaty variation on the old favorite. This has been my husband's favorite chili for years.

—LAURA MANNING LILBURN, GA

PREP: 20 MIN. • **COOK:** 4 HOURS
MAKES: 16 SERVINGS (4 QUARTS)

- 2 pounds ground beef
- 1 medium onion, chopped
- 2 cans (16 ounces each) kidney beans, rinsed and drained
- 2 cans (15 ounces each) black beans, rinsed and drained
- 2 cans (15 ounces each) pinto beans, rinsed and drained
- 3 cans (7 ounces each) white or shoepeg corn, drained
- 1 can (14½ ounces) diced tomatoes, undrained
- 1 can (10 ounces) diced tomatoes and green chilies
- 1 can (11½ ounces) V8 juice
- 2 envelopes ranch salad dressing mix
- 2 envelopes taco seasoning
  Sour cream, shredded cheddar cheese and corn chips, optional

1. In a large skillet, cook the beef and onion over medium heat until the meat is no longer pink; drain. Transfer to a 5- or 6-qt. slow cooker. Stir in the beans, corn, tomatoes, juice, salad dressing mix and taco seasoning.

2. Cover and cook on high for 4-6 hours or until heated through. Serve with sour cream, cheese and corn chips if desired.

GLAZED CORNED BEEF SANDWICHES

Fans of good food will cheer when you bring out these full-flavored, hearty sandwiches! Made of tender corned beef and a special sweet and spicy seasoning, they're always a hit.

—RITA REIFENSTEIN EVANS CITY, PA

PREP: 30 MIN. • **COOK:** 4 HOURS
MAKES: 12-16 SERVINGS

- 1 corned beef brisket (3 to 4 pounds) with spice packet
- 12 peppercorns
- 4 bay leaves
- 3 garlic cloves, minced
- 2 cinnamon sticks (3 inches), broken
- 1 tablespoon crushed red pepper flakes

GLAZE

- ½ cup packed brown sugar
- ½ teaspoon ground cloves
- ½ teaspoon ground ginger
- ½ teaspoon ground mustard
- ¼ teaspoon celery salt
- ¼ teaspoon caraway seeds
  Sandwich buns

1. Place corned beef with seasoning packet in a Dutch oven; cover with water. Add peppercorns, bay leaves, garlic, cinnamon and red pepper flakes and bring to a boil. Reduce heat; cover and simmer for 4 to 4¼ hours or until the meat is tender. Drain, discarding the juices; blot brisket dry.

2. In a small bowl, combine glaze ingredients. Rub glaze top of warm meat. Grill or broil for 5- 10 minutes on each side until glazed. Slice the meat and serve warm or chilled on buns.

WINTER HARVEST VEGETABLE SOUP

Rich, earthy root vegetables blend with savory spices and the tartness of apples in this wonderful soup. A friend gave me this low-fat recipe after my husband's cardiac surgery and now it's our favorite. It gets even better with reheating!

—BARBARA MARAKOWSKI LOYSVILLE, PA

PREP: 25 MIN. • **COOK:** 50 MIN.
MAKES: 12 SERVINGS (3 QUARTS)

-   3 medium carrots, halved and thinly sliced
-   ¾ cup chopped celery
-   1 medium onion, chopped
-   2 green onions, thinly sliced
-   1 tablespoon butter
-   1 tablespoon olive oil
-   1 garlic clove, minced
-   7 cups reduced-sodium chicken broth or vegetable broth
-   3 cups cubed peeled potatoes
-   2 cups cubed peeled butternut squash
-   2 large tart apples, peeled and chopped
-   2 medium turnips, peeled and chopped
-   2 parsnips, peeled and sliced
-   1 bay leaf
-   ½ teaspoon dried basil
-   ¼ teaspoon dried thyme
-   ¼ teaspoon pepper
    Additional thinly sliced green onions, optional

1. In a Dutch oven over medium heat, cook and stir the carrots, celery and onions in butter and oil until tender. Add garlic; cook 1 minute longer.

2. Add the broth, potatoes, squash, apples, turnips, parsnips and bay leaf. Bring to a boil. Reduce heat; simmer, uncovered, for 20 minutes.

3. Stir in the basil, thyme and pepper; simmer 15 minutes longer or until the vegetables are tender. Discard the bay leaf before serving. Garnish with additional green onions if desired.

CARAMELIZED HAM & SWISS BUNS

My next-door neighbor shared this recipe with me, and now I make it regularly. You can make it ahead and cook it quickly when company arrives. The combo of poppy seeds, ham and cheese, horseradish and brown sugar is simply delicious!

—IRIS WEIHEMULLER BAXTER, MN

PREP: 25 MIN. + CHILLING • **BAKE:** 30 MIN.
MAKES: 1 DOZEN

-   1 package (12 ounces) Hawaiian sweet rolls, split
-   ½ cup horseradish sauce
-   12 slices deli ham
-   6 slices Swiss cheese, halved
-   ½ cup butter, cubed
-   2 tablespoons finely chopped onion
-   2 tablespoons brown sugar
-   1 tablespoon spicy brown mustard
-   2 teaspoons poppy seeds
-   1½ teaspoons Worcestershire sauce
-   ¼ teaspoon garlic powder

1. Spread the bottoms of the rolls with horseradish sauce. Layer with ham and cheese; replace the tops. Arrange the filled rolls in a single layer in a greased 9-in. square baking pan.

2. In a small skillet, heat butter over medium-high heat. Add onion; cook and stir 1-2 minutes or until tender. Stir in remaining ingredients. Pour over rolls. Refrigerate, covered, several hours or overnight.

3. Preheat oven to 350°. Bake the dish, covered, for 25 minutes. Bake, uncovered, 5-10 minutes longer or until golden brown.

TEST KITCHEN TIP
If you want a thicker body to your vegetable soup, try adding a sweet potato. Before you make the soup, peel, cube, cook and mash a sweet potato and add it to the soup stock or broth. This gives the soup a thicker body and richer flavor.

**BRISKET SLIDERS WITH
CARAMELIZED ONIONS**

SLOW COOKER 🍲
BRISKET SLIDERS WITH CARAMELIZED ONIONS

For a dear friend's going-away party, I made a juicy brisket and turned it into sliders. If you cook the brisket ahead, slider assembly will be a breeze.

—**MARLIES COVENTRY** NORTH VANCOUVER, BC

PREP: 25 MIN. + MARINATING • **COOK:** 7 HOURS
MAKES: 2 DOZEN

- 2 tablespoons plus ⅛ teaspoon salt, divided
- 2 tablespoons sugar
- 2 tablespoons whole peppercorns, crushed
- 5 garlic cloves, minced
- 1 fresh beef brisket (about 4 pounds)
- 1 cup mayonnaise
- ½ cup crumbled blue cheese
- 2 teaspoons horseradish
- ⅛ teaspoon cayenne pepper
- 3 medium carrots, cut into 1-inch pieces
- 2 medium onions, chopped
- 2 celery ribs, chopped
- 1 cup dry red wine or beef broth
- ¼ cup stone-ground mustard
- 3 bay leaves
- 1 tablespoon olive oil
- 3 medium onions, sliced
- 24 mini buns
  Arugula and tomato slices, optional

1. In a small bowl, combine 2 tablespoons salt, sugar, peppercorns and garlic; rub onto all sides of the brisket. Wrap in plastic; refrigerate 8 hours or overnight. In a small bowl, combine mayonnaise, blue cheese, horseradish and cayenne. Refrigerate until assembling.

2. Place carrots, chopped onions and celery in a 6- or 7-qt. slow cooker. Unwrap the brisket; place on top of the vegetables. In a small bowl, combine red wine, mustard and bay leaves; pour over the brisket. Cook, covered, on low for 7-9 hours or until the meat is fork-tender. Meanwhile, in a large skillet, heat oil over medium heat. Add sliced onions and remaining salt; cook and stir until softened. Reduce heat to medium-low; cook 30-35 minutes or until deep golden brown, stirring occasionally.

3. Remove the brisket; let it cool slightly. Reserve 1 cup of the cooking juices; discard the rest. Skim fat from the reserved juices. Thinly slice brisket across the grain; return meat to slow cooker. Pour the reserved juices over the brisket.

4. Serve brisket on buns with the mayonnaise mixture and caramelized onions and, if desired, arugula and tomato slices.

SPICED-UP HEALTHY SOUP

My spiced-up soup has been a hit with family and friends. It's low in fat and filled with good-for-you ingredients.

—**DIANE TAYMAN** DIXON/GRAND DETOUR, IL

PREP: 15 MIN. • **COOK:** 40 MIN.
MAKES: 14 SERVINGS (3½ QUARTS)

- 1 medium onion, chopped
- ⅓ cup medium pearl barley
- 2 tablespoons canola oil
- 4 garlic cloves, minced
- 5 cans (14½ ounces each) reduced-sodium chicken broth
- 2 boneless skinless chicken breast halves (4 ounces each)
- 1 cup dried lentils, rinsed
- 1 jar (16 ounces) picante sauce
- 1 can (15 ounces) chickpeas, rinsed and drained
- ½ cup minced fresh cilantro
- 8 cups chopped fresh spinach

1. In a Dutch oven, saute onion and barley in oil until the onion is tender. Add garlic; cook 1 minute longer. Add the broth, chicken and lentils; bring to a boil. Reduce heat; cover and simmer for 15 minutes or until the chicken is no longer pink. Remove the chicken and set it aside.

2. Add the picante sauce, garbanzo beans and cilantro to the soup; cover and simmer 10 minutes longer or until the barley and lentils are tender.

3. Shred the chicken with two forks. Add spinach and chicken to soup. Simmer, uncovered, for 5 minutes or until the spinach is wilted.

ANTIPASTO BRAID

We're fans of Mediterranean food in our house, so this play on antipasto is a favorite in my family. Meat and cheese make it a nice, hearty appetizer.

—PATRICIA HARMON BADEN, PA

PREP: 25 MIN. • **BAKE:** 30 MIN. + STANDING
MAKES: 12 SERVINGS

- ⅓ cup pitted Greek olives, chopped
- ¼ cup marinated quartered artichoke hearts, drained and chopped
- ¼ cup julienned oil-packed sun-dried tomatoes
- 2 tablespoons plus 2 teaspoons grated Parmesan cheese, divided
- 3 tablespoons olive oil, divided
- 1 tablespoon chopped fresh basil or 1 teaspoon dried basil
- 1 tube (11 ounces) refrigerated crusty French loaf
- 6 thin slices prosciutto or deli ham
- 4 slices provolone cheese
- ¾ cup julienned roasted sweet red peppers

1. Preheat oven to 350°. In a small bowl, toss olives, artichokes, tomatoes, 2 tablespoons Parmesan cheese, 2 tablespoons oil and basil until combined.

2. On a lightly floured surface, carefully unroll the French loaf dough; roll into a 15x10-in. rectangle. Transfer to a greased 15x10x1-in. baking pan. Layer prosciutto, provolone cheese and red peppers lengthwise down the center third of the dough. Top with the olive mixture.

3. On each long side, cut 10 strips about 3½ in. into the center. Starting at one end, fold alternating strips at an angle across the filling, pinching ends to seal. Brush with the remaining oil and sprinkle with the remaining Parmesan cheese.

4. Bake for 30-35 minutes or until golden brown. Let stand 10 minutes before cutting. Serve warm.

FAVORITE FISH CHOWDER

Economics had a lot to do with what we ate when I was growing up in New Hampshire during the Depression. Fish was plentiful and affordable, so that's how we began eating this dish. When meat rationing came along in World War II, fish chowder again became a staple in our household. Fortunately, my family loved it…it's still one of my favorites!

—FRAN GUSTAFSON BETHESDA, MD

PREP: 10 MIN. • **COOK:** 25 MIN.
MAKES: 4 QUARTS

- 1 large onion, chopped
- ½ cup butter, cubed
- 4 cups water
- 6 cups cubed peeled potatoes
- 2 pounds cod fillets, cut into large chunks
- 3 tablespoons lemon juice
- 2 cups milk
- 2 cans (12 ounces each) evaporated milk
- 2½ teaspoons salt
- 2 teaspoons pepper
  Minced fresh parsley

In a Dutch oven, saute the onion in butter. Add water and bring to a boil. Add the potatoes; cook for 10 minutes. Add the fish and lemon juice; reduce heat and simmer for 10 minutes. Add the milk, evaporated milk, salt and pepper. Sprinkle with parsley.

CHIPOTLE PULLED
CHICKEN

MAKE AHEAD / SLOW COOKER

CHIPOTLE PULLED CHICKEN

I love chicken that has a smoky chipotle kick to it.
This is a go-to meal when I'm looking for something
extra tasty, and it always goes over well with friends.
—**TAMRA PARKER** MANLIUS, NY

PREP: 15 MIN. • **COOK:** 3 HOURS
MAKES: 12 SERVINGS

- 2 **cups ketchup**
- 1 **small onion, finely chopped**
- ¼ **cup Worcestershire sauce**
- 3 **tablespoons reduced-sodium soy sauce**
- 2 **tablespoons brown sugar**
- 2 **tablespoons cider vinegar**
- 3 **garlic cloves, minced**
- 1 **tablespoon molasses**
- 2 **teaspoons dried oregano**
- 2 **teaspoons minced chipotle pepper in adobo sauce plus 1 teaspoon sauce**
- 1 **teaspoon ground cumin**
- 1 **teaspoon smoked paprika**
- ¼ **teaspoon salt**
- ¼ **teaspoon crushed red pepper flakes**
- 2½ **pounds boneless skinless chicken breasts**
- 12 **sesame seed hamburger buns, split and toasted**

1. In a 3-qt. slow cooker, combine the first 14 ingredients; add the chicken. Cook, covered, on low for 3-4 hours or until the chicken is tender (a thermometer should read at least 165°).
2. Remove the chicken from the slow cooker. Shred with two forks; return to slow cooker. Using tongs, place chicken mixture in the buns.
FREEZE OPTION *Freeze the cooled meat mixture and sauce in freezer containers. To use, partially thaw in refrigerator overnight. Heat through in a saucepan, stirring occasionally.*

CURRIED CHICKEN POCKETS

I served these pitas stuffed with zippy chicken filling for a picnic the day my husband and I got engaged. Now our children enjoy them.

—**LISA SCANDRETTE** EVELETH, MN

PREP: 35 MIN. + RISING • **BAKE:** 10 MIN.
MAKES: 12 SANDWICHES

- ½ cup mayonnaise
- ½ cup chutney
- 1 tablespoon curry powder
- 6 cups cubed cooked chicken

PITA BREAD

- 1 package (¼ ounce) active dry yeast
- 1⅓ cups warm water (110° to 115°), divided
- 3 to 3½ cups all-purpose flour
- 1 tablespoon vegetable oil
- 1 teaspoon salt
- ¼ teaspoon sugar
- 3 tablespoons cornmeal
  Lettuce leaves

1. In a large bowl, combine the mayonnaise, chutney, curry powder and chicken; refrigerate until serving.

2. In a large bowl, dissolve the yeast in ⅓ cup warm water. Add 1½ cups of flour, oil, salt, sugar and the remaining water; beat until smooth. Add enough of the remaining flour to form a soft dough. Turn dough onto a floured surface; knead until smooth and elastic, about 10 minutes. Place in a greased bowl, turning once to grease top. Cover and let rise in a warm place until doubled, about 1 hour.

3. Punch the dough down; shape into six balls. Let rise for 30 minutes. Sprinkle three ungreased baking sheets with cornmeal. Roll out each ball into a 7-in. circle. Place two circles on each baking sheet. Let rise for 30 minutes.

4. Bake at 500° for 10 minutes or until lightly browned. Cool. Cut pitas in half. Line each with lettuce; fill with ⅓ cup chicken mixture.

SLOW COOKER

SHRIMP CHOWDER

I simmer my rich and creamy shrimp soup in the slow cooker. Because the chowder is ready in less than 4 hours, it can be prepared in the afternoon and served to dinner guests that night.

—**WILL ZUNIO** GRETNA, LA

PREP: 15 MIN. • **COOK:** 3½ HOURS
MAKES: 12 SERVINGS (3 QUARTS)

- ½ cup chopped onion
- 2 teaspoons butter
- 2 cans (12 ounces each) evaporated milk
- 2 cans (10¾ ounces each) condensed cream of potato soup, undiluted
- 2 cans (10¾ ounces each) condensed cream of chicken soup, undiluted
- 1 can (7 ounces) white or shoepeg corn, drained
- 1 teaspoon Creole seasoning
- ½ teaspoon garlic powder
- 2 pounds peeled and deveined cooked small shrimp
- 3 ounces cream cheese, cubed

1. In a small skillet, saute the onion in butter until tender. In a 5-qt. slow cooker, combine the onion, milk, soups, corn, Creole seasoning and garlic powder.

2. Cover and cook on low for 3 hours. Stir in shrimp and cream cheese. Cook 30 minutes longer or until shrimp are heated through and cheese is melted. Stir to blend.

NOTE *The following spice mix may be substituted for 1 teaspoon Creole seasoning: ¼ teaspoon each salt, garlic powder and paprika; and a pinch each of dried thyme, ground cumin and cayenne pepper.*

★ ★ ★ ★ ★ **READER REVIEW**

"Simple to make. Warm to enjoy. Cleanup simple. Excellent!"

REDCAR2 TASTEOFHOME.COM

SHRIMP CHOWDER

refrigerate ½ cup of the mixture for sauce; pour the remaining mixture over the beef. Cover and cook on low for 8-10 hours or until the meat is tender.

refrigerate ½ cup of the mixture for sauce; pour the remaining mixture over the beef. Cover and cook on low for 8-10 hours or until the meat is tender.

2. Remove the beef and let it cool slightly. Skim the fat from the cooking juices. Shred the meat using two forks and return it to the slow cooker; heat through.

3. In a small saucepan, combine the ketchup, brown sugar, butter, pepper sauce and reserved water mixture. Bring to a boil; reduce heat. Simmer, uncovered, for 2-3 minutes to allow the flavors to blend. Using a slotted spoon, place beef on rolls; drizzle with sauce.

NOTE *This is a fresh beef brisket, not corned beef.*

SLOW COOKER
PULLED BRISKET SANDWICHES

Don't let the number of ingredients in this recipe scare you; I'll bet you have most of them in your pantry already. The sauce is what makes this dish special. It's hard not to like ketchup, brown sugar and a little butter drizzled over tender beef brisket.
—JANE GUILBEAU NEW ORLEANS, LA

PREP: 25 MIN. • **COOK:** 8 HOURS
MAKES: 12 SERVINGS

- 1 fresh beef brisket (4 to 5 pounds)
- 1½ cups water
- ½ cup Worcestershire sauce
- 2 tablespoons cider vinegar
- 2 garlic cloves, minced
- 1½ teaspoons beef bouillon granules
- 1½ teaspoons chili powder
- 1 teaspoon ground mustard
- ½ teaspoon cayenne pepper
- ¼ teaspoon garlic salt
- ½ cup ketchup
- 2 tablespoons brown sugar
- 2 tablespoons butter
- ½ teaspoon hot pepper sauce
- 12 kaiser rolls, split

1. Cut brisket in half; place in a 5-qt. slow cooker. In a small bowl, combine water, Worcestershire sauce, vinegar, garlic, bouillon, chili powder, mustard, cayenne and garlic salt. Cover and

GOLDEN SQUASH SOUP

I enjoy making this special recipe from my mother-in-law every fall. The soup is so pretty that it dresses up the table. We enjoy it on crisp evenings.
—MARY ANN KLEIN WASHINGTON TOWNSHIP, NJ

PREP: 35 MIN. • **COOK:** 30 MIN. + COOLING
MAKES: 12-14 SERVINGS (3½ QUARTS)

- 3 leeks (white portion only), sliced
- 4 medium carrots, chopped
- 5 tablespoons butter
- 3 pounds butternut squash, peeled and cubed
- 6 cups chicken broth
- 3 medium zucchini, peeled and sliced
- 2 teaspoons salt
- ½ teaspoon dried thyme
- ¼ teaspoon white pepper
- 1 cup half-and-half cream
- ½ cup 2% milk
  Grated Parmesan cheese and chives, optional

1. In a Dutch oven, saute the leeks and carrots in butter for 5 minutes, stirring occasionally. Add the squash, broth, zucchini, salt, thyme and pepper; bring to a boil. Reduce heat; cover and simmer for 30-35 minutes or until the vegetables are tender. Cool until lukewarm.

2. In a blender, puree the soup in small batches until smooth; return to pan. Stir in cream and milk; heat through (do not boil). Sprinkle with cheese and chives if desired.

SUMMER VEGGIE SUBS

Every Sunday night during the summer, a local park near us holds free outdoor concerts. We've been going for years. These subs are perfect for picnics, and I've taken them to the park several times.

—**JENNIE TODD** LANCASTER, PA

PREP: 30 MIN. + STANDING
MAKES: 12 SERVINGS

- 4 medium sweet red peppers
- ½ cup fat-free mayonnaise
- 2 tablespoons minced fresh basil
- 1 tablespoon minced fresh parsley
- 1 tablespoon minced fresh tarragon
- 2 loaves French bread (1 pound each), halved lengthwise
- 2 cups fresh baby spinach
- 2 cups thinly sliced cucumbers
- 2 cups alfalfa sprouts
- 4 medium tomatoes, sliced
- 2 medium ripe avocados, peeled and sliced
- ¾ pound thinly sliced deli turkey
- 6 slices reduced-fat Swiss cheese, halved

1. Broil the peppers 4 in. from the heat until the skins blister, about 5 minutes. With tongs, rotate peppers a quarter turn. Broil and rotate until all sides are blistered and blackened. Remove from the heat and immediately place in a large bowl; cover and let stand for 15-20 minutes.

2. Peel off the charred skin from the peppers and discard. Remove stems and seeds. Julienne the peppers.

3. Combine the mayonnaise, basil, parsley and tarragon; spread over the bottom halves of the bread. Top with spinach, cucumbers, sprouts, roasted peppers, tomatoes, avocados, turkey and cheese. Replace tops. Cut each loaf into six slices.

TEST KITCHEN TIP
To keep fresh parsley in the refrigerator for several weeks, wash the entire bunch in warm water, shake off excess moisture, wrap in a paper towel, and seal in a plastic bag.

BEEF AND BARLEY SOUP

I came across this recipe years ago at a recipe exchange through a church group. The contributor didn't sign her name, so I don't know whom to thank—but my husband and son thank me by helping themselves to seconds and thirds!

—**ELLEN MCCLEARY** SCOTLAND, ON

PREP: 10 MIN. • **COOK:** 1 HOUR
MAKES: 12 SERVINGS (3 QUARTS)

- 1½ pounds ground beef
- 3 celery ribs, sliced
- 1 medium onion, chopped
- 3 cans (10½ ounces each) condensed beef consomme, undiluted
- 1 can (28 ounces) diced tomatoes, undrained
- 4 medium carrots, sliced
- 2 cups water
- 1 can (10¾ ounces) condensed tomato soup, undiluted
- ½ cup medium pearl barley
- 1 bay leaf

In a Dutch oven, cook the beef, celery and onion over medium heat until the meat is no longer pink; drain. Add the remaining ingredients; bring to a boil. Reduce heat; simmer, uncovered, for 45-50 minutes or until barley is tender. Discard bay leaf.

**MINI ROSEMARY-
ROAST BEEF
SANDWICHES**
Susan Hein
Burlington, WI

MINI ROSEMARY-ROAST BEEF SANDWICHES

Roast beef sandwiches never last long at a party, especially if you dollop them with mayo, mustard, horseradish and pickled giardiniera relish.

—SUSAN HEIN BURLINGTON, WI

PREP: 25 MIN. + CHILLING • **BAKE:** 50 MIN. + CHILLING
MAKES: 2 DOZEN

- 1 beef top round roast (3 pounds)
- 3 teaspoons kosher salt
- 2 teaspoons crushed dried rosemary
- 2 tablespoons olive oil, divided
- 2 teaspoons pepper
- 2 cups mild giardiniera, drained
- 1 cup reduced-fat mayonnaise
- 2 tablespoons stone-ground mustard
- 1 to 2 tablespoons prepared horseradish
- 24 Hawaiian sweet rolls, split

1. Sprinkle the roast with salt and rosemary; wrap tightly in plastic wrap. Refrigerate at least 8 hours or up to 24 hours.

2. Preheat oven to 325°. Unwrap the roast and pat dry. Rub the roast with 1 tablespoon oil; sprinkle with pepper. In a large ovenproof skillet, heat the remaining oil over medium-high heat. Brown the meat on both sides.

3. Transfer to oven; roast 50-60 minutes or until a thermometer reads 135° for medium-rare. (The temperature of the roast will continue to rise about 10° upon standing.) Remove the roast from the pan; let stand 1 hour. Refrigerate, covered, at least 2 hours or until cold.

4. Place giardiniera in a food processor; pulse until finely chopped. In a small bowl, mix mayonnaise, mustard and horseradish.

5. To serve, thinly slice the cold beef. Serve on rolls with the mayonnaise mixture and giardiniera.

EMILY'S BEAN SOUP

Served with thick slices of warm homemade bread, my soup makes a wonderful fall or winter meal. The recipe has evolved over the years as I added to it. I often double it and freeze what we don't eat.

—EMILY CHANEY PENOBSCOT, ME

PREP: 25 MIN. + STANDING • **COOK:** 3 HOURS
MAKES: 22 SERVINGS (ABOUT 5½ QUARTS)

- ½ cup each dried great northern beans, kidney beans, navy beans, lima beans, butter beans, split green or yellow peas, pinto beans and lentils
    Water
- 1 meaty ham bone
- 2 teaspoons chicken bouillon granules
- 1 can (28 ounces) tomatoes with liquid, quartered
- 1 can (6 ounces) tomato paste
- 1 large onion, chopped
- 3 celery ribs, chopped
- 4 medium carrots, sliced
- 2 garlic cloves, minced
- ¼ cup minced chives
- 3 bay leaves
- 2 tablespoons dried parsley flakes
- 1 teaspoon dried thyme
- 1 teaspoon ground mustard
- ½ teaspoon cayenne pepper

1. Wash all beans thoroughly; drain and place in a large saucepan. Add 5 cups of water. Bring to a rapid boil; boil for 2 minutes. Remove from the heat; cover and let stand for 1 hour.

2. Meanwhile, place ham bone and 3 qts. of water in a stockpot. Simmer until the beans have stood for 1 hour.

3. Drain the beans and add them to the ham stock; add the remaining ingredients. Simmer for 2-3 hours or until the beans are tender. Cut meat from ham bone; discard bone. Add additional water to soup if desired.

APRICOT
GINGER
MUSTARD-
GLAZED HAM,
PAGE 115

CLASSIC MAIN DISHES

"The generous will themselves be blessed, for they share their food with the poor."

PROVERBS 22:9

FLAVORFUL POT ROAST
Arlene Butler
Ogden, UT

SLOW COOKER 🍲

FLAVORFUL POT ROAST

Slow cooking makes this pot roast incredibly tender. I use packages of dressing and gravy, so the sauce isn't just delicious—it's convenient and easy, too!

—ARLENE BUTLER OGDEN, UT

PREP: 10 MIN. • **COOK:** 7 HOURS
MAKES: 15 SERVINGS

- 2 boneless beef chuck roasts (2½ pounds each)
- 1 envelope ranch salad dressing mix
- 1 envelope Italian salad dressing mix
- 1 envelope brown gravy mix
- ½ cup water
  Chopped fresh parsley, optional

Place the chuck roasts in a 5-qt. slow cooker. In a small bowl, combine the salad dressings and gravy mix; stir in water. Pour over meat. Cover and cook on low for 7-8 hours or until tender. If desired, sprinkle with parsley and thicken the cooking juices for gravy.

CHEESY MANICOTTI CREPES

This entree may lack meat but it's loaded with three cheeses, so you won't miss it! Using homemade crepes instead of manicotti shells makes it a special treat whenever it's served.

—LORI HENRY ELKHART, IN

PREP: 2 HOURS + CHILLING • **BAKE:** 45 MIN.
MAKES: 12 SERVINGS

- 2 cans (28 ounces each) diced tomatoes, undrained
- 1½ cups finely chopped onion
- 1 can (6 ounces) tomato paste
- ⅓ cup olive oil
- 4 garlic cloves, minced
- 2 tablespoons dried parsley flakes
- 1 tablespoon sugar
- 1 tablespoon salt
- 1 teaspoon minced fresh oregano
- 1 teaspoon minced fresh basil
- ¼ teaspoon pepper

CREPES
- 6 large eggs
- 1½ cups water
- 1½ cups all-purpose flour
  Dash salt
- 2 tablespoons canola oil, divided

FILLING
- 2 cartons (15 ounces each) ricotta cheese
- 2 cups shredded part-skim mozzarella cheese
- 1 cup shredded Parmesan cheese
- 2 large eggs
- 1 tablespoon dried parsley flakes
- 1 teaspoon salt
- ¼ teaspoon pepper

1. In a large saucepan, combine the first 11 ingredients. Bring to a boil. Reduce heat; simmer, uncovered, for 1½ to 2 hours or until the sauce is reduced to 5 cups, stirring occasionally.

2. Meanwhile, in a large bowl, beat eggs and water. Combine flour and salt; add to egg mixture and mix well. Cover and refrigerate for 1 hour. In a large bowl, combine filling ingredients. Cover and refrigerate the batter.

3. Heat ¾ teaspoon oil in an 8-in. nonstick skillet. Stir the crepe batter; pour a scant 3 tablespoons into the center of the skillet. Lift and tilt the pan to coat the bottom evenly. Cook until the top appears dry; turn and cook 15-20 seconds longer. Remove to a wire rack. Repeat with the remaining batter, using the remaining oil as needed. When the crepes are cool, stack them with waxed paper or paper towels in between.

4. Spread about ¼ cup filling down the center of each crepe; roll up and place 12 crepes in each of two greased 13x9-in. baking dishes. Spoon the sauce over top. Cover and bake at 350° for 45-50 minutes or until a thermometer reads 160°.

SLOW COOKER

BLACK BEAN, CHORIZO & SWEET POTATO CHILI

Chili is one of my all-time favorite dishes. This recipe takes chili to the next level by changing up the flavors and adding a surprise—sweet potatoes!

—JULIE MERRIMAN SEATTLE, WA

PREP: 20 MIN. • **COOK:** 6 HOURS
MAKES: 16 SERVINGS (4 QUARTS)

- 1 pound uncooked chorizo, casings removed, or spicy bulk pork sausage
- 1 large onion, chopped
- 2 poblano peppers, finely chopped
- 2 jalapeno peppers, seeded and finely chopped
- 3 tablespoons tomato paste
- 3 large sweet potatoes, peeled and cut into ½-inch cubes
- 4 cans (14½ ounces each) fire-roasted diced tomatoes, undrained
- 2 cans (15 ounces each) black beans, rinsed and drained
- 2 cups beef stock
- 2 tablespoons chili powder
- 1 tablespoon dried oregano
- 1 tablespoon ground coriander
- 1 tablespoon ground cumin
- 1 tablespoon smoked paprika
- ¼ cup lime juice

1. In a large skillet, cook and stir the chorizo, onion, poblanos and jalapenos over medium heat for 8-10 minutes or until chorizo is cooked. Using a slotted spoon, transfer to a 6-qt. slow cooker.
2. Stir in the tomato paste. Add the potatoes, tomatoes, beans, stock and spices; stir to combine. Cover and cook on low for 6-7 hours or until the potatoes are tender. Stir in lime juice.

FAST FIX

GREEK TACOS

Try a surprising twist on tacos by trading taco seasoning, lettuce and cheddar for Greek flavors, spinach and feta. You'll be impressed.

—*TASTE OF HOME* TEST KITCHEN

START TO FINISH: 30 MIN.
MAKES: 12 SERVINGS.

- 1 pound lean ground beef (90% lean)
- 1 can (14½ ounces) diced tomatoes, undrained
- 2 teaspoons Greek seasoning
- ½ teaspoon minced garlic
- ¼ teaspoon pepper
- 2 cups fresh baby spinach
- 1 can (2¼ ounces) sliced ripe olives, drained
- 1 package (4½ ounces) taco shells
- ½ cup crumbled feta cheese
- ¼ cup chopped red onion

1. In a large skillet, cook beef over medium heat until no longer pink; drain. Stir in the tomatoes, Greek seasoning, garlic and pepper. Bring to a boil. Reduce heat; simmer for 8-10 minutes or until thickened. Add spinach and olives; cook and stir for 2-3 minutes or until the spinach is wilted.
2. Meanwhile, place taco shells on an ungreased baking sheet. Bake at 300° for 3-5 minutes or until heated through. Spoon about ¼ cup of the beef mixture into each shell. Top with feta cheese and onion.
NOTE *For a substitute for 1 tablespoon Greek seasoning, use ½ teaspoon each dried oregano, dried marjoram, garlic powder, lemon-pepper seasoning, ground mustard and salt. Omit the salt from recipes that call for it.*

PAELLA

A big pan of paella is the perfect choice when cooking for a crowd. All you need to round out the meal is fresh bread and a green salad.

—**JANE MONTGOMERY** HILLIARD, OH

PREP: 55 MIN. • **COOK:** 35 MIN.
MAKES: 24 SERVINGS

- 3 pounds uncooked skinless turkey breast, cubed
- 4 pounds uncooked chorizo, cut into 1½-inch pieces, or bulk spicy pork sausage
- 3 tablespoons olive oil
- 2 medium onions, chopped
- 1 medium sweet red pepper, chopped
- 4 garlic cloves, minced
- ½ teaspoon cayenne pepper
- 2 cups tomato puree
- 1 cup white wine or chicken broth
- 5 cups water
- 4 cups uncooked long grain rice
- 3½ cups chicken broth
- 2 teaspoons salt
- 1 teaspoon dried thyme
- ¾ teaspoon saffron threads or 2 teaspoons ground turmeric
- 1 bay leaf
- 2 pounds uncooked medium shrimp, peeled and deveined
- ¾ cup pitted Greek olives
- ½ cup minced fresh parsley

1. In a large skillet, cook turkey and chorizo in oil in batches until browned. Remove with a slotted spoon and keep warm.
2. In the same skillet, saute onions and red pepper until tender. Add garlic and cayenne; cook 1 minute longer. Stir in tomato puree and wine. Bring to a boil; cook and stir for 2 minutes or until thickened.
3. Transfer to a stock pot. Stir in the water, rice, broth, salt, thyme, saffron, bay leaf, turkey and chorizo. Bring to a boil. Reduce heat; cover and simmer for 20 minutes or until rice is tender.
4. Add shrimp; cook for 2-3 minutes or until shrimp turn pink. Remove from the heat; discard bay leaf. Stir in olives and parsley.

SOUTH CAROLINA CHICKEN & RICE

Chicken Bog is the traditional name for this South Carolina Low Country dish. We always make a big batch the day after Thanksgiving, when we're busy working on our family's Christmas tree farm.

—**JEAN COCHRAN** LEXINGTON, SC

PREP: 10 MIN. • **COOK:** 50 MIN.
MAKES: 12 SERVINGS

- 2½ pounds boneless skinless chicken thighs
- 8 cups chicken broth, divided
- 2 packages (13 to 14 ounces each) smoked sausage, sliced
- 1 large onion, finely chopped
- 3 cups uncooked long grain rice
  Salt and pepper to taste

1. In a 6-quart stockpot, cook chicken in 2 cups broth over medium heat until a thermometer reads 170°, turning halfway through cooking. Remove the chicken; set aside to cool. Add sausage, onion and the remaining broth to stockpot; bring to a boil. Add rice. Reduce heat; simmer, uncovered, 15-18 minutes or until rice is almost tender (the mixture may be soupy).
2. Shred chicken; add to rice. Cook, covered, until rice is tender. Season with salt and pepper to taste.

GARDEN VEGGIE LASAGNA

Stroll the farmers market and you'll see veggies and cheeses galore. Why not pull them together in one harmonious bunch and make this your go-to lasagna when you crave a twist on an Italian favorite?

—SAMANTHA NEAL MORGANTOWN, WV

PREP: 50 MIN. • **BAKE:** 35 MIN. + STANDING
MAKES: 12 SERVINGS

- 2 medium zucchini, sliced diagonally ¼-in. thick
- 2 cups fresh broccoli florets
- 2 large carrots, julienned
- 2 medium sweet red peppers, julienned
- ¼ cup olive oil
- 2 garlic cloves, minced
- ¾ teaspoon dried thyme
- ½ teaspoon salt
- ½ teaspoon pepper

SAUCE
- 2 cups finely chopped baby portobello mushrooms
- 1 large onion, finely chopped
- 2 garlic cloves, minced
- 2 tablespoons olive oil
- 2 cans (28 ounces each) crushed tomatoes
- 3 teaspoons Italian seasoning
- ¾ teaspoon salt
- ¾ teaspoon pepper

FILLING
- 1¼ cups ricotta cheese
- 1 package (8 ounces) cream cheese, softened
- ¾ cup grated Parmesan cheese
- 1 large egg, lightly beaten
- 2 teaspoons dried basil

ASSEMBLY
- 12 no-cook lasagna noodles
- 3 cups shredded Italian cheese blend

1. Preheat oven to 425°. Place the first nine ingredients in a large bowl; toss to coat. Arrange on two greased 15x10x1-in baking pans. Bake 10-15 minutes or until tender, stirring occasionally. Reduce oven to 350°.
2. Meanwhile, in a Dutch oven, saute mushrooms, onion and garlic in oil until tender. Stir in the remaining sauce ingredients; bring to a boil. Reduce

heat; simmer, uncovered, 10-12 minutes, stirring sauce occasionally.
3. In a large bowl, combine the filling ingredients. Spread 1 cup of the sauce into a greased 13x9-in. baking dish. Layer a third of the noodles, a third of the ricotta cheese mixture, half of the vegetables, a third of the remaining sauce and a third of the cheese blend; repeat. Top with the remaining noodles, ricotta mixture, sauce and cheese blend.
4. Cover and bake for 35-40 minutes or until bubbly. Let stand 15 minutes before cutting.

SAVORY PORK ROAST

I love this herbed roast so much that I make it as often as I can. It's wonderful for special occasions, particularly when served with sweet potatoes and corn muffins.

—EDIE DESPAIN LOGAN, UT

PREP: 5 MIN. • **BAKE:** 80 MIN. + STANDING
MAKES: 12 SERVINGS

- 1 garlic clove, minced
- 2 teaspoons dried marjoram
- 1 teaspoon salt
- 1 teaspoon rubbed sage
- 1 boneless whole pork loin roast (4 pounds)

1. Combine the seasonings; rub over roast. Place on a rack in a shallow roasting pan.
2. Bake, uncovered, at 350° for 80 minutes or until a meat thermometer reads 145°. Let stand for 10-15 minutes before slicing.

TEST KITCHEN TIP
Stop overcooking your pork! The USDA recently changed the guidelines for cooking fresh pork to a recommended internal temperature of 145° with a minimum 3-minute rest time. The internal color of boneless roasts may be faint pink, and bone-in roasts may be slightly pink near the bone, but if the juices run clear, the meat is properly cooked. Ground meat should still be cooked to an internal temperature of 160°.

**SAVORY
PORK ROAST**

BEST SPAGHETTI AND MEATBALLS

We had unexpected company one evening, so I warmed up some of these meatballs I had in the freezer. Everyone raved! This classic recipe makes a big batch and is perfect for entertaining.
—**MARY LOU KOSKELLA** PRESCOTT, AZ

PREP: 30 MIN. • **COOK:** 2 HOURS
MAKES: 16 SERVINGS

- 1½ cups chopped onions
- 2 tablespoons olive oil
- 3 garlic cloves, minced
- 3 cups water
- 1 can (29 ounces) tomato sauce
- 2 cans (12 ounces each) tomato paste
- ⅓ cup minced fresh parsley
- 1 tablespoon dried basil
- 1 tablespoon salt
- ½ teaspoon pepper

MEATBALLS

- 4 large eggs, lightly beaten
- 2 cups soft bread cubes (¼-inch pieces)
- 1½ cups milk
- 1 cup grated Parmesan cheese
- 3 garlic cloves, minced
- 1 tablespoon salt
- ½ teaspoon pepper
- 3 pounds ground beef
- 2 tablespoons canola oil
  Hot cooked spaghetti

1. In a Dutch oven over medium heat, saute onions in oil. Add garlic; cook 1 minute longer. Add the water, tomato sauce and paste, parsley, basil, salt and pepper; bring to a boil. Reduce heat; cover and simmer for 50 minutes.

2. In a large bowl, combine the first seven meatball ingredients. Crumble the beef over the mixture and mix well. Shape into 1½-in. balls.

3. In a large skillet over medium heat, brown the meatballs in batches in oil until no longer pink; drain. Add meatballs to sauce; bring to a boil. Reduce heat; cover and simmer for 1 hour or until flavors are blended, stirring occasionally. Serve with spaghetti.

TURKEY PECAN ENCHILADAS

A friend passed along this recipe, and I've served it at church potlucks many times since. It's creamy, just a little spicy and a change from the norm.
—**CATHY HUPPE** GEORGETOWN, MA

PREP: 25 MIN. • **BAKE:** 45 MIN.
MAKES: 12 SERVINGS

- 1 medium onion, chopped
- 4 ounces reduced-fat cream cheese
- 1 tablespoon water
- 1 teaspoon ground cumin
- ¼ teaspoon pepper
- ⅛ teaspoon salt
- 4 cups cubed cooked turkey breast
- ¼ cup chopped pecans, toasted
- 12 flour tortillas (6 inches), warmed
- 1 can (10¾ ounces) reduced-fat reduced-sodium condensed cream of chicken soup, undiluted
- 1 cup reduced-fat sour cream
- 1 cup fat-free milk
- 2 tablespoons canned chopped green chilies
- ½ cup shredded reduced-fat cheddar cheese
- 2 tablespoons minced fresh cilantro

1. In a small nonstick skillet coated with cooking spray, cook and stir the onion over medium heat until tender. Set aside.

2. In a large bowl, beat the cream cheese, water, cumin, pepper and salt until smooth. Stir in the onion, turkey and pecans.

3. Spoon ⅓ cup turkey mixture down the center of each tortilla. Roll up tortillas and place seam side down in a 13x9-in. baking dish coated with cooking spray. Combine the soup, sour cream, milk and chilies; pour over enchiladas.

4. Cover and bake at 350° for 40 minutes. Uncover; sprinkle with cheese. Bake 5 minutes longer or until heated through and cheese is melted. Sprinkle with cilantro.

CHICKEN MOLE
Darlene Morris
Franklinton, LA

MAKE AHEAD | **SLOW COOKER**

CHICKEN MOLE

Chocolate with chicken? If you're not familiar with mole, don't be afraid of this versatile Mexican sauce. I love sharing this recipe because it's a great one to experiment with.

—**DARLENE MORRIS** FRANKLINTON, LA

PREP: 25 MIN. • **COOK:** 6 HOURS
MAKES: 12 SERVINGS

 12 bone-in chicken thighs (about 4½ pounds), skin removed
  1 teaspoon salt
MOLE SAUCE
  1 can (28 ounces) whole tomatoes, drained
  1 medium onion, chopped
  2 dried ancho chilies, stems and seeds removed
  ½ cup sliced almonds, toasted
  ¼ cup raisins
  3 ounces bittersweet chocolate, chopped
  3 tablespoons olive oil
  1 chipotle pepper in adobo sauce
  3 garlic cloves, peeled and halved
  ¾ teaspoon ground cumin
  ½ teaspoon ground cinnamon
     Fresh cilantro leaves, optional

1. Sprinkle chicken with salt; place in a 5- or 6-qt. slow cooker. Place the tomatoes, onion, chilies, almonds, raisins, chocolate, oil, chipotle pepper, garlic, cumin and cinnamon in a food processor; cover and process until blended. Pour over chicken.
2. Cover and cook on low for 6-8 hours or until the chicken is tender; skim fat. Serve the chicken with sauce, and if desired, sprinkle with cilantro.
FREEZE OPTION *Cool chicken in mole sauce. Freeze in freezer containers. To use, partially thaw in refrigerator overnight. Heat through slowly in a covered skillet or Dutch oven until a thermometer inserted in chicken reads 165°, stirring occasionally and adding a little broth or water if necessary.*

**SPINACH BEEF
MACARONI BAKE**

BIEROCKS

This is an old German recipe handed down from generation to generation, using foods grown or raised on the family farm. I remember helping my grandmother make these when I could barely see over the kitchen table!

—**ELLEN BATT** HOISINGTON, KS

PREP: 30 MIN. + RISING • **BAKE:** 30 MIN.
MAKES: 24 SERVINGS

DOUGH

- 10 to 11 cups all-purpose flour, divided
- 1 package (¼-ounce) active dry yeast
- ½ cup sugar
- 2 teaspoons salt
- 2½ cups water
- 1 cup whole milk
- ½ cup butter, cubed
- 2 large eggs

FILLING

- 2 pounds ground beef
- 1 large onion, chopped
- 2 teaspoons salt
- 1 teaspoon ground white pepper
- 2 pounds shredded cabbage, cooked and drained

1. For dough, in a large bowl, combine 4 cups of flour, yeast, sugar and salt; mix well and set aside.
2. In a saucepan, heat water, milk and butter just until butter melts. Remove from heat and cool to 120°-130°. Combine with the flour mixture; add eggs. Using an electric mixer, blend at low speed until moistened, then beat at medium speed for 3 minutes. By hand, gradually stir in enough of the remaining flour to make a firm dough.
3. Knead dough on a floured surface for about 10 minutes. Place in a greased bowl, turning once to grease top. Cover and let rise in a warm place until doubled, about 1 hour. Punch dough down; let rise again until almost doubled.
4. Meanwhile, for the filling, brown beef with onion, salt and pepper; drain. Mix together with cabbage; set aside. Divide the dough into fourths. Roll each piece into a 15x10-in. rectangle. Cut into 5-inch squares. Spoon ⅓ to ½ cup filling onto each square.

Bring the four corners up over the filling; pinch together to seal. Repeat with remaining dough and filling. Place on greased baking sheets.
5. Bake at 375° for 30 minutes or until brown.

SPINACH BEEF MACARONI BAKE

I serve this dish at family gatherings and church suppers and sometimes cut the recipe in half for smaller family dinners. My grandson-in-law and great-grandson often ask me to serve it when they stop by to visit.

—**LOIS LAUPPE** LAHOMA, OK

PREP: 55 MIN. • **BAKE:** 25 MIN.
MAKES: 2 CASSEROLES (12 SERVINGS EACH)

- 5¼ cups uncooked elbow macaroni
- 2½ pounds ground beef
- 2 large onions, chopped
- 3 large carrots, shredded
- 3 celery ribs, chopped
- 2 cans (28 ounces each) Italian diced tomatoes, undrained
- 4 teaspoons salt
- 1 teaspoon garlic powder
- 1 teaspoon pepper
- ½ teaspoon dried oregano
- 2 packages (10 ounces each) frozen chopped spinach, thawed and squeezed dry
- 1 cup grated Parmesan cheese

1. Cook macaroni according to package directions. Meanwhile, in a large Dutch oven, cook the beef, onions, carrots and celery over medium heat until the meat is no longer pink; drain. Add the tomatoes, salt, garlic powder, pepper and oregano. Bring to a boil. Reduce heat; cover and simmer for 30 minutes or until the vegetables are tender.
2. Drain macaroni; add macaroni and spinach to the beef mixture. Pour into two greased 3-qt. baking dishes. Sprinkle with cheese. Bake, uncovered, at 350° for 25-30 minutes or until heated through.

HALIBUT ENCHILADAS

To create a dish where North meets South of the Border, I roll our local Alaskan halibut into tortillas. It's one of my most requested recipes.

—**CAROLE DERIFIELD** VALDEZ, AK

PREP: 45 MIN. • **BAKE:** 40 MIN.
MAKES: 12 SERVINGS

- 3 pounds halibut fillets
- ½ teaspoon salt
- ⅛ teaspoon pepper
- ⅛ teaspoon cayenne pepper
- 1 medium onion, finely chopped
- 1 medium green pepper, finely chopped
- 1 tablespoon canola oil
- 2 garlic cloves, minced
- 1 can (10 ounces) hot enchilada sauce
- 1 can (10 ounces) green enchilada sauce
- 1 cup (8 ounces) sour cream
- 1 cup mayonnaise
- 2 cans (4 ounces each) chopped green chilies
- 2 cans (10 ounces each) mild enchilada sauce
- 4 cups shredded Colby-Monterey Jack cheese
- 24 flour tortillas (6 inches), warmed
- 1 bunch green onions, thinly sliced
- 2 tablespoons chopped ripe olives

1. Place fillets on a greased baking sheet. Sprinkle with salt, pepper and cayenne. Bake, uncovered, at 350° for 15-20 minutes or until the fish flakes easily with a fork.

2. In a large skillet, saute onion and green pepper in oil until tender. Add garlic; cook 1 minute longer.

3. Flake the fish with two forks; set aside. In a large bowl, combine the hot enchilada sauce, green enchilada sauce, sour cream, mayonnaise, chilies, onion mixture and fish. Spread ½ cup mild enchilada sauce into each of two greased 13x9-in. baking dishes. Sprinkle each with 1 cup cheese.

4. Place a heaping ⅓ cup of the halibut mixture down the center of each tortilla. Roll up each and place seam side down over the cheese in the baking dish. Pour remaining sauce over top.

5. Cover and bake at 350° for 30 minutes. Sprinkle with the green onions, olives and remaining cheese. Bake, uncovered, 10-15 minutes to melt cheese.

BALSAMIC PORK SCALLOPINE

I developed this delightful dish by tweaking my veal scallopine recipe. Thinly sliced pork is an economical alternative to veal and a tasty success!

—**MARY COKENOUR** MONTICELLO, UT

PREP: 25 MIN. • **COOK:** 30 MIN.
MAKES: 12 SERVINGS

- 3 pounds pork sirloin cutlets
- 1½ cups all-purpose flour
- ½ cup olive oil
- 2 tablespoons butter
- 1 medium onion, chopped
- ½ cup chopped roasted sweet red peppers
- 6 garlic cloves, minced
- 1 can (14½ ounces) reduced-sodium chicken broth
- ½ cup minced fresh basil or 2 tablespoons dried basil
- ½ cup balsamic vinegar
- ½ teaspoon pepper

NOODLES
- 1 package (16 ounces) egg noodles
- ½ cup half-and-half cream
- ¼ cup grated Romano cheese
- ¼ cup butter, cubed
- ½ teaspoon pepper
- ¼ teaspoon garlic powder

1. Dredge pork cutlets in flour. Heat oil and butter in a large skillet over medium-high heat; add the pork and brown in batches. Set aside.

2. Add onion and red peppers to the pan; saute until the onion is tender. Add garlic; cook 1 minute longer. Add the broth, basil, vinegar and pepper. Return the pork to the pan, layering if necessary.

3. Cover and cook over low heat for 15-20 minutes or until the meat is tender.

4. Meanwhile, in a Dutch oven, cook noodles according to package directions. Drain; stir in the cream, cheese, butter, pepper and garlic powder. Serve with the pork.

FIREFIGHTER'S CHICKEN SPAGHETTI

My husband is a firefighter in our town, and I'm often in the kitchen most of the day making some kind of dish for the local fire department, neighbors or family to pass around. This spaghetti casserole is a firehouse favorite.

—KRISTA DAVIS-KEITH NEW CASTLE, IN

PREP: 20 MIN. • **BAKE:** 45 MIN.
MAKES: 14 SERVINGS

- 12 ounces uncooked spaghetti, broken in half
- 1 can (10¾ ounces) condensed cream of chicken soup, undiluted
- 1 can (10¾ ounces) condensed cream of mushroom soup, undiluted
- 1 cup sour cream
- ½ cup whole milk
- ¼ cup butter, melted, divided
- 2 tablespoons dried parsley flakes
- ½ teaspoon garlic powder
- ½ teaspoon salt
- ¼ teaspoon pepper
- 2 cups shredded part-skim mozzarella cheese
- 1 cup grated Parmesan cheese
- 2 to 3 celery ribs, chopped
- 1 medium onion, chopped
- 1 can (4 ounces) mushroom stems and pieces, drained
- 5 cups cubed cooked chicken
- 1½ cups crushed cornflakes

1. Preheat oven to 350°. Cook spaghetti according to package directions; drain.
2. In a large bowl, combine soups, sour cream, milk, 2 tablespoons butter and seasonings. Add the cheeses, celery, onion and mushrooms. Stir in the chicken and spaghetti.
3. Transfer to a greased 3-qt. baking dish (the dish will be full). Combine cornflakes and remaining butter; sprinkle over the top.
4. Bake, uncovered, 45-50 minutes or until bubbly.

APRICOT GINGER MUSTARD-GLAZED HAM

I decided to do a home-baked ham with a gingery glaze for a holiday meal. This is how you do special-occasion dining!

—ALLY PHILLIPS MURRELLS INLET, SC

PREP: 15 MIN. • **BAKE:** 2 HOURS
MAKES: 16 SERVINGS

- 1 fully cooked bone-in ham (7 to 9 pounds)
- ½ cup apricot halves, drained
- ½ cup stone-ground mustard
- ⅓ cup packed brown sugar
- 2 tablespoons grated fresh gingerroot
- 1 tablespoon whole peppercorns
- ½ teaspoon sea salt
- ½ teaspoon coarsely ground pepper

1. Preheat oven to 325°. Place ham on a rack in a shallow roasting pan. Using a sharp knife, score the surface of the ham with ¼-in.-deep cuts in a diamond pattern. Cover and bake 1¾ to 2¼ hours or until a thermometer reads 130°.
2. Meanwhile, place the remaining ingredients in a food processor; process until blended. Remove ham from the oven. Increase oven setting to 425°. Spread the apricot mixture over the ham.
3. Bake ham, uncovered, 15-20 minutes longer or until a thermometer reads 140°. If desired, increase oven setting to broil; broil for 2-4 minutes or until golden brown.

CHICAGO-STYLE DEEP-DISH PIZZA

My husband and I tried to duplicate the pizza from a popular Chicago restaurant, and I think our recipe turned out even better! The secret is baking it in a cast-iron skillet.

—**LYNN HAMILTON** NAPERVILLE, IL

PREP: 20 MIN. + RISING • **BAKE:** 40 MIN.
MAKES: 2 PIZZAS (8 SLICES EACH)

- 3½ cups all-purpose flour, divided
- ¼ cup cornmeal
- 1 package (¼ ounce) quick-rise yeast
- 1½ teaspoons sugar
- ½ teaspoon salt
- 1 cup water
- ⅓ cup olive oil

TOPPINGS

- 6 cups shredded part-skim mozzarella cheese, divided
- 1 can (28 ounces) diced tomatoes, well drained
- 1 can (8 ounces) tomato sauce
- 1 can (6 ounces) tomato paste
- ½ teaspoon salt
- ¼ teaspoon each garlic powder, dried oregano, dried basil and pepper
- 48 slices pepperoni
- 1 pound bulk Italian sausage, cooked and crumbled
- ½ pound sliced fresh mushrooms
- ¼ cup grated Parmesan cheese

1. In a large bowl, combine 1½ cups flour, cornmeal, yeast, sugar and salt. In a saucepan, heat water and oil to 120°-130°. Add to dry ingredients; beat just until moistened. Add the remaining flour to form a stiff dough.

2. Turn dough onto a floured surface; knead until smooth and elastic, 6-8 minutes. Place in a greased bowl, turning once to grease top. Cover and let rise in warm place until doubled, about 30 minutes.

3. Punch dough down; divide in half. Roll each portion into an 11-in. circle. Press dough onto the bottom and up the sides of two greased 10-in. ovenproof skillets. Sprinkle each with 2 cups of mozzarella cheese.

4. In a large bowl, combine the tomatoes, tomato sauce, tomato paste and seasonings. Spoon 1½ cups over each pizza. Layer each with half of the sausage, pepperoni and mushrooms; 1 cup mozzarella; and 2 tablespoons Parmesan cheese.

5. Cover and bake at 450° for 35 minutes. Uncover; bake 5 minutes longer or until pizzas are lightly browned.

NOTE *Two 9-in. springform pans may be used in place of the skillets. Place pans on baking sheets. After baking, run a knife around the inner edge of the pan to loosen the crust before removing the sides of the pan.*

MAKE AHEAD **FAST FIX** ▶

MAKE-AHEAD MEATBALLS

My husband and I have company often. Keeping a supply of these frozen meatballs on hand means I can easily prepare a quick, satisfying meal. This versatile meatball mix makes about 12 dozen meatballs; I freeze them in batches for future use.

—**RUTH ANDREWSON** LEAVENWORTH, WA

START TO FINISH: 25 MIN.
MAKES: 5 BATCHES (ABOUT 30 MEATBALLS PER BATCH)

- 4 large eggs, lightly beaten
- 2 cups dry bread crumbs
- ½ cup finely chopped onion
- 1 tablespoon salt
- 2 teaspoons Worcestershire sauce
- ½ teaspoon white pepper
- 4 pounds lean ground beef (90% lean)

1. In a large bowl, combine the first six ingredients. Crumble the beef over the mixture and mix well. Shape into 1-in. balls, about 12 dozen.

2. Place meatballs on greased racks in shallow baking pans. Bake at 400° for 10-15 minutes or until no longer pink, turning often; drain. Cool.

FREEZE OPTION *Freeze cooled meatballs in freezer containers. To use, partially thaw in the refrigerator overnight. Reheat on a greased 15x10x1-in. baking pan in a preheated 350° oven until heated through.*

CHICAGO-STYLE
DEEP-DISH PIZZA

BLACK-AND-BLUE PIZZAS

Here, blue cheese, shiitake mushrooms and blackened seasoning lend a tasty change to traditional pizza. Add a mixed green salad to make the meal complete.

—**MICHELLE HUELSKAMP** MARION, NC

PREP: 40 MIN. • **BAKE:** 15 MIN.
MAKES: 2 PIZZAS (12 PIECES EACH)

- 2 loaves (1 pound each) frozen bread dough, thawed
- 8 bacon strips, chopped
- 1 pound boneless skinless chicken breasts, cut into strips
- 5 teaspoons blackened seasoning
- 3 shallots, finely chopped
- 2 garlic cloves, minced
- 1 jar (15 ounces) Alfredo sauce
- 2½ cups sliced fresh shiitake mushrooms
- 1 can (3.8 ounces) sliced ripe olives, drained
- ½ cup finely chopped sun-dried tomatoes (not packed in oil)
- 1¼ cups crumbled blue cheese
- 3 tablespoons minced fresh basil or 3 teaspoons dried basil
- 2 tablespoons minced fresh thyme or 2 teaspoons dried thyme
- 12 slices provolone cheese
- 3 ounces Parmesan cheese, shaved into strips, or ¾ cup grated Parmesan cheese

1. Roll dough into two 16x10-in. rectangles; transfer to ungreased baking sheets and build up edges slightly.

2. In a large skillet, cook bacon over medium heat until crisp. Remove to paper towels with a slotted spoon; drain, reserving 2 tablespoons drippings. Sprinkle chicken with blackened seasoning; cook chicken in the drippings until no longer pink. Add shallots and garlic; cook 1 minute longer. Set aside.

3. Spread sauce over crusts; top with chicken mixture, bacon, mushrooms, olives and tomatoes. Sprinkle with blue cheese, basil and thyme; top with provolone and Parmesan cheeses.

4. Bake at 450° for 14-18 minutes or until bubbly and cheese is melted.

BRUNSWICK STEW

Brunswick Stew dates back to the 1860s when it was served as a complete meal. It's delicious picnic fare when served with country ribs, coleslaw or potato salad. When I make this stew, I double the recipe and freeze small portions so we can enjoy it at several meals.

—**ALYCE RAY** FOREST PARK, GA

PREP: 1½ HOURS + CHILLING • **COOK:** 1 HOUR
MAKES: 6 QUARTS

- 1 pound bone-in pork loin chops
- 2 bone-in chicken breast halves, skin removed
- 1 pound beef top round steak, cut into bite-size pieces
- 6 cups water
- 2 cans (14½ ounces each) diced tomatoes, undrained
- 2 cups chopped onion
- 1 can (8 ounces) tomato sauce
- ½ cup cider vinegar
- ¼ cup sugar
- 4 to 5 garlic cloves, minced
- 2 teaspoons hot pepper sauce
- 2 cans (15¼ ounces each) whole kernel corn, drained
- 2 cans (14¾ ounces each) cream-style corn
- 1 cup dry bread crumbs, toasted
  Salt and pepper to taste

1. Place the pork chops, chicken and round steak in a large Dutch oven; cover with water. Cover and cook for 1½ hours or until the meat is tender.

2. Strain stock into another large kettle; refrigerate overnight. Remove any bones from the meat; dice and place in a separate bowl. Cover and refrigerate meat overnight.

3. The next day, skim fat from the stock. Add the tomatoes, onion, tomato sauce, vinegar, sugar, garlic and pepper sauce. Simmer, uncovered, for 45 minutes.

4. Add the whole kernel corn, cream-style corn, reserved meat; heat through. Stir in bread crumbs; season with salt and pepper.

SPINACH-PESTO
SPIRAL CHICKEN

SPINACH-PESTO SPIRAL CHICKEN

Homemade pesto sets this recipe apart. Elegant enough for a special dinner, simple enough for an evening at home, and impressive enough to share with friends, it's a main dish you can make anytime.
—**AMY BLOM** MARIETTA, GA

PREP: 20 MIN. • **BAKE:** 40 MIN.
MAKES: 12 SERVINGS

- 12 **boneless skinless chicken thighs (about 3 pounds)**
- 2 **cups fresh baby spinach**
- 1 **cup packed basil leaves**
- 6 **garlic cloves**
- 2 **teaspoons olive oil**
- 2 **tablespoons grated Parmesan cheese**
- 2 **tablespoons chopped walnuts**
- 2 **tablespoons reduced-sodium chicken broth**
- ½ **cup chopped oil-packed sun-dried tomatoes**
- ⅓ **cup chopped water-packed artichoke hearts, rinsed and drained**
- ½ **teaspoon salt, divided**
- ¼ **teaspoon pepper, divided**

1. Preheat oven to 375°. Pound chicken breasts with a meat mallet to ¼-in. thickness.
2. In a food processor, combine spinach, basil, garlic, oil, cheese, walnuts and broth. Cover and process until blended. Stir in tomatoes, artichoke hearts, ¼ teaspoon salt and ⅛ teaspoon pepper. Spread over chicken. Starting at a short side, roll up and secure with toothpicks.
3. Place in two greased 11x7-in. baking dishes, seam side down. Sprinkle with remaining salt and pepper. Bake 40-45 minutes or until a thermometer reads 170°. Discard toothpicks before serving.

CHICKEN & CHEDDAR
BISCUIT CASSEROLE

MAKE AHEAD

CHICKEN & CHEDDAR BISCUIT CASSEROLE

I always get rave reviews when I bring this casserole to my son's Cub Scouts meetings. We think it's also the perfect comfort meal after a long day.

—SARAH PHILLIPS EAST LANSING, MI

PREP: 40 MIN. • **BAKE:** 35 MIN.
MAKES: 12 SERVINGS

- ⅓ cup butter, cubed
- 1 large onion, chopped
- 2 celery ribs, chopped
- 2 medium carrots, chopped
- 2 garlic cloves, minced
- ½ cup all-purpose flour
- 1 teaspoon salt
- ½ teaspoon pepper
- 4 cups chicken broth or stock
- 5 cups cubed cooked chicken
- 3 cups biscuit/baking mix
- ¾ cup 2% milk
- 1 cup shredded cheddar cheese
- 1 cup roasted sweet red peppers, drained and chopped

1. Preheat oven to 425°. In a 6-qt. stockpot, heat butter over medium-high heat. Add onion, celery and carrots; cook and stir 3-5 minutes or until tender. Add garlic; cook and stir 1 minute longer. Stir in flour, salt and pepper; gradually whisk in broth. Bring to a boil, stirring constantly; cook and stir over medium heat 4-6 minutes or until thickened. Add chicken. Transfer to a greased 13x9-in. baking dish. Bake, uncovered, 20 minutes.
2. In a large bowl, combine biscuit mix and milk just until moistened. Turn onto a lightly floured surface; knead gently 8-10 times. Roll into a 12x8-in. rectangle. Sprinkle with cheese and peppers. Roll up jelly-roll style, starting with a long side; pinch seam to seal. Cut roll crosswise into 1-in.-thick slices. Place on top of hot chicken mixture. Return dish to oven and bake, uncovered, 15-20 minutes or until biscuits are golden brown.
FREEZE OPTION *Cool baked casserole; cover and freeze. To use, partially thaw in refrigerator overnight. Remove from refrigerator 30 minutes before baking. Preheat oven to 425°. Bake casserole, covered, 40 minutes or until heated through and a thermometer inserted in center reads 165°.*

GOLDEN BAKED CHICKEN

This recipe makes a delicious crispy chicken without frying, and the paprika gives the chicken pieces a pleasant punch and a pretty color.

—HARRIET STICHTER MILFORD, IN

PREP: 20 MIN. • **BAKE:** 50 MIN.
MAKES: 12 SERVINGS

- 2 cups mashed potato flakes
- ¾ cup grated Parmesan cheese
- 2 tablespoons dried parsley flakes
- 1 tablespoon paprika
- ¾ teaspoon garlic salt
- ¾ teaspoon onion powder
- ½ teaspoon pepper
- 1 cup butter, melted
- 3 broiler/fryer chicken (3 to 4 pounds each), cut up and skin removed

1. In a shallow bowl, combine the potato flakes, cheese, parsley, paprika, garlic salt, onion powder and pepper. In another shallow bowl, add butter. Dip chicken in the butter, then into the seasoned potato-flake mixture.
2. Place on two greased 15x10x1-in. baking pans. Bake at 375° for 50-60 minutes or until chicken juices run clear.

★ ★ ★ ★ ★ **READER REVIEW**

"This baked chicken recipe is excellent. My whole family loved it!"

VESBACH TASTEOFHOME.COM

SAVORY RUBBED ROAST CHICKEN

A blend of paprika, onion powder, garlic and cayenne creates a delicious, slightly spicy roast chicken. The aroma of this dish while it's cooking drives my family nuts!

—MARGARET COLE IMPERIAL, MO

PREP: 20 MIN. • **BAKE:** 2 HOURS + STANDING
MAKES: 12 SERVINGS

- 2 teaspoons paprika
- 1 teaspoon salt
- 1 teaspoon onion powder
- 1 teaspoon white pepper
- 1 teaspoon cayenne pepper
- 1 teaspoon dried thyme
- ¾ teaspoon garlic powder
- ½ teaspoon pepper
- 1 roasting chicken (6 to 7 pounds)
- 1 large onion, cut into wedges

1. Preheat oven to 350°. In a small bowl, mix the first eight ingredients.
2. Pat chicken dry and place on a rack in a roasting pan, breast side up. Rub the seasoning mixture over the outside and inside of chicken. Place onion inside the cavity. Tuck wings under chicken; tie drumsticks together.
3. Roast 2 to 2½ hours or until a thermometer inserted in thickest part of thigh reads 170°-175°. (Cover loosely with foil if chicken browns too quickly.) Remove chicken from oven; tent with foil. Let stand 15 minutes before carving.

SLOW COOKER

SOUTHWEST BEEF STEW

I made this stew for my ladies group at church, and everyone loved it! Best of all, I could start the soup before I left for work in the morning and and have it ready to go when I got home.

—ANITA ROBERSON WILLIAMSTON, NC

PREP: 30 MIN. • **COOK:** 7 HOURS
MAKES: 11 SERVINGS (2¾ QUARTS)

- 1½ pounds lean ground beef (90% lean)
- 1 large onion, chopped
- 2 cans (14½ ounces each) diced tomatoes, undrained
- 1 package (16 ounces) frozen corn
- 1 can (15 ounces) black beans, rinsed and drained
- 1 can (14½ ounces) chicken broth
- 1 can (10 ounces) diced tomatoes and green chilies, undrained
- 1 teaspoon garlic powder
- 1½ teaspoons salt-free Southwest chipotle seasoning blend
- 1½ cups cooked rice
- ¼ cup shredded cheddar cheese

1. In a large skillet, cook the beef and onion over medium heat until the meat is no longer pink; drain.
2. Transfer to a 5-qt. slow cooker. Stir in the tomatoes, corn, black beans, broth, tomatoes, garlic powder and seasoning blend. Cover and cook on low for 6-8 hours or until heated through.
3. Stir in rice; heat through. Sprinkle each serving with cheese.

TEST KITCHEN TIP
If you're using a frozen chicken, make sure the bird is completely thawed before roasting it. If it isn't, increase the roasting time and check the internal temperature often. We recommend thawing it in the refrigerator: Allow 24 hours per five pounds of chicken. For faster thawing, place the chicken in a leakproof bag and immerse it in cold tap water. Change the water every 30 minutes, allowing 30 minutes for every pound.

MAKE AHEAD
GOLDEN CHICKEN POTPIES

The golden crust and creamy sauce make this veggie-packed pie a sure hit. Frozen vegetables work extremely well in this mild and comforting family favorite.

—*TASTE OF HOME* TEST KITCHEN

PREP: 20 MIN. • **BAKE:** 35 MIN.
MAKES: 2 POTPIES (6 SERVINGS EACH)

- 4 cups cubed cooked chicken
- 4 cups frozen cubed hash brown potatoes, thawed
- 1 package (16 ounces) frozen mixed vegetables, thawed and drained
- 1 can (10¾ ounces) condensed cream of chicken soup, undiluted
- 1 can (10¾ ounces) condensed cream of onion soup, undiluted
- 1 cup whole milk
- 1 cup sour cream
- 2 tablespoons all-purpose flour
- ½ teaspoon salt
- ½ teaspoon pepper
- ¼ teaspoon garlic powder
- 1 package (15 ounces) refrigerated pie pastry

1. Preheat oven to 400°. In a large bowl, combine the first 11 ingredients. Divide between two 9-in. deep-dish pie plates. Roll out pastry to fit the top of each pie. Place pastry over the filling; trim, seal and flute the edges. Cut slits in the top or make decorative cutouts in pastry.

2. Bake 35-40 minutes or until golden brown.

FREEZE OPTION: *Cover and freeze unbaked pies up to 3 months. To use, remove from freezer 30 minutes before baking (do not thaw). Preheat oven to 425°. Place pie on a baking sheet; cover edges loosely with foil. Bake 30 minutes. Reduce heat to 350°; remove foil and bake 50-55 minutes longer or until golden brown, or until heated through and a thermometer inserted in the center reads 165°.*

POTLUCK SPARERIBS

When I want to bring home an empty pan from a potluck, I turn to this recipe. The ribs always disappear in minutes!

—**SHERI KIRKMAN** LANCASTER, NY

PREP: 10 MIN. • **BAKE:** 1¾ HOURS
MAKES: 12 SERVINGS

- 6 pounds pork spareribs
- 1½ cups ketchup
- ¾ cup packed brown sugar
- ½ cup white vinegar
- ½ cup honey
- ⅓ cup soy sauce
- 1½ teaspoons ground ginger
- 1 teaspoon salt
- ¾ teaspoon ground mustard
- ½ teaspoon garlic powder
- ¼ teaspoon pepper

1. Cut ribs into serving-size pieces; place with the meaty side up on racks in two greased 13x9-in. baking pans. Cover tightly with foil. Bake at 350° for 1¼ hours or until the meat is tender.

2. Remove racks; drain and return the ribs to pans. Combine the remaining ingredients; pour over the ribs. Bake, uncovered, for 30-40 minutes or until the sauce coats ribs, basting occasionally. Ribs can also be grilled over medium-hot heat for the last 30-40 minutes instead of baking.

SOUTHWESTERN POTPIE WITH CORNMEAL BISCUITS

My southwestern-inspired potpie is full of sweet and spicy pork, corn, beans and chilies. It's a sure-fire winner for any gathering. The cornmeal gives the biscuits a delightful little crunch.

—**ANDREA BOLDEN** UNIONVILLE, TN

PREP: 35 MIN. + SIMMERING
BAKE: 15 MIN. + STANDING
MAKES: 12 SERVINGS

- ¼ cup all-purpose flour
- 1½ pounds boneless pork loin roast, cut into ½-inch cubes
- 2 tablespoons butter
- 1 jalapeno pepper, seeded and chopped
- 2 garlic cloves, minced
- 2 cups beef broth
- 1 can (14½ ounces) diced tomatoes, undrained
- 1 teaspoon ground cumin
- ½ teaspoon chili powder
- ¼ to ½ teaspoon ground cinnamon
- 1 can (15¼ ounces) whole kernel corn, drained
- 1 can (15 ounces) pinto beans, rinsed and drained
- 1 can (4 ounces) chopped green chilies

BISCUITS

- 3 cups biscuit/baking mix
- ¾ cup cornmeal
- ½ cup shredded cheddar cheese
- 4½ teaspoons sugar
- 1 cup 2% milk

1. Place flour in a large resealable plastic bag. Add the pork, a few pieces at a time, and shake to coat. In a Dutch oven, brown pork in butter in batches. Remove and set aside.

2. In the same pan, saute jalapeno and garlic in the drippings for 1 minute. Stir in broth, tomatoes, cumin, chili powder, cinnamon and pork. Bring to a boil. Reduce heat; cover and simmer 1 hour or until the pork is tender.

3. Preheat oven to 400°. Add corn, beans and chilies; heat through. Transfer to a greased 13x9-in. baking dish.

4. In a large bowl, combine the biscuit mix, cornmeal, cheese and sugar; stir in milk just until moistened. Turn dough onto a lightly floured surface; knead 8-10 times.

5. Pat or roll out to ½-in. thickness; cut with a floured 2½-in. biscuit cutter. Arrange over meat mixture. Bake for 15-18 minutes or until biscuits are golden brown. Let stand 10 minutes before serving.

NOTE *Wear disposable gloves when cutting hot peppers; the oils can burn skin. Avoid touching your face.*

GARLIC HERBED BEEF TENDERLOIN

You don't need much seasoning to add flavor to this tender beef roast. The mild blend of rosemary, basil and garlic does the trick in this recipe.

—**RUTH ANDREWSON** LEAVENWORTH, WA

PREP: 5 MIN. • **BAKE:** 40 MIN. + STANDING
MAKES: 12 SERVINGS

- 1 beef tenderloin roast (3 pounds)
- 2 teaspoons olive oil
- 2 garlic cloves, minced
- 1½ teaspoons dried basil
- 1½ teaspoons dried rosemary, crushed
- 1 teaspoon salt
- 1 teaspoon pepper

1. Tie tenderloin at 2-in. intervals with kitchen string. Combine oil and garlic; brush over meat. Combine the basil, rosemary, salt and pepper; sprinkle evenly over meat. Place on a rack in a shallow roasting pan.

2. Bake, uncovered, at 425° for 40-50 minutes or until the meat reaches desired doneness (for medium-rare, a meat thermometer should read 145°; medium, 160°; well-done, 170°). Let stand for 10 minutes before slicing.

**GARLIC HERBED
BEEF TENDERLOIN**

SWEET 'N' SOUR BEANS, PAGE 146

SLOW-COOKED FAVORITES

||||||||||||||||||||||||||||||||||||||||||||||||||||||||||||||||||||||||||||||||||||||||||

*"A generous person will prosper;
whoever refreshes others
will be refreshed."*

PROVERBS 11:25

SLOW COOKER 🍲

SAVORY SAUSAGE STUFFING

I used to make the same old stuffing every year for Thanksgiving. About 10 years ago, I decided to jazz up my recipe by adding pork sausage. Now folks ask for this for every holiday meal.
—**URSULA HERNANDEZ** WALTHAM, MN

PREP: 30 MIN. • **COOK:** 2 HOURS
MAKES: 16 SERVINGS

- 1 pound sage pork sausage
- ½ cup butter, cubed
- ½ pound fresh mushrooms, finely chopped
- 6 celery ribs, finely chopped
- 2 small onions, finely chopped
- 2 garlic cloves, minced
- 1 loaf (13 ounces) French bread, cut into ½-inch cubes (about 17 cups)
- 4 cups cubed multigrain bread (½ inch)
- 1 tablespoon rubbed sage
- 1 cup chicken stock
- ½ cup white wine or chicken stock
- 1 cup dried cranberries
- ½ cup sunflower kernels, optional

1. In a large skillet, cook the sausage over medium heat 4-6 minutes or until no longer pink, breaking into crumbles; drain. In a stockpot, melt butter over medium heat. Add mushrooms, celery and onions; cook and stir 3-4 minutes or until tender. Add garlic; cook 1 minute longer. Remove from heat.
2. Stir in the sausage. Add bread cubes and sage; toss to combine. Add chicken stock and wine. Stir in cranberries and, if desired, sunflower kernels. Transfer to a greased 6-qt. slow cooker. Cook, covered, on low for 2-3 hours or until heated through, stirring once.

TEST KITCHEN TIP
Sage is the go-to herb for traditional stuffing recipes, but what if you don't like sage? You can still enjoy delicious stuffing by swapping a generous amount of parsley for the sage.

SLOW COOKER 🍲

ASIAN PORK ROAST

Slow-cooked dishes are a favorite in our home, and this pork roast with honey, soy and spices is perfect for chilly evenings. The aroma fills the house with a scent that cries out, "Welcome home."
—**SHEREE SHOWN** JUNCTION CITY, OR

PREP: 25 MIN. • **COOK:** 4 HOURS
MAKES: 12 SERVINGS

- 2 large onions, thinly sliced
- 3 garlic cloves, minced
- ½ teaspoon salt
- ½ teaspoon pepper
- 1 boneless pork loin roast (3 pounds)
- 1 tablespoon canola oil
- 3 bay leaves
- ¼ cup hot water
- ¼ cup honey
- ¼ cup reduced-sodium soy sauce
- 2 tablespoons rice vinegar
- 1 teaspoon ground ginger
- ½ teaspoon ground cloves
- 3 tablespoons cornstarch
- ¼ cup cold water
  Hot cooked rice
- 2 tablespoons sesame seeds, toasted
  Sliced green onions, optional

1. Place the onions in a 5-qt. slow cooker. Mix garlic, salt and pepper. Cut roast in half; rub with garlic mixture. In a large nonstick skillet coated with cooking spray, brown the pork in oil on all sides. Transfer to slow cooker; add bay leaves.
2. In a small bowl, mix hot water and honey; stir in soy sauce, vinegar and spices. Pour over pork. Cook, covered, on low for 4-5 hours or until the meat is tender.
3. Remove pork from slow cooker; keep warm. Discard bay leaves. Mix cornstarch and cold water until smooth; gradually stir into slow cooker. Cover and cook on high for 30 minutes or until thickened, stirring twice.
4. Coarsely shred pork into bite-size pieces; serve with sauce over rice. Sprinkle with sesame seeds and, if desired, green onions.

ASIAN PORK ROAST

SLOW COOKER 🍲

SMOKY BAKED BEANS

They'll be standing in line for this saucy bean recipe, full of campfire flavor. A variation on colorful calico beans, it makes a great side dish with many of your favorite dishes.

—LYNNE GERMAN WOODLAND HILLS, CA

PREP: 25 MIN. • **COOK:** 7 HOURS
MAKES: 16 SERVINGS

- 1 pound bulk spicy pork sausage
- 1 medium onion, chopped
- 2 15-oz. cans pork and beans
- 1 can (16 ounces) kidney beans, rinsed and drained
- 1 can (16 ounces) butter beans, rinsed and drained
- 1 can (15½ ounces) navy beans, rinsed and drained
- 1 can (15 ounces) black beans, rinsed and drained
- 1 can (10 ounces) diced tomatoes and green chilies, drained
- ½ cup hickory smoke-flavored barbecue sauce
- ½ cup ketchup
- ½ cup packed brown sugar
- 1 teaspoon ground mustard
- 1 teaspoon steak seasoning
- 1 teaspoon liquid smoke, optional

1. In a large skillet, cook sausage and onion over medium heat until the meat is no longer pink; drain.
2. In a 5-qt. slow cooker, combine the beans, tomatoes and sausage mixture. In a small bowl, combine the barbecue sauce, ketchup, brown sugar, mustard, steak seasoning and Liquid Smoke if desired. Stir into the bean mixture.
3. Cover and cook on low for 7-8 hours or until heated through.

SLOW COOKER 🍲

BEEF STROGANOFF

This slow cooker recipe makes a traditional dinner completely fuss-free. Serve tender sirloin steak with a flavorful gravy over noodles for a home-style meal that your whole family is bound to request time and time again.

—LISA VANEGMOND ANNAPOLIS, IL

PREP: 25 MIN. • **COOK:** 7 HOURS
MAKES: 16 SERVINGS

- 3 to 4 pounds beef top sirloin steak, cubed
- 2 cans (14½ ounces each) chicken broth
- 1 pound sliced fresh mushrooms
- 1 can (12 ounces) regular cola
- ½ cup chopped onion
- 1 envelope onion soup mix
- 1 to 2 teaspoons garlic powder
- 2 teaspoons dried parsley flakes
- ½ teaspoon pepper
- 2 envelopes country gravy mix
- 2 cups sour cream
  Hot cooked noodles

1. In a 5-qt. slow cooker, combine the first nine ingredients. Cover and cook on low for 7-8 hours or until the beef is tender.
2. With a slotted spoon, remove the beef and mushrooms. Place gravy mix in a large saucepan; gradually whisk in the cooking liquid. Bring to a boil; cook and stir for 2 minutes or until thickened. Remove from the heat; stir in sour cream. Add beef and mushrooms to the gravy. Serve with noodles.

SLOW COOKER

MEATY SUN-DRIED TOMATO SAUCE

Marinated artichokes, celery and sweet green pepper are wonderful additions to this hearty spaghetti sauce. Don't worry about leftovers—this tangy sauce is even better the next day.

—**AYSHA SCHURMAN** AMMON, ID

PREP: 35 MIN. • **COOK:** 8 HOURS
MAKES: 12 SERVINGS (2¼ QUARTS)

- 1 pound bulk Italian sausage
- ½ pound ground beef
- 1 medium red onion, chopped
- 1 medium green pepper, chopped
- 2 celery ribs, chopped
- 3 garlic cloves, minced
- 3 cans (14½ ounces each) diced tomatoes
- 1 can (6 ounces) Italian tomato paste
- 1 jar (7½ ounces) marinated quartered artichoke hearts, drained and chopped
- 1 cup sun-dried tomatoes (not packed in oil), chopped
- 3 tablespoons minced fresh parsley
- 1½ teaspoons minced fresh rosemary or ½ teaspoon dried rosemary, crushed
- 1 bay leaf
- 1 teaspoon pepper
- ½ teaspoon salt

1. In a large skillet, cook the sausage, beef, onion, green pepper, celery and garlic over medium heat until the meat is no longer pink; drain. Transfer to a 4-qt. slow cooker.
2. Stir in the remaining ingredients. Cover and cook on low for 8-10 hours. Discard the bay leaf.

TEST KITCHEN TIP
If you find the texture of dried rosemary harsh, try grinding it with a mortar and pestle. Or you can freeze rosemary from your garden for use in the winter. Simply wrap sprigs of rosemary in foil, place them in a freezer bag, and freeze for up to 3 months. When using, remember that frozen rosemary has a stronger flavor than fresh.

SLOW COOKER

CHOCOLATE ESPRESSO LAVA CAKE

My aunt inspired this cake, sure to satisfy the strongest chocolate craving. It's gooey and saucy but not crazy sweet. It's also potluck perfect.

—**LISA RENSHAW** KANSAS CITY, MO

PREP: 15 MIN. • **COOK:** 3 HOURS + STANDING
MAKES: 16 SERVINGS

- 1 package chocolate fudge cake mix (regular size)
- 1 tablespoon instant espresso powder
- 3 cups 2% milk
- 1 package (3.9 ounces) instant chocolate pudding mix
- 1 cup (6 ounces) semisweet chocolate chips
- 1 cup white baking chips

1. Prepare cake mix batter according to package directions, adding espresso powder before mixing. Transfer to a greased 4-qt. slow cooker.
2. In a small bowl, whisk milk and pudding mix for 2 minutes. Let stand 2 minutes or until soft-set. Pour over the batter. Cook, covered, on low for 3 to 3½ hours or until a toothpick inserted in the cake portion comes out with moist crumbs.
3. Sprinkle with chocolate chips and baking chips. Turn off the slow cooker; remove insert. Let stand, uncovered, 15-30 minutes or until the chips are softened. Serve warm.

SLOW COOKER SPAGHETTI & MEATBALLS
Jane Whittaker
Pensacola, FL

SLOW COOKER 🍲

SLOW COOKER SPAGHETTI & MEATBALLS

I've been cooking 50 years, and this dish is still one that guests ask for frequently. My No.1 standby recipe, it also makes amazing meatball sandwiches, and the sauce works for any pasta.

—**JANE WHITTAKER** PENSACOLA, FL

PREP: 50 MIN. • **COOK:** 5 HOURS
MAKES: 12 SERVINGS (ABOUT 3½ QUARTS SAUCE)

- 1 cup seasoned bread crumbs
- 2 tablespoons grated Parmesan and Romano cheese blend
- 1 teaspoon pepper
- ½ teaspoon salt
- 2 large eggs, lightly beaten
- 2 pounds ground beef

SAUCE

- 1 large onion, finely chopped
- 1 medium green pepper, finely chopped
- 3 cans (15 ounces each) tomato sauce
- 2 cans (14½ ounces each) diced tomatoes, undrained
- 1 can (6 ounces) tomato paste
- 6 garlic cloves, minced
- 2 bay leaves
- 1 teaspoon each dried basil, oregano and parsley flakes
- 1 teaspoon salt
- ½ teaspoon pepper
- ¼ teaspoon crushed red pepper flakes
  Hot cooked spaghetti

1. In a large bowl, mix the bread crumbs, cheese, pepper and salt; stir in eggs. Add the beef; mix lightly but thoroughly. Shape into 1½-in. balls. In a large skillet over medium heat, brown the meatballs in batches; drain.

2. Place the first five sauce ingredients in a 6-qt. slow cooker; stir in garlic and seasonings. Add the meatballs, stirring gently to coat. Cook, covered, on low for 5-6 hours or until the meatballs are cooked through.

3. Remove bay leaves. Serve with spaghetti.

SLOW COOKER 🍲

CHICKEN SLIDERS WITH SESAME SLAW

These tangy, spicy chicken sliders have an Asian style that tingles the taste buds. At our potlucks, they quickly vanish.

—**PRISCILLA YEE** CONCORD, CA

PREP: 25 MIN. • **COOK:** 6 HOURS
MAKES: 20 SERVINGS

- 1 medium onion, coarsely chopped
- 3 pounds boneless skinless chicken thighs
- ½ cup ketchup
- ¼ cup reduced-sodium teriyaki sauce
- 2 tablespoons dry sherry or reduced-sodium chicken broth
- 2 tablespoons minced fresh gingerroot
- ½ teaspoon salt

SESAME SLAW

- ¼ cup mayonnaise
- 1 tablespoon rice wine vinegar
- 1 tablespoon sesame oil
- 1 teaspoon Sriracha Asian hot chili sauce
- 3 cups coleslaw mix
- ⅓ cup dried cherries or cranberries
- 2 tablespoons minced fresh cilantro
- 20 slider buns or dinner rolls, split

1. Place the onion and chicken in a 4-qt. slow cooker. In a small bowl, mix ketchup, teriyaki sauce, sherry, ginger and salt. Pour over the chicken. Cook, covered, on low for 6-7 hours or until a thermometer reads 170°.

2. Remove the chicken; cool slightly. Skim fat from the cooking juices. Shred the chicken with two forks and return the meat to the slow cooker. In a small bowl, whisk mayonnaise, vinegar, sesame oil and Sriracha sauce until blended. Stir in coleslaw mix, cherries and cilantro. Using a slotted spoon, place ¼ cup chicken mixture on the bottom half of each bun; top with about 2 tablespoons slaw. Replace the top halves of the buns.

PARTY SAUSAGES

Don't want any leftovers from your party? Serve these tempting sausages in a sweet and savory sauce. I've never had even one piece go uneaten.
—**JO ANN RENNER** XENIA, OH

PREP: 15 MIN. • **COOK:** 1 HOUR
MAKES: 16 SERVINGS

2 **pounds smoked sausage links**
1 **bottle (8 ounces) Catalina salad dressing**
1 **bottle (8 ounces) Russian salad dressing**
½ **cup packed brown sugar**
½ **cup pineapple juice**
 Sliced green onions, optional

1. Cut sausages into ½-in. slices; cook in a skillet over medium heat until lightly browned. Transfer to a 3-qt. slow cooker; discard the pan drippings.
2. Add dressings, brown sugar and juice to the same skillet; cook and stir over medium-low until the sugar is dissolved. Pour over the sausages. Cover and cook on low for 1-2 hours or until heated through. If desired, sprinkle with green onions.
NOTE *French salad dressing may be substituted for one or both dressings.*
SIMMERED SMOKED LINKS *Omit dressings and pineapple juice. Increase brown sugar to 1 cup; add ½ cup ketchup and ¼ cup prepared horseradish. Cook as directed.*

SLOW COOKER BACON MAC & CHEESE

I'm all about easy slow cooker meals. Using more cheese than ever, I've developed an addictive spin on this casserole favorite.
—**KRISTEN HEIGL** STATEN ISLAND, NY

PREP: 20 MIN. • **COOK:** 3 HOURS + STANDING
MAKES: 18 SERVINGS (½ CUP EACH)

2 **large eggs, lightly beaten**
4 **cups whole milk**
1 **can (12 ounces) evaporated milk**
¼ **cup butter, melted**
1 **tablespoon all-purpose flour**
1 **teaspoon salt**
1 **package (16 ounces) small pasta shells**
1 **cup shredded provolone cheese**
1 **cup shredded Manchego or Monterey Jack cheese**
1 **cup shredded white cheddar cheese**
8 **bacon strips, cooked and crumbled**

1. In a large bowl, whisk the first six ingredients until blended. Stir in pasta and cheeses; transfer to a 4- or 5-qt. slow cooker.
2. Cook, covered, on low 3-3½ hours or until the pasta is tender. Turn off slow cooker; remove insert. Let stand, uncovered, 15 minutes before serving. Top with bacon.

★ ★ ★ ★ ★ **READER REVIEW**

"This mac & cheese is amazing! And so easy—I just did it all in the slow cooker. No muss, no fuss."

BETHHUGHES TASTEOFHOME.COM

MINI TERIYAKI
TURKEY
SANDWICHES

SLOW COOKER 🍲
MINI TERIYAKI TURKEY SANDWICHES

Preparing the pulled turkey in a delicious teriyaki sauce for these snack-size sandwiches is a breeze using a slow cooker. Serve them on lightly toasted sweet dinner rolls for the finishing touch.

—**AMANDA HOOP** SEAMAN, OH

PREP: 20 MIN. • **COOK:** 5½ HOURS
MAKES: 20 SERVINGS

- 2 boneless skinless turkey breast halves (2 pounds each)
- ⅔ cup packed brown sugar
- ⅔ cup reduced-sodium soy sauce
- ¼ cup cider vinegar
- 3 garlic cloves, minced
- 1 tablespoon minced fresh gingerroot
- ½ teaspoon pepper
- 2 tablespoons cornstarch
- 2 tablespoons cold water
- 20 Hawaiian sweet rolls
- 2 tablespoons butter, melted

1. Place turkey in a 5- or 6-qt. slow cooker. In a small bowl, combine brown sugar, soy sauce, vinegar, garlic, ginger and pepper; pour over the turkey. Cook, covered, on low for 5-6 hours or until the meat is tender.

2. Remove the turkey from the slow cooker. In a small bowl, mix cornstarch and cold water until smooth; gradually stir into the cooking liquid. When cool enough to handle, shred the turkey with two forks and return the meat to the slow cooker. Cook, covered, on high 30-35 minutes or until the sauce is thickened.

3. Preheat oven to 325°. Split the rolls and brush cut sides with butter; place on an ungreased baking sheet, cut side up. Bake 8-10 minutes or until toasted and golden brown. Spoon ⅓ cup turkey mixture on the roll bottoms. Replace tops.

SLOW COOKER 🍲
POTATO MINESTRONE

Even the die-hard meat lovers in your family won't be able to get enough of this savory meatless soup. If you prefer a thicker consistency, mash half of the chickpeas before adding them to the slow cooker.

—PAULA ZSIRAY LOGAN, UT

PREP: 10 MIN. • **COOK:** 8½ HOURS
MAKES: 12 SERVINGS (ABOUT 3 QUARTS)

- 2 cans (14½ ounces each) chicken or vegetable broth
- 1 can (28 ounces) crushed tomatoes
- 1 can (16 ounces) kidney beans, rinsed and drained
- 1 can (15 ounces) chickpeas, rinsed and drained
- 1 can (14½ ounces) beef broth
- 2 cups frozen cubed hash brown potatoes, thawed
- 1 tablespoon dried minced onion
- 1 tablespoon dried parsley flakes
- 1 teaspoon salt
- 1 teaspoon dried oregano
- ½ teaspoon garlic powder
- ½ teaspoon dried basil
- ½ teaspoon dried marjoram
- 1 package (10 ounces) frozen chopped spinach, thawed and drained
- 2 cups frozen peas and carrots, thawed

In a 5-qt. slow cooker, combine the first 13 ingredients. Cover and cook on low for 8 hours. Stir in the spinach and the peas and carrots; cook for 30 minutes or until heated through.

SLOW COOKER 🍲
SLOW-COOKED TURKEY WITH BERRY COMPOTE

This delicious dish is a great way to get all that yummy turkey flavor without heating up the house, and the berries make the perfect summer chutney. For a browner turkey, just broil for a few minutes before serving.

—MARGARET BRACHER ROBERTSDALE, AL

PREP: 35 MIN. • **COOK:** 3 HOURS
MAKES: 12 SERVINGS (3¼ CUP COMPOTE)

- 1 teaspoon salt
- ½ teaspoon garlic powder
- ½ teaspoon dried thyme
- ½ teaspoon pepper
- 2 boneless turkey breast halves (2 pounds each)
- ⅓ cup water

COMPOTE
- 2 medium apples, peeled and finely chopped
- 2 cups fresh raspberries
- 2 cups fresh blueberries
- 1 cup white grape juice
- ¼ teaspoon crushed red pepper flakes
- ¼ teaspoon ground ginger

1. Mix salt, garlic powder, thyme and pepper; rub over turkey breasts. Place in a 5- or 6-qt. slow cooker. Pour water around turkey. Cook, covered, on low for 3-4 hours (a thermometer inserted in turkey should read at least 165°).
2. Remove turkey from the slow cooker; tent with foil. Let stand 10 minutes before slicing.
3. Meanwhile, in a large saucepan, combine the compote ingredients. Bring to a boil. Reduce heat to medium; cook, uncovered, 15-20 minutes or until slightly thickened and the apples are tender, stirring occasionally. Serve turkey with compote.

**SLOW-COOKED TURKEY
WITH BERRY COMPOTE**

SOUTHWESTERN PULLED PORK CROSTINI

A fresh take on crostini, these hearty appetizers are great for potlucks and other casual parties. These spicy, sweet and salty bites surprise and delight.

—RANDY CARTWRIGHT LINDEN, WI

PREP: 45 MIN. • **COOK:** 6 HOURS
MAKES: 32 APPETIZERS

- 1 boneless pork shoulder butt roast (about 2 pounds)
- ½ cup lime juice
- 2 envelopes mesquite marinade mix
- ¼ cup sugar
- ¼ cup olive oil

SALSA
- 1 cup frozen corn, thawed
- 1 cup canned black beans, rinsed and drained
- 1 small tomato, finely chopped
- 2 tablespoons finely chopped seeded jalapeno pepper
- 2 tablespoons lime juice
- 2 tablespoons olive oil
- 1½ teaspoons ground cumin
- 1 teaspoon chili powder
- ½ teaspoon salt
- ¼ teaspoon crushed red pepper flakes

SAUCE
- 1 can (4 ounces) chopped green chilies
- ⅓ cup apricot preserves
- ⅛ teaspoon salt

CROSTINI
- 32 slices French bread baguette (¼ inch thick)
- ¼ cup olive oil
- ⅔ cup crumbled queso fresco or feta cheese
  Lime wedges, optional

1. Place roast in a 3-qt. slow cooker. In a small bowl, whisk lime juice, marinade mix, sugar and oil until blended; pour over the roast. Cook, covered, on low for 6-8 hours or until the meat is tender.

2. For the salsa, in a small bowl, combine corn, beans, tomato and jalapeno. Stir in lime juice, oil and seasonings.

3. In a small saucepan, combine the sauce ingredients; cook and stir over low heat until blended.

4. For crostini, preheat broiler. Brush bread slices on both sides with oil; place on ungreased baking sheets. Broil 3-4 in. from heat 1-2 minutes on each side or until golden brown.

5. Remove roast from slow cooker; cool slightly. Shred the meat with two forks. To serve, layer toasts with salsa, pork and cheese. Top with sauce. If desired, serve with lime wedges.

SLOW COOKER 🍲

SLOW-COOKED GREEN BEANS

I spent hours looking up side dishes for a cooking demo to present to women from my church. These easy green beans became my star attraction.

—ALICE WHITE WILLOW SPRING, NC

PREP: 10 MIN. • **COOK:** 2 HOURS
MAKES: 12 SERVINGS

- 16 cups frozen french-style green beans (about 48 ounces), thawed
- ½ cup butter, melted
- ½ cup packed brown sugar
- 1½ teaspoons garlic salt
- ¾ teaspoon reduced-sodium soy sauce

Place green beans in a 5-qt. slow cooker. Mix the remaining ingredients; pour over beans and toss to coat. Cook, covered, on low until heated through, 2-3 hours. Serve with a slotted spoon.

SLOW COOKER 🍲
WHERE'S THE BEEF?

These juicy sandwiches are particularly irresistible while staying in during winter months for sporting events, game nights or movies. And they save the day for going out to potlucks and gatherings.

—CATHERINE CASSIDY MILWAUKEE, WI

PREP: 30 MIN. • **COOK:** 7 HOURS
MAKES: 18 SERVINGS

- 1 boneless beef chuck roast (4 to 5 pounds)
- 4 teaspoons Montreal steak seasoning
- 3 tablespoons butter
- 1 medium onion, chopped
- 2 celery ribs, chopped
- 1 small carrot, finely chopped
- ½ cup seeded and chopped pepperoncini
- ½ cup fresh basil leaves, thinly sliced
- 4 garlic cloves, minced
- 2 cups beef broth
- 1½ cups chili sauce
- 1 bottle (12 ounces) beer
- 3 tablespoons reduced-sodium soy sauce
- 1 tablespoon dried rosemary, crushed
- 1 bay leaf
- ¼ teaspoon salt
- ¼ teaspoon pepper

ASSEMBLY
- 18 mini buns, split
  Additional chopped pepperoncini, sliced red onion, dill pickle slices and stone-ground mustard, optional

1. Trim roast; sprinkle with steak seasoning. Cut roast in half. In a large skillet, heat butter over medium heat; brown meat in batches. Transfer meat and drippings to a 6-qt. slow cooker. Add the remaining ingredients. Cook, covered, on low for 7-8 hours or until the meat is tender.

2. Remove roast; cool slightly. Strain the cooking juices, discarding vegetables and bay leaf; skim fat. Shred the roast with two forks. Return meat and cooking juices to slow cooker; heat through. Using tongs, place meat on bun bottoms. Serve with cooking juices for dipping and top as desired.

SLOW COOKER 🍲
CHAMPIONSHIP BEAN DIP

When I arrive at any gathering, my friends and neighbors ask, "You brought your bean dip, didn't you?" It's irresistable. I've given out this recipe a hundred times.

—WENDI WAVRIN LAW OMAHA, NE

PREP: 10 MIN. • **COOK:** 2 HOURS
MAKES: 4½ CUPS

- 1 can (16 ounces) refried beans
- 1 cup picante sauce
- 1 cup shredded Monterey Jack cheese
- 1 cup shredded cheddar cheese
- ¾ cup sour cream
- 3 ounces cream cheese, softened
- 1 tablespoon chili powder
- ¼ teaspoon ground cumin
  Tortilla chips and salsa

In a large bowl, combine the first eight ingredients; transfer to a 1½-qt. slow cooker. Cover and cook on high for 2 hours or until heated through, stirring once or twice. Serve with tortilla chips and salsa.

CARIBBEAN BREAD
PUDDING

SLOW COOKER
CARIBBEAN BREAD PUDDING

A completely unexpected dessert from the slow cooker, this pudding is moist and sweet with plump, juicy raisins and the wonderful tropical flavors of pineapple and coconut.

—ELIZABETH DOSS CALIFORNIA CITY, CA

PREP: 30 MIN. • **COOK:** 4 HOURS
MAKES: 16 SERVINGS

- 1 cup raisins
- 1 can (8 ounces) crushed pineapple, undrained
- 2 large firm bananas, halved
- 1 can (12 ounces) evaporated milk
- 1 can (10 ounces) frozen non-alcoholic pina colada mix
- 1 can (6 ounces) unsweetened pineapple juice
- 3 large eggs
- ½ cup cream of coconut
- ¼ cup light rum, optional
- 1 loaf (1 pound) French bread, cut into 1-inch cubes
  Whipped cream and maraschino cherries, optional

1. In a small bowl, combine the raisins and pineapple; set aside. In a blender, combine the bananas, milk, pina colada mix, pineapple juice, eggs, cream of coconut and, if desired, rum. Cover and process until smooth.

2. Place two-thirds of the bread in a greased 6-qt. slow cooker. Top with 1 cup of the raisin mixture. Layer with the remaining bread and raisin mixture. Pour the banana mixture into slow cooker. Cover and cook on low for 4-5 hours or until a knife inserted in the center comes out clean. Serve warm and, if desired, with whipped cream and cherries.

SLOW COOKER
POTLUCK CANDIED SWEET POTATOES

It's hard to go wrong with candied sweet potatoes when it comes to pleasing a crowd. To make it easier to bring this traditional Southern staple to a potluck or gathering, I updated it so that it can be made in a slow cooker.

—DEIRDRE COX KANSAS CITY, MO

PREP: 20 MIN. • **COOK:** 5 HOURS
MAKES: 12 SERVINGS

- 1 cup packed brown sugar
- 1 cup sugar
- 8 medium sweet potatoes, peeled and cut into ½-inch slices
- ¼ cup butter, melted
- 2 teaspoons vanilla extract
- ¼ teaspoon salt
- 2 tablespoons cornstarch
- 2 tablespoons cold water
  Minced fresh parsley, optional

1. In a small bowl, combine the sugars. In a greased 5-qt. slow cooker, layer a third of the sweet potatoes; sprinkle with a third of the sugar mixture. Repeat layers twice.

2. In another small bowl, combine the butter, vanilla and salt; drizzle over the potatoes. Cover and cook on low for 5-6 hours or until the sweet potatoes are tender.

3. Using a slotted spoon, transfer the potatoes to a serving dish; keep warm. Pour the cooking juices into a small saucepan; bring to a boil. In a small bowl, combine cornstarch and water until smooth; stir into pan. Return to a boil, stirring constantly; cook and stir for 1-2 minutes or until thickened. Spoon over the sweet potatoes. If desired, sprinkle with parsley.

SLOW COOKER 🍲

OLD-FASHIONED TAPIOCA

My family loves old-fashioned tapioca, but I don't always have time to make it. So I came up with this simple recipe. It lets us enjoy one of our favorites without all the hands-on time.

—**RUTH PETERS** BEL AIR, MD

PREP: 10 MIN. • **COOK:** 4½ HOURS
MAKES: 18 SERVINGS

- 8 cups 2% milk
- 1 cup pearl tapioca
- 1 cup plus 2 tablespoons sugar
- ⅛ teaspoon salt
- 4 large eggs
- 1½ teaspoons vanilla extract
  Sliced fresh strawberries and whipped cream, optional

1. In a 4- to 5-qt. slow cooker, combine the milk, tapioca, sugar and salt. Cover and cook on low for 4-5 hours.

2. In a large bowl, beat the eggs; stir in a small amount of hot tapioca mixture. Return all to the slow cooker, stirring to combine. Cover and cook 30 minutes longer or until a thermometer reads 160°. Stir in vanilla.

3. If desired, serve with sliced strawberries and whipped cream.

★ ★ ★ ★ ★ **READER REVIEW**

"I made this casserole for a pasta night for my daughter's volleyball team. They loved it! I'll definitely make it again."

FRITSCH5 TASTEOFHOME.COM

SLOW COOKER 🍲

SLOW COOKER PIZZA CASSEROLE

A comforting casserole with mass appeal is just what you need when you are cooking for a crowd. For added convenience, it stays warm in a slow cooker.

—**VIRGINIA KRITES** CRIDERSVILLE, OH

PREP: 20 MIN. • **COOK:** 2 HOURS
MAKES: 14 SERVINGS

- 1 package (16 ounces) rigatoni or large tube pasta
- 1½ pounds ground beef
- 1 small onion, chopped
- 4 cups shredded part-skim mozzarella cheese
- 2 cans (15 ounces each) pizza sauce
- 1 can (10¾ ounces) condensed cream of mushroom soup, undiluted
- 1 package (8 ounces) sliced pepperoni

1. Cook pasta according to package directions. Meanwhile, in a skillet, cook beef and onion over medium heat until the meat is no longer pink; drain.

2. Drain pasta; place in a 5-qt. slow cooker. Stir in the beef mixture, cheese, pizza sauce, soup and pepperoni. Cover and cook on low for 2-3 hours or until heated through.

SLOW COOKER SPINACH & ARTICHOKE DIP
Jennifer Stowell
Montezuma, IA

SLOW COOKER 🍲

SLOW COOKER SPINACH & ARTICHOKE DIP

With this creamy dip, I can get my daughters to eat spinach and artichokes. Serve it with chips, toasted pita bread or fresh veggies.

—**JENNIFER STOWELL** MONTEZUMA, IA

PREP: 10 MIN. • **COOK:** 2 HOURS
MAKES: 32 SERVINGS

- 2 cans (14 ounces each) water-packed artichoke hearts, drained and chopped
- 2 packages (10 ounces each) frozen chopped spinach, thawed and squeezed dry
- 1 jar (15 ounces) Alfredo sauce
- 1 package (8 ounces) cream cheese, cubed
- 2 cups shredded Italian cheese blend
- 1 cup shredded part-skim mozzarella cheese
- 1 cup shredded Parmesan cheese
- 1 cup 2% milk
- 2 garlic cloves, minced
  Assorted crackers and/or cucumber slices

In a greased 4-qt. slow cooker, combine the first nine ingredients. Cook, covered, on low for 2-3 hours or until heated through. Serve with crackers and/or cucumber slices.

SLOW COOKER
LOADED POTATO SOUP

I like to put a twist on my grandmother's recipes, as I did with her recipe for potato soup. I look forward my kids making their own changes to mine.

—JAMIE CHASE RISING SUN, IN

PREP: 30 MIN. • **COOK:** 8¼ HOURS
MAKES: 12 SERVINGS (4 QUARTS)

- 5 pounds potatoes, peeled and cubed (about 10 cups)
- 1 medium onion, finely chopped
- 5 cans (14½ ounces each) chicken broth
- 1 garlic clove, minced
- 1½ teaspoons salt
- ¼ teaspoon pepper
- 2 packages (8 ounces each) cream cheese, softened and cubed
- 1 cup half-and-half cream
- ¼ cup butter, cubed

TOPPINGS
- 1 pound bacon strips, cooked and crumbled
- ¾ cup shredded sharp cheddar cheese
- ¼ cup minced chives

1. Place potatoes and onion in a 6-qt. slow cooker; add broth, garlic, salt and pepper. Cook, covered, on low 8-10 hours or until the potatoes are tender.
2. Mash potatoes to desired consistency. Stir in cream cheese, cream and butter. Cook, covered, 15 minutes longer or until heated through.
3. Just before serving, whisk soup to combine. Top servings with bacon, cheese and chives.

TEST KITCHEN TIP
Pot roasts are done when a long-handled fork can be inserted into the thickest part of the roast easily. If the pot roast is cooked until it falls apart, the meat is actually overcooked and will be stringy, tough and dry.

SLOW COOKER
SWEET 'N' TANGY POT ROAST

I made this roast the first time I cooked for my husband-to-be more than 20 years ago. He thought he'd died and gone to heaven!

—CAROL MULLIGAN HONEOYE FALLS, NY

PREP: 10 MIN. • **COOK:** 9½ HOURS
MAKES: 12 SERVINGS

- 1 boneless beef chuck roast (3 pounds)
- ½ teaspoon salt
- ½ teaspoon pepper
- 1 cup cold water
- 1 cup ketchup
- ¼ cup red wine or beef broth
- 1 envelope brown gravy mix
- 2 teaspoons Dijon mustard
- 1 teaspoon Worcestershire sauce
- ⅛ teaspoon garlic powder
- 3 tablespoons cornstarch
- ¼ cup cold water

1. Cut meat in half and place in a 5-qt. slow cooker. Season with salt and pepper. Combine the water, ketchup, wine or broth, gravy mix, mustard, Worcestershire sauce and garlic powder; pour over the meat.
2. Cover and cook on low for 9-10 hours or until the meat is tender.
3. Combine cornstarch and water until smooth. Stir into slow cooker. Cover and cook on high for 30 minutes or until the gravy is thickened. Remove meat from slow cooker. Slice and serve with gravy.

**SWEET 'N' TANGY
POT ROAST**

paper towels. Drain, reserving 2 tablespoons of the drippings. Saute onions in the drippings until tender. Add brown sugar, vinegar, salt, mustard and garlic powder. Bring to a boil.

2. In a 5-qt. slow cooker, combine the beans and peas. Add the onion mixture and bacon; mix well. Cover and cook on high for 3-4 hours or until heated through.

SLOW COOKER 🍲

ANYTHING GOES SAUSAGE SOUP

I call this recipe anything goes because you can add or take out a variety of ingredients, and the soup still turns out absolutely delicious. It's impossible to have just one bowl—unless your first bowl is huge and filled to the brim.

—SHEENA WELLARD NAMPA, ID

PREP: 40 MIN. • **COOK:** 9½ HOURS
MAKES: 15 SERVINGS (ABOUT 4 QUARTS)

- 1 pound bulk pork sausage
- 4 cups water
- 1 can (10¾ ounces) condensed cream of mushroom soup, undiluted
- 1 can (10¾ ounces) condensed cheddar cheese soup, undiluted
- 5 medium red potatoes, cubed
- 4 cups chopped cabbage
- 3 large carrots, thinly sliced
- 4 celery ribs, chopped
- 1 medium zucchini, chopped
- 1 large onion, chopped
- 5 chicken bouillon cubes
- 1 tablespoon dried parsley flakes
- ¾ teaspoon pepper
- 1 can (12 ounces) evaporated milk

1. In a large skillet, cook the sausage over medium heat until no longer pink; drain. Transfer to a 6-qt. slow cooker. Stir in the water and soups until blended. Add the vegetables, bouillon, parsley and pepper.

2. Cover and cook on low for 9-10 hours or until the vegetables are tender. Stir in milk; cover and cook 30 minutes longer.

SLOW COOKER 🍲

SWEET 'N' SOUR BEANS

This recipe came from a friend in Alaska, traveled with me to Mexico, where I lived for five years, and is now a potluck favorite in my Arkansas community.

—BARBARA SHORT MENA, AR

PREP: 20 MIN. • **COOK:** 3 HOURS
MAKES: 20 SERVINGS

- 8 bacon strips, diced
- 2 medium onions, halved and thinly sliced
- 1 cup packed brown sugar
- ½ cup cider vinegar
- 1 teaspoon salt
- 1 teaspoon ground mustard
- ½ teaspoon garlic powder
- 1 can (28 ounces) baked beans, undrained
- 1 can (16 ounces) kidney beans, rinsed and drained
- 1 can (15 ounces) pinto beans, rinsed and drained
- 1 can (15 ounces) lima beans, rinsed and drained
- 1 can (15½ ounces) black-eyed peas, rinsed and drained

1. In a large skillet, cook the bacon over medium heat until crisp. Remove with slotted spoon to

SLOW COOKER 🍲

ITALIAN MEATBALLS

These meatballs can be served as an appetizer right out of the slow cooker or with your favorite pasta as a main dish. I bet you'll find other uses for them, too.

—JASON ROMANO DOWNINGTOWN, PA

PREP: 50 MIN. • **COOK:** 3 HOURS
MAKES: ABOUT 5 DOZEN

- 2 tablespoons olive oil
- 1 small onion, finely chopped
- 3 garlic cloves, minced
- 1 cup Italian-style panko (Japanese) bread crumbs
- 2 large eggs, lightly beaten
- ½ cup grated Parmesan cheese
- ½ cup minced fresh parsley
- ¼ cup water
- ¼ cup minced fresh basil
- 2 tablespoons Worcestershire sauce
- ½ teaspoon salt
- ½ teaspoon pepper
- 1 pound ground beef
- ½ pound ground pork
- ½ pound ground veal
- 4 cups spaghetti sauce
  Minced fresh parsley, optional

1. Preheat oven to 400°. In a small skillet, heat oil over medium heat. Add the onion and garlic; cook 5-9 minutes or until the onion is tender and golden brown. Cool slightly.

2. In a large bowl, combine the bread crumbs, eggs, cheese, parsley, water and seasonings. Add the ground meats; mix lightly but thoroughly. Shape into 1-in. balls. Place meatballs on greased racks in shallow baking pans. Bake 20-25 minutes or until browned.

3. Transfer the meatballs to a 4- or 5-qt. slow cooker. Pour the spaghetti sauce over top. Cook, covered, on low for 3-4 hours or until the meatballs are cooked through. If desired, serve with minced fresh parsley.

SLOW COOKER 🍲

CREAMY HASH BROWN POTATOES

I like to fix a batch of these cheesy slow cooker potatoes for potlucks and other big gatherings. Frozen hash browns, canned soup and flavored cream cheese make this wildly popular dish quick to put together.

—JULIANNE HENSON STREAMWOOD, IL

PREP: 5 MIN. • **COOK:** 3½ HOURS
MAKES: 14 SERVINGS

- 1 package (32 ounces) frozen cubed hash brown potatoes
- 1 can (10¾ ounces) condensed cream of potato soup, undiluted
- 2 cups shredded Colby-Monterey Jack cheese
- 1 cup sour cream
- ¼ teaspoon pepper
- ⅛ teaspoon salt
- 1 carton (8 ounces) spreadable chive and onion cream cheese

1. Place potatoes in a lightly greased 4-qt. slow cooker. In a large bowl, combine the soup, cheese, sour cream, pepper and salt. Pour mixture over the potatoes and mix well.

2. Cover and cook on low for 3½ to 4 hours or until the potatoes are tender. Stir in cream cheese.

CITRUS
TURKEY
ROAST

SLOW COOKER 🍲
CITRUS TURKEY ROAST

At first, I was skeptical of the idea that you could make turkey in the slow cooker. But once I tasted this dish, I was hooked.

—KATHY KITTELL LENEXA, KS

PREP: 15 MIN. • **COOK:** 5¼ HOURS
MAKES: 12 SERVINGS

- 1 frozen boneless turkey roast, thawed (3 pounds)
- 1 tablespoon garlic powder
- 1 tablespoon paprika
- 1 tablespoon olive oil
- 2 teaspoons Worcestershire sauce
- ½ teaspoon salt
- ½ teaspoon pepper
- 8 garlic cloves, peeled
- 1 cup chicken broth, divided
- ¼ cup water
- ¼ cup white wine or additional chicken broth
- ¼ cup orange juice
- 1 tablespoon lemon juice
- 2 tablespoons cornstarch

1. Cut the roast in half. Combine garlic powder, paprika, oil, Worcestershire sauce, salt and pepper; rub over the turkey. Place in a 5-qt. slow cooker. Add the garlic, ½ cup of the broth, water, wine, orange juice and lemon juice. Cover and cook on low for 5-6 hours or until a thermometer reads 175°.

2. Remove the turkey and keep it warm. Discard the garlic cloves. For gravy, combine cornstarch and remaining broth until smooth; stir into the cooking juices. Cover and cook on high for 15 minutes or until thickened. Slice the turkey; serve with gravy.

SLOW COOKER 🍲
SLOW-COOKED PEACH SALSA

Fresh peaches and tomatoes with a little jalapeno pepper makes my salsa a hands-down winner over store versions. Jars of it make perfect gifts.

—PEGGI STAHNKE CLEVELAND, OH

PREP: 20 MIN. • **COOK:** 3 HOURS + COOLING
MAKES: 11 CUPS

- 4 pounds tomatoes (about 12 medium), chopped
- 1 medium onion, chopped
- 4 jalapeno peppers, seeded and finely chopped
- ½ to ⅔ cup packed brown sugar
- ¼ cup minced fresh cilantro
- 4 garlic cloves, minced
- 1 teaspoon salt
- 4 cups chopped peeled fresh peaches (about 4 medium), divided
- 1 can (6 ounces) tomato paste

1. In a 5-qt. slow cooker, combine the first seven ingredients; stir in 2 cups peaches. Cook, covered, on low for 3-4 hours or until the onion is tender.

2. Stir tomato paste and the remaining peaches into the slow cooker. Cool. Transfer to covered containers. (If freezing, use freezer-safe containers and fill to within ½ in. of tops.) Refrigerate up to 1 week or freeze up to 12 months. Thaw frozen salsa in refrigerator before serving.

NOTE *Wear disposable gloves when cutting hot peppers; the oils can burn skin. Avoid touching your face.*

★ ★ ★ ★ ★ **READER REVIEW**

"My future son-in-law adores this and begs for it every other week. It's one of the best turkey roast recipes I've ever come across."

WICADRAGON TASTEOFHOME.COM

**HAM & SWISS EGG
CASSEROLE, PAGE 167**

CROWD-PLEASING CASSEROLES

"...For the Lord your God will bless you in all your harvest and in all the work of your hands, and your joy will be complete."

DEUTERONOMY 16:15

SOUTHWESTERN CASSEROLE
Joan Hallford
North Richland Hills, TX

SOUTHWESTERN CASSEROLE

I've made this family-pleasing casserole for years. It's bold and budget-friendly—and you get a second casserole to freeze and keep for up to three months.

—JOAN HALLFORD NORTH RICHLAND HILLS, TX

PREP: 15 MIN. • **BAKE:** 40 MIN.
MAKES: 2 CASSEROLES (6 SERVINGS EACH)

- 2 cups (8 ounces) uncooked elbow macaroni
- 2 pounds ground beef
- 1 large onion, chopped
- 2 garlic cloves, minced
- 2 cans (14½ ounces each) diced tomatoes, undrained
- 1 can (16 ounces) kidney beans, rinsed and drained
- 1 can (6 ounces) tomato paste
- 1 can (4 ounces) chopped green chilies, drained
- 1½ teaspoons salt
- 1 teaspoon chili powder
- ½ teaspoon ground cumin
- ½ teaspoon pepper
- 2 cups shredded Monterey Jack cheese
- 2 jalapeno peppers, seeded and chopped

1. Cook macaroni according to package directions. In a large saucepan, cook beef and onion over medium heat, crumbling beef, until no longer pink. Add garlic; cook 1 minute longer. Drain. Stir in next eight ingredients. Bring to a boil. Reduce heat; simmer, uncovered, for 10 minutes. Drain macaroni; stir into beef mixture.
2. Preheat oven to 375°. Transfer macaroni mixture to two greased 2-qt. baking dishes. Top with cheese and jalapenos. Cover; bake for 30 minutes. Uncover; bake until bubbly and heated through, about 10 minutes longer.
TO USE FROZEN CASSEROLE *Thaw in refrigerator 8 hours. Remove from refrigerator 30 minutes before baking. Cover and bake at 375° until heated through and a thermometer inserted in center reads 165°, 20-25 minutes.*
NOTE *Wear disposable gloves when cutting hot peppers; the oils can burn skin. Avoid touching your face.*

COCONUT-BOURBON SWEET POTATOES

The rich addition of coconut, bourbon, raisins and spices might win over even those who firmly state they are not fans of sweet potatoes.

—REBECCA ANDERSON DRIFTWOOD, TX

PREP: 25 MIN. • **BAKE:** 35 MIN.
MAKES: 14 SERVINGS

- 8 cups mashed sweet potatoes
- ¾ cup half-and-half cream
- ½ cup packed brown sugar
- ½ cup bourbon
- 2 large eggs
- ¼ cup honey
- 3 teaspoons vanilla extract
- 1¼ teaspoons ground cinnamon
- ¼ teaspoon salt
- 1 tablespoon molasses, optional
- ½ teaspoon ground cardamom, optional
- 1 cup flaked coconut
- ¾ cup golden raisins
- 1½ cups miniature marshmallows

TOPPING
- ½ cup all-purpose flour
- ½ cup packed brown sugar
- 1 teaspoon ground cinnamon
- ⅓ cup butter, melted
- 1 cup chopped pecans

1. In a large bowl, combine first nine ingredients; add molasses and cardamom if desired. Stir in the coconut and raisins. Transfer to a greased 13x9-in. baking dish; sprinkle with marshmallows.
2. In a small bowl, combine the flour, brown sugar and cinnamon. Add butter; mix until crumbly. Stir in pecans; sprinkle over marshmallows.
3. Bake, uncovered, at 350° for 35-40 minutes or until heated through and topping is golden brown.

EGGPLANT SAUSAGE CASSEROLE

If you want your kids to happily eat their eggplant, serve it in this lovely layered casserole. Our whole family enjoys it. Always a popular potluck item, it's a great company dish, as well.

—**CAROL MIESKE** RED BLUFF, CA

PREP: 45 MIN. • **BAKE:** 45 MIN. + STANDING
MAKES: 12 SERVINGS

- 1 package (16 ounces) penne pasta
- 2 pounds bulk Italian sausage
- 1 medium eggplant, peeled and cubed
- 1 large onion, chopped
- 2 tablespoons olive oil
- 2 garlic cloves, minced
- 1 can (28 ounces) diced tomatoes, undrained
- 1 can (6 ounces) tomato paste
- 1 teaspoon salt
- 1 teaspoon dried basil
- 1 teaspoon paprika
- 1 carton (15 ounces) ricotta cheese
- 4 cups shredded part-skim mozzarella cheese, divided

1. Cook pasta according to package directions. Meanwhile, in a large skillet, cook sausage over medium heat until no longer pink; drain. Set sausage aside.

2. In the same skillet, saute eggplant and onion in oil. Add garlic; cook 1 minute longer. Stir in the tomatoes, tomato paste, salt, basil and paprika; simmer, partially covered, for 15 minutes. Remove from the heat. Drain pasta; stir into eggplant mixture. Add sausage.

3. Spread half of the sausage mixture in a greased 13x9-in. baking dish. Spread with ricotta cheese. Top with half of the cheese and the remaining sausage mixture.

4. Cover, bake casserole at 350° for 40 minutes. Uncover; sprinkle with the remaining cheese. Bake 5 minutes longer or until cheese is melted. Let stand for 10 minutes before serving.

MAKE AHEAD

RICH POTATO CASSEROLE

A friend in my country line-dance club gave me this recipe several years ago. When I married my husband, this dish was on the wedding menu.

—**PAT COFFEE** KINGSTON, WA

PREP: 15 MIN. • **BAKE:** 55 MIN.
MAKES: 2 CASSEROLES (12-15 SERVINGS EACH)

- 2 packages (30 ounces each) frozen shredded hash brown potatoes, thawed
- ¾ cup butter, melted, divided
- 4 cups sour cream
- 2 cans (10¾ ounces each) condensed cream of chicken soup, undiluted
- 1 bunch green onions, sliced
- 4 cups shredded cheddar cheese
- 1 teaspoon salt
- ¼ teaspoon pepper
- 1½ cups cornflakes, crushed

In a large bowl, combine the potatoes, ½ cup butter, sour cream, soup, onions, cheese, salt and pepper. Transfer to two greased shallow 3-qt. baking dishes. Combine cornflakes and remaining butter; sprinkle evenly over tops. Bake, uncovered, at 350° for 55-60 minutes or until bubbly.

NOTE *You can prepare this casserole the day before. Cover and refrigerate the assembled, unbaked casserole. Remove from the refrigerator 30 minutes before baking.*

MAKE AHEAD FAST FIX
WILD RICE CHICKEN DINNER

We raised nine children, so I know how to put together a quick dinner. I make two dishes of this bake to satisfy my large family, but you can also freeze one casserole for later. If you're cooking for a large crowd, skip the instructions for freezing, and serve up the whole batch!

—**LORRAINE HANSON** INDEPENDENCE, IA

START TO FINISH: 30 MIN.
MAKES: 2 CASSEROLES (8 SERVINGS EACH)

- 2 packages (8.8 ounces each) ready-to-serve long grain and wild rice
- 2 packages (16 ounces each) frozen French-style green beans, thawed
- 2 cans (10¾ ounces each) condensed cream of celery soup, undiluted
- 2 cans (8 ounces each) sliced water chestnuts, drained
- ⅔ cup chopped onion
- 2 jars (4 ounces each) sliced pimientos, drained
- 1 cup mayonnaise
- ½ cup 2% milk
- 1 teaspoon pepper
- 6 cups cubed cooked chicken
- 1 cup slivered almonds, divided

1. Heat rice according to package directions. Meanwhile, in a Dutch oven, combine the green beans, soup, water chestnuts, onion, pimientos, mayonnaise, milk and pepper. Bring to a boil. Reduce heat; cover and simmer for 5 minutes. Stir in chicken and rice; cook 3-4 minutes longer or until chicken is heated through.

2. Transfer half of the mixture to a serving dish; sprinkle with ½ cup almonds. Serve immediately. Pour the remaining mixture into a greased 13x9-in. baking dish; cool. Sprinkle with remaining almonds. Cover and freeze for up to 3 months.

TO USE FROZEN CASSEROLE *Thaw in the refrigerator overnight. Cover and bake at 350° for 40-45 minutes or until heated through.*

CHRISTMAS CAULIFLOWER CASSEROLE

This creamy casserole is filled with tender cauliflower and topped with a sprinkling of crispy herb stuffing. The holiday classic appeals to both kids and adults.

—**CAROL REX** OCALA, FL

PREP: 20 MIN. • **BAKE:** 20 MIN.
MAKES: 12 SERVINGS

- 3 packages (16 ounces each) frozen cauliflower
- 2 cups sour cream
- 2 cups shredded cheddar cheese
- 3 teaspoons chicken bouillon granules
- 1½ teaspoons ground mustard
- ¼ cup butter, cubed
- 1 cup stuffing mix
- ¾ cup chopped walnuts

1. Preheat oven to 375°. Cook cauliflower according to package directions; drain.

2. In a large bowl, mix sour cream, cheese, bouillon and mustard until blended. Stir in cauliflower; transfer to a greased 13x9-in. baking dish.

3. In a large skillet, heat butter over medium heat. Add stuffing mix and walnuts; cook and stir until lightly toasted. Sprinkle over casserole. Bake, uncovered, 17-20 minutes or until heated through and topping is browned.

ARGENTINE LASAGNA

My family is from Argentina, which has a strong Italian heritage and large cattle ranches. This all-in-one lasagna is packed with meat, cheese and veggies.

—**SYLVIA MAENENR** OMAHA, NE

PREP: 30 MIN. • **BAKE:** 55 MIN. + STANDING
MAKES: 12 SERVINGS

- 1 pound ground beef
- 1 large sweet onion, chopped
- ½ pound sliced fresh mushrooms
- 1 garlic clove, minced
- 1 can (15 ounces) tomato sauce
- 1 can (6 ounces) tomato paste
- ¼ teaspoon pepper
- 4 cups shredded part-skim mozzarella cheese, divided
- 1 jar (15 ounces) Alfredo sauce
- 1 carton (15 ounces) ricotta cheese
- 2½ cups frozen peas, thawed
- 1 package (10 ounces) frozen chopped spinach, thawed and squeezed dry
- 1 package (9 ounces) no-cook lasagna noodles
  Fresh basil leaves and grated Parmesan cheese, optional

1. In a Dutch oven, cook the beef, onion, mushrooms and garlic over medium heat until meat is no longer pink; drain. Stir in the tomato sauce, tomato paste, pepper and 2 cups mozzarella cheese; set aside.

2. In a large bowl, combine the Alfredo sauce, ricotta cheese, peas and spinach.

3. Spread 1 cup meat sauce into a greased 13x9-in. baking dish. Layer with four noodles, 1¼ cups meat sauce and 1¼ cups spinach mixture. Repeat layers three times. Sprinkle with remaining mozzarella cheese. (Pan will be full.)

4. Cover and bake at 350° for 45 minutes. Uncover; bake 10 minutes longer or until cheese is melted. Let stand for 10 minutes before cutting. Garnish with basil and serve with Parmesan cheese.

GREEK ZUCCHINI & FETA BAKE

Looking to highlight your meal with something light, indulgent and golden on top? Turn to this Greek-style egg bake.

—**GABRIELA STEFANESCU** WEBSTER, TX

PREP: 40 MIN. • **BAKE:** 30 MIN. + STANDING
MAKES: 12 SERVINGS

- 2 tablespoons olive oil, divided
- 5 medium zucchini, cut into ½-in. cubes (about 6 cups)
- 2 large onions, chopped (about 4 cups)
- 1 teaspoon dried oregano, divided
- ½ teaspoon salt
- ¼ teaspoon pepper
- 6 large eggs
- 2 teaspoons baking powder
- 1 cup reduced-fat plain yogurt
- 1 cup all-purpose flour
- 2 packages (8 ounces each) feta cheese, cubed
- ¼ cup minced fresh parsley
- 1 teaspoon paprika

1. Preheat oven to 350°. In a Dutch oven, heat 1 tablespoon oil over medium-high heat. Add half of the zucchini, half of the onions and ½ teaspoon oregano; cook and stir 8-10 minutes or until the zucchini is crisp-tender. Remove from pan. Repeat with remaining vegetables. Return previously cooked vegetables to pan. Stir in salt and pepper. Cool slightly.

2. In a large bowl, whisk eggs and baking powder until blended; whisk in yogurt and flour just until blended. Stir in the cheese, parsley and zucchini mixture. Transfer to a greased 13x9-in. baking dish. Sprinkle with paprika.

3. Bake, uncovered, 30-35 minutes or until golden brown and set. Let stand 10 minutes before cutting.

TEST KITCHEN TIP
The shelf life for baking powder is about 6 months. To test for freshness, place 1 teaspoon baking powder in a cup and add ⅓ cup hot tap water. If it actively bubbles, it's fine to use. If not, replace it.

GREEK ZUCCHINI
& FETA BAKE

EGGSQUISITE BREAKFAST CASSEROLE

I developed this recipe more than 20 years ago. The rich, warm sauce tastes especially great on cold winter mornings. I hope your family enjoys it as much as mine!

—BEE FISCHER JEFFERSON, WI

PREP: 20 MIN. • **BAKE:** 55 MIN.
MAKES: 16 SERVINGS

- 1 pound sliced bacon, diced
- 2 packages (4½ ounces each) sliced dried beef, cut into thin strips
- 1 can (4 ounces) sliced mushrooms
- ½ cup all-purpose flour
- ⅛ teaspoon pepper
- 4 cups whole milk
- 16 large eggs
- 1 cup evaporated milk
- ¼ teaspoon salt
- ¼ cup butter, cubed
  Chopped fresh parsley, optional

1. In a large skillet, cook bacon until crisp. Remove bacon to paper towel to drain; discard all but ¼ cup of the drippings. In the same skillet, add the beef, mushrooms, flour and pepper to the drippings; cook until thoroughly combined. Gradually add whole milk; cook and stir until thickened. Stir in bacon; set aside.

2. In a large bowl, whisk the eggs, evaporated milk and salt. In another large skillet, heat butter until hot. Add the egg mixture; cook and stir over medium heat until the eggs are completely set.

3. Place half of the eggs in a greased 13x9-in. baking dish; pour half the sauce over the eggs. Repeat layers. Cover and bake at 350° for 55-65 minutes or until a knife inserted near the center comes out clean. Let stand 5 minutes before serving.

TOMATO, SAUSAGE & CHEDDAR BREAD PUDDING

This savory dish is the perfect excuse to have bread pudding as the entire meal, not merely afterward as dessert.

—HOLLY JONES KENNESAW, GA

PREP: 30 MIN. • **BAKE:** 45 MIN.
MAKES: 12 SERVINGS

- 3 cups shredded sharp cheddar cheese
- 1 can (28 ounces) diced tomatoes, drained
- 1 pound bulk Italian sausage, cooked and crumbled
- 4 green onions, thinly sliced
- ¼ cup minced fresh basil or 1 tablespoon dried basil
- ¼ cup packed brown sugar
- 1 teaspoon dried oregano
- 1 teaspoon garlic powder
- 3 cups cubed French bread
- 6 large eggs
- 1½ cups heavy whipping cream
- ½ teaspoon salt
- ½ teaspoon pepper
- ½ cup grated Parmesan cheese

1. Preheat oven to 350°. In a large bowl, combine first eight ingredients. Stir in bread. Transfer to a greased 13x9-in. baking dish.

2. In the same bowl, whisk eggs, cream, salt and pepper; pour over bread mixture. Sprinkle with Parmesan cheese. Bake 45-50 minutes or until a knife inserted near the center comes out clean.

SWEET POTATO & CHIPOTLE CASSEROLE

SWEET POTATO & CHIPOTLE CASSEROLE

Sweet potato marshmallow casserole is old-school. My recipe—sweet potatoes with a streusel topping— is a blockbuster! Everyone who tries it gives it double thumbs up.

—**DIANA MALACH** VANCOUVER, WA

PREP: 45 MIN. • **BAKE:** 35 MIN.
MAKES: 18 SERVINGS

- 6 pounds sweet potatoes, peeled and cubed (about 20 cups)
- 1 to 2 chipotle peppers in adobo sauce, finely chopped
- 1 cup heavy whipping cream
- 4 large eggs, beaten
- 1 teaspoon salt

TOPPING

- 1 cup packed brown sugar
- ¾ cup all-purpose flour
- ¾ teaspoon ground ginger
- ¾ teaspoon ground cumin
- ½ teaspoon ground cloves
- ¼ teaspoon cayenne pepper
- ⅓ cup cold butter
- 1½ cups chopped pecans

1. Preheat oven to 350°. Place sweet potatoes in a large stockpot; cover with water. Bring to a boil. Reduce heat; cook, uncovered, 15-20 minutes or until tender.

2. Drain; return to pot. Mash potatoes with chipotle pepper to reach desired consistency. Cool slightly. Stir in the cream, eggs and salt. Transfer to a greased 13x9-in. baking dish (dish will be full).

3. For topping, in a large bowl, mix brown sugar, flour and spices; cut in butter until crumbly. Stir in pecans. Sprinkle over casserole. Bake, uncovered, 35-40 minutes or until a thermometer reads 160°.

PESTO CHICKEN
STRATA

MAKE AHEAD
PESTO CHICKEN STRATA

I like this rustic strata for its hearty flavors. It's great for a morning potluck because it's nice to have something savory along with sweeter brunch dishes.
—**MICHAEL COHEN** LOS ANGELES, CA

PREP: 25 MIN. + CHILLING • **BAKE:** 40 MIN.
MAKES: 12 SERVINGS

- 1 pound boneless skinless chicken thighs, cut into 1-inch pieces
- ¾ teaspoon salt, divided
- ¾ teaspoon coarsely ground pepper, divided
- 1 tablespoon plus ½ cup olive oil, divided
- 1 cup chopped fresh basil
- 1½ cups grated Parmesan cheese, divided
- 1 cup shredded part-skim mozzarella cheese
- ⅔ cup pine nuts, toasted
- 5 garlic cloves, minced
- 10 large eggs
- 3 cups 2% milk
- 8 cups cubed Italian bread
  Additional chopped fresh basil leaves

1. Sprinkle chicken with ¼ teaspoon salt and ¼ teaspoon pepper. In a large skillet, heat 1 tablespoon oil over medium heat. Add the chicken; cook and stir 6-8 minutes or until no longer pink. Drain.
2. Mix the basil, 1 cup Parmesan cheese, mozzarella cheese, pine nuts and garlic. In another bowl, whisk the eggs, milk and the remaining oil, salt and pepper.
3. In a greased 13x9-in. baking dish, layer half of the bread cubes, a third of the cheese mixture and half of the chicken. Repeat layers. Top with remaining cheese mixture. Pour egg mixture over top; sprinkle with remaining Parmesan cheese. Refrigerate, covered, several hours or overnight.
4. Remove strata from refrigerator. Preheat oven to 350°. Bake, uncovered, 40-50 minutes or until golden brown and a knife inserted near the center comes out clean. Let stand 5-10 minutes before serving. Sprinkle with additional basil.
NOTE *To toast nuts, bake in a shallow pan in a 350° oven for 5-10 minutes or cook in a skillet over low heat until lightly browned, stirring occasionally.*

CHEESE GRITS & SAUSAGE BREAKFAST CASSEROLE

I can't resist this breakfast casserole. It brings all my favorites into one dish: creamy grits, tangy cheese, rich eggs and flavorful sausage. It's the perfect alternative to traditional breakfast casseroles.
—**MANDY RIVERS** LEXINGTON, SC

PREP: 30 MIN. • **BAKE:** 40 MIN. + STANDING
MAKES: 12 SERVINGS

- 2 pounds bulk Italian sausage
- 2 cups water
- 2 cups chicken broth
- ½ teaspoon salt
- 1¼ cups quick-cooking grits
- 1 pound sharp cheddar cheese, shredded
- 1 cup 2% milk
- 1½ teaspoons garlic powder
- 1 teaspoon rubbed sage
- 6 large eggs, beaten
  Paprika, optional

1. In a large skillet, cook sausage over medium heat until no longer pink; drain.
2. In a large saucepan, bring the water, broth and salt to a boil. Slowly stir in grits. Reduce heat; cook and stir for 5-7 minutes or until thickened. Remove from the heat. Add the cheese, milk, garlic powder and sage, stirring until cheese is melted. Stir in sausage and eggs. Transfer to a greased 13x9-in. baking dish; sprinkle with paprika if desired.
3. Bake, uncovered, at 350° for 40-45 minutes or until a knife inserted near the center comes out clean. Let stand for 10 minutes before serving.

TEST KITCHEN TIP
You'll pay a premium for pre-shredded cheese, so why not buy in bulk and shred your own? Shred cheddar, Monterey Jack and mozzarella in a food processor, then store the cheese in the freezer in heavy-duty resealable plastic bags.

FIVE-CHEESE MACARONI WITH PROSCIUTTO BITS

Pasta baked with smoked Gouda, Swiss, white cheddar, goat cheese and Parmesan and topped with crispy prosciutto—so worth it!

—**MYA ZERONIS** PITTSBURGH, PA

PREP: 25 MIN. • **BAKE:** 15 MIN.
MAKES: 12 SERVINGS

- 1 package (16 ounces) elbow macaroni
- ⅓ cup unsalted butter, cubed
- 1 medium onion, halved and thinly sliced
- 1 garlic clove, minced
- ⅓ cup all-purpose flour
- ½ cup white wine or reduced-sodium chicken broth
- 4 cups heavy whipping cream
- 1 teaspoon white pepper
- ¼ teaspoon salt
- 5 ounces fresh goat cheese, crumbled
- 5 ounces white cheddar cheese, shredded
- 5 ounces Swiss cheese, shredded
- 3 ounces smoked Gouda cheese, shredded
- ¾ cup grated Parmesan cheese
- ½ cup panko (Japanese) bread crumbs
- 4 ounces thinly sliced prosciutto, chopped

1. Cook macaroni according to package directions for al dente.

2. In a Dutch oven, heat butter over medium-high heat. Add onion; cook and stir for 4-6 minutes or until golden brown. Add garlic; cook 1 minute longer. Stir in flour until blended; gradually stir in wine. Add cream, pepper and salt; bring to a boil, stirring constantly. Cook and stir for 2 minutes or until thickened.

3. Reduce heat to medium-low. Add goat cheese; stir gently until melted. Gradually stir in remaining cheeses; cook until melted. Remove from the heat.

4. Drain macaroni; stir into sauce. Transfer to a greased 13x9-in. baking dish. Sprinkle with bread crumbs. Bake, uncovered, at 375° for 15-20 minutes or until lightly browned.

5. In a small nonstick skillet, cook prosciutto over medium heat for 5-7 minutes or until crisp, stirring frequently. Sprinkle over macaroni before serving.

SPICY NACHO BAKE

I made this hearty, layered Southwestern casserole for a dinner meeting, and now I'm asked to bring it to every potluck. Everybody savors the ground beef and bean filling and crunchy, cheesy topping. The recipe makes two casseroles to feed a crowd, but you can easily halve it for a smaller guest list.

—**ANITA WILSON** MANSFIELD, OH

PREP: 1 HOUR • **BAKE:** 20 MIN.
MAKES: 2 CASSEROLES (15 SERVINGS EACH)

- 2 pounds ground beef
- 2 large onions, chopped
- 2 large green peppers, chopped
- 2 cans (28 ounces each) diced tomatoes, undrained
- 2 cans (16 ounces each) hot chili beans, undrained
- 2 cans (15 ounces each) black beans, rinsed and drained
- 2 cans (11 ounces each) whole kernel corn, drained
- 2 cans (8 ounces each) tomato sauce
- 2 envelopes taco seasoning
- 2 packages (13 ounces each) spicy nacho-flavored tortilla chips
- 4 cups shredded cheddar cheese

1. In a Dutch oven, cook the beef, onions and green peppers over medium heat until the meat is no longer pink; drain. Stir in the tomatoes, beans, corn, tomato sauce and taco seasoning. Bring to a boil. Reduce heat; simmer, uncovered, for 30 minutes (the mixture will be thin).

2. In each of two greased 13x9-in. baking dishes, layer 5 cups of chips and 4⅔ cups of meat mixture. Repeat layers. Top each with 4 cups of chips and 2 cups of cheese.

3. Bake, uncovered, at 350° for 20-25 minutes or until golden brown.

MAKE AHEAD

SPINACH AND ARTICHOKE BREAD PUDDING

Bread pudding is usually considered a dessert, but this savory version packed with spinach, artichokes and cheese is a perfect side for both dinner and brunch.

—**KATHLEEN FRAHER** FLORISSANT, MO

PREP: 20 MIN. + CHILLING • **BAKE:** 35 MIN. + STANDING
MAKES: 15 SERVINGS

- 2 packages (9 ounces each) fresh spinach
- 2 cans (14 ounces each) water-packed artichoke hearts, rinsed, drained and quartered
- 9 large eggs, beaten
- 2¾ cups heavy whipping cream
- 1 cup shredded Monterey Jack cheese
- 1 cup shredded cheddar cheese
- ½ cup shredded Parmesan cheese
- ½ cup shredded Romano cheese
  Dash salt
- 8 cups day-old cubed French bread

1. In a large saucepan, bring ½ in. of water to a boil. Add the spinach; cover and cook for 3-5 minutes or until wilted. Drain.

2. In a large bowl, combine the artichokes, eggs, cream, cheeses and salt. Gently stir in the bread cubes and spinach. Transfer to a greased 13x9-in. baking dish. Cover and refrigerate overnight.

3. Remove from the refrigerator 30 minutes before baking. Bake, uncovered, at 350° for 35-40 minutes or until a knife inserted in the center comes out clean. Let stand 10 minutes before cutting.

★ ★ ★ ★ ★ **READER REVIEW**

"I've made this bread pudding twice for my church Bible study group breakfast...I've gotten rave reviews both times!"

NOODLENEL TASTEOFHOME.COM

BAKED POTATO CASSEROLE

I created this baked potato casserole with input from friends and neighbors. It makes a great side dish for special meals.

—**KAREN BERLEKAMP** MAINEVILLE, OH

PREP: 15 MIN. • **BAKE:** 50 MIN.
MAKES: 24 SERVINGS

- 5 pounds red potatoes, cooked and cubed
- 1 pound sliced bacon, cooked and crumbled
- 1 pound cheddar cheese, cubed
- 4 cups shredded cheddar cheese
- 1 large onion, finely chopped
- 1 cup mayonnaise
- 1 cup sour cream
- 1 tablespoon minced chives
- 1 teaspoon salt
- ½ teaspoon pepper

1. In a very large bowl, combine potatoes and bacon. In another large bowl, combine remaining ingredients; add to the potato mixture and gently toss to coat.

2. Transfer to a greased 4½-qt. baking dish. Bake, uncovered, at 325° for 50-60 minutes or until bubbly and lightly browned.

NEW ENGLAND BAKED BEANS

For a potluck or picnic, you can't beat this classic side that starts with a pound of dried beans. Molasses and maple syrup give it a slight sweetness.

—**PAT MEDEIROS** TIVERTON, RI

PREP: 1½ HOURS + SOAKING • **BAKE:** 2½ HOURS
MAKES: 12 SERVINGS

- 1 pound dried great northern beans
- ½ pound thick-sliced bacon strips, chopped
- 2 large onions, chopped
- 3 garlic cloves, minced
- 2 cups ketchup
- 1½ cups packed dark brown sugar
- ⅓ cup molasses
- ⅓ cup maple syrup
- ¼ cup Worcestershire sauce
- ½ teaspoon salt
- ¼ teaspoon coarsely ground pepper

1. Sort beans and rinse with cold water. Place the beans in a Dutch oven; add enough water to cover by 2 in. Bring to a boil; boil for 2 minutes. Remove from the heat; cover and let stand for 1 hour or until the beans are softened.

2. Drain and rinse the beans, discarding the liquid. Return beans to Dutch oven; add 6 cups water. Bring to a boil. Reduce heat; cover and simmer for 1 hour or until the beans are almost tender.

3. In a large skillet, cook bacon over medium heat until crisp. Remove to paper towels with a slotted spoon; drain, reserving 2 tablespoons drippings. Saute onions in the drippings until tender. Add garlic; cook 1 minute longer. Stir in the ketchup, brown sugar, molasses, syrup, Worcestershire sauce, salt and pepper.

4. Drain the beans, reserving the cooking liquid; place in an ungreased 3-qt. baking dish. Stir in the onion mixture and bacon. Cover and bake at 300° for 2½ hours or until the beans are tender and reach desired consistency, stirring every 30 minutes. Add the reserved cooking liquid as needed.

CREAMY PARMESAN SPINACH BAKE

This creamy, comforting side dish wonderfully rounds out Thanksgiving dinner. Just a little of this rich casserole goes a long way.

—**JENNIFER BLEY** AUSTIN, TX

PREP: 35 MIN. • **BAKE:** 20 MIN.
MAKES: 12 SERVINGS

- 3 packages (9 ounces each) fresh baby spinach
- 1 small red onion, chopped
- 1 tablespoon butter
- 1 package (8 ounces) cream cheese, cubed
- 1 cup sour cream
- ½ cup half-and-half cream
- ⅓ cup plus 3 tablespoons grated Parmesan cheese, divided
- 3 garlic cloves, minced
- ⅛ teaspoon pepper
- 2 cans (14 ounces each) water-packed artichoke hearts, rinsed, drained and chopped
- 1 tablespoon snipped fresh dill
- ¼ teaspoon seasoned salt
- 8 butter-flavored crackers, coarsely crushed

1. Preheat oven to 350°. Place half of the spinach in a steamer basket; place in a large saucepan over 1 in. of water. Bring to a boil; cover and steam for 3-4 minutes or just until wilted. Transfer to a large bowl. Repeat with the remaining spinach; set aside.

2. In a large saucepan, saute the onion in butter until tender. Reduce heat to low; stir in the cream cheese, sour cream, half-and-half, ⅓ cup Parmesan cheese, garlic and pepper. Cook and stir until the cream cheese is melted. Stir in the artichokes, dill, seasoned salt and spinach.

3. Transfer to an ungreased 2-qt. baking dish. Sprinkle with cracker crumbs and the remaining Parmesan cheese. Bake, uncovered, for 20-25 minutes or until the edges are bubbly.

CREAMY PARMESAN
SPINACH BAKE

DURANGO POTATO CASSEROLE

If you like it spicy, it's easy to turn up the heat on these potatoes by adding more chili powder or jalapenos.

—**PATRICIA HARMON** BADEN, PA

PREP: 35 MIN. • **BAKE:** 25 MIN.
MAKES: 12 SERVINGS

- 2½ pounds potatoes (about 8 medium), peeled and cut into 1-inch cubes
- 8 thick-sliced bacon strips
- 1 can (14½ ounces) diced tomatoes and green chilies, drained
- 3 cups shredded Mexican cheese blend
- 4 green onions, chopped
- ⅓ cup chopped green pepper
- ⅓ cup chopped sweet red pepper
- 1½ cups reduced-fat mayonnaise
- 2 tablespoons lime juice
- 1 teaspoon seasoned salt
- ¼ teaspoon pepper
- 1½ teaspoons chili powder
- 2 tablespoons minced fresh cilantro

1. Place the potatoes in a large saucepan and cover with water. Bring to a boil. Reduce heat; cover and simmer for 10-15 minutes or until tender.
2. In a large skillet, cook the bacon over medium heat until partially cooked but not crisp. Remove to paper towels to drain; set aside.
3. Drain the potatoes and transfer to a large bowl; add the tomatoes, cheese, onions and peppers.
4. In a small bowl, whisk the mayonnaise, lime juice, seasoned salt and pepper; add to the potatoes and gently stir to coat. Transfer to a greased 13x9-in. baking dish. Coarsely chop the bacon; sprinkle over the top. Sprinkle casserole with chili powder.
5. Bake, uncovered, at 350° for 25-30 minutes or until heated through. Sprinkle with cilantro. Let stand for 5 minutes before serving.

SCALLOPED CARROTS

After my mother died, I found this recipe of hers. It's a crowd-pleasing side dish with a comforting sauce and a pretty, golden crumb topping.

—**CHERYL HOLLAND** ORTONVILLE, MI

PREP: 25 MIN. • **BAKE:** 45 MIN.
MAKES: 4 CASSEROLES (12-13 SERVINGS EACH)

- 1½ cups butter, cubed
- 1½ cups all-purpose flour
- 3 quarts milk
- ½ cup lemon juice
- 4 teaspoons celery salt
- 2 teaspoons pepper
- 6 pounds carrots, diced and cooked
- 2½ pounds shredded cheddar cheese
- 6 cups crushed butter-flavored crackers

1. Preheat oven to 350°. In a saucepan over medium heat, cook and stir butter and flour until smooth and bubbly, about 2 minutes. Gradually add milk and lemon juice; cook and stir until thickened. Add celery salt, pepper; mix well. Remove from heat.
2. In four greased 2½-qt. baking dishes, layer half the carrots, sauce, cheese and crackers. Repeat layers. Bake, uncovered, 45-50 minutes or until top is golden brown. Serve immediately.

HAM & SWISS EGG CASSEROLE
Kathy Harding
Richmond, MO

MAKE AHEAD

HAM & SWISS EGG CASSEROLE

Breakfast for a crew doesn't get easier than this mix of buttery croissants, smooth Swiss and tender eggs.

—**KATHY HARDING** RICHMOND, MO

PREP: 20 MIN. • **BAKE:** 35 MIN.
MAKES: 12 SERVINGS

- 16 **large eggs**
- 2 **cups 2% milk**
- ½ **teaspoon salt**
- ¼ **teaspoon ground nutmeg**
- 4 **cups shredded Swiss cheese**
- 8 **ounces sliced deli ham, chopped**
- 4 **croissants, torn into 1½ inch pieces**
- 1 **tablespoon minced chives**

1. Preheat oven to 350°. Whisk together eggs, milk, salt and nutmeg. Sprinkle cheese and ham into a greased 13x9-in. baking dish or pan; pour in egg mixture. Sprinkle croissant pieces over top.
2. Bake, uncovered, until puffed and golden brown, about 35-40 minutes. Sprinkle with chives. Let stand 5-10 minutes before serving.

NOTE *To make ahead, refrigerate the unbaked casserole, covered, several hours or overnight. To use, preheat oven to 350°. Remove casserole from refrigerator while oven heats. Bake as directed.*

WHITE SEAFOOD LASAGNA

WHITE SEAFOOD LASAGNA

We make lasagna with shrimp and scallops as part of the traditional Italian Feast of the Seven Fishes. Every bite delivers a tasty jewel from the sea.

—JOE COLAMONICO NORTH CHARLESTON, SC

PREP: 1 HOUR • **BAKE:** 40 MIN. + STANDING
MAKES: 12 SERVINGS

- 9 uncooked lasagna noodles
- 1 tablespoon butter
- 1 pound uncooked shrimp (31-40 per pound), peeled and deveined
- 1 pound bay scallops
- 5 garlic cloves, minced
- ¼ cup white wine
- 1 tablespoon lemon juice
- 1 pound fresh crabmeat

CHEESE SAUCE
- ¼ cup butter, cubed
- ¼ cup all-purpose flour
- 3 cups 2% milk
- 1 cup shredded part-skim mozzarella cheese
- ½ cup grated Parmesan cheese
- ½ teaspoon salt
- ¼ teaspoon pepper
- Dash ground nutmeg

RICOTTA MIXTURE
- 1 carton (15 ounces) part-skim ricotta cheese
- 1 package (10 ounces) frozen chopped spinach, thawed and squeezed dry
- 1 cup shredded part-skim mozzarella cheese
- ½ cup grated Parmesan cheese
- ½ cup seasoned bread crumbs
- 1 large egg, lightly beaten

TOPPING
- 1 cup shredded part-skim mozzarella cheese
- ¼ cup grated Parmesan cheese
- Minced fresh parsley

1. Preheat oven to 350°. Cook lasagna noodles according to the package directions; drain.

2. Meanwhile, in a large skillet, heat butter over medium heat. Add shrimp and scallops in batches; cook 2-4 minutes or until shrimp turn pink and scallops are firm and opaque. Remove from pan.

3. Add garlic to same pan; cook 1 minute. Add wine and lemon juice, stirring to loosen any browned bits from the pan. Bring to a boil; cook 1-2 minutes or until the liquid is reduced by half. Add crab; heat through. Stir in the shrimp and scallops.

4. For cheese sauce, melt butter over medium heat in a large saucepan. Stir in flour until smooth; gradually whisk in milk. Bring to a boil, stirring constantly; cook and stir 1-2 minutes or until thickened. Remove from heat; stir in the remaining cheese sauce ingredients. In a large bowl, combine the ricotta mixture ingredients; stir in 1 cup of the cheese sauce.

5. Spread ½ cup cheese sauce into a greased 13x9-in. baking dish. Layer with three noodles, half the ricotta mixture, half the seafood mixture and ⅔ cup cheese sauce. Repeat layers. Top with the remaining noodles and cheese sauce. Sprinkle with remaining mozzarella cheese and Parmesan cheese.

6. Bake, uncovered, 40-50 minutes or until bubbly and the top is golden brown. Let stand 10 minutes before serving. Sprinkle with parsley.

★ ★ ★ ★ ★ **READER REVIEW**

"This is so good that I threw away my seafood lasagna recipe that I have used for the past 25 years."

DARJUR TASTEOFHOME.COM

4. Drain raisins. In a small saucepan, melt butter over medium heat; stir in raisins. Add brown sugar and orange juice, stirring to dissolve sugar. Pour over the vegetables.

5. Bake, uncovered, 25-30 minutes or until vegetables are heated through and sauce is bubbly; if desired, baste occasionally with sauce. Let stand 10 minutes; toss before serving.

CHEESY SPAGHETTI BAKE

With the favorite ingredients of spaghetti and meat sauce, this recipe makes two hearty family-style casseroles. It's great for entertaining or a potluck.
—SUE BRAUNSCHWEIG DELAFIELD, WI

PREP: 45 MIN. • **BAKE:** 40 MIN.
MAKES: 2 CASSEROLES (12 SERVINGS EACH)

1   pound uncooked spaghetti, broken into
    3-inch pieces
4   pounds ground beef
2   large onions, chopped
1   large green pepper, chopped
4   cups milk
4   cans (10¾ ounces each) condensed
    tomato soup, undiluted
2   cans (10¾ ounces each) condensed cream
    of mushroom soup, undiluted
4   cups shredded sharp cheddar cheese, divided

1. Cook the spaghetti according to the package directions. Drain and place in two greased 13x9-in. baking dishes; set aside.

2. In two Dutch ovens or stock pots, cook the beef, onions and green pepper over medium heat until the meat is no longer pink; drain. To each pot, add 2 cups of milk, two cans of tomato soup, one can of mushroom soup and 1 cup of cheese. Bring to a boil.

3. Spoon over the spaghetti (spaghetti will absorb liquid during baking). Sprinkle with the remaining cheese. Bake, uncovered, at 350° for 40-45 minutes or until bubbly and top is lightly browned.

SWEET POTATO & CARROT CASSEROLE

This tangy and sweet casserole is full of flavor. We've served it at many celebrations over the years and it's always been popular.
—GLORIA MEZIKOFSKY WAKEFIELD, MA

PREP: 55 MIN. • **BAKE:** 25 MIN. + STANDING
MAKES: 12 SERVINGS

½   cup golden raisins
3½ pounds medium sweet potatoes
    (about 6 potatoes)
4   large carrots, cut into 1½-inch pieces
¼   cup butter or nondairy margarine
1½ cups packed brown sugar
⅓   cup orange juice

1. Preheat oven to 375°. In a small bowl, cover raisins with hot water; let stand 30 minutes.

2. Place the potatoes in a 6-qt. stockpot; add water to cover. Bring to a boil. Reduce heat; cook, uncovered, 15-20 minutes or just until tender. Remove the potatoes and cool slightly. Add the carrots to same pot of boiling water; cook, uncovered, 15-20 minutes or until tender; drain.

3. Peel sweet potatoes and cut crosswise into 1½-in.-thick slices. Arrange potatoes and carrots in a greased 13x9-in. baking dish, cut sides down.

ITALIAN CASSEROLE

I come from a huge family, and it seems there's always a potluck occasion. Graduation parties are the perfect place for this hearty main dish. It's easy to make and serve.

—RITA GOSHAW SOUTH MILWAUKEE, WI

PREP: 40 MIN. • **BAKE:** 25 MIN.
MAKES: 2 CASSEROLES (10 SERVINGS EACH)

- 1½ pounds bulk Italian sausage
- 1½ pounds ground beef
- 1 cup chopped onion
- 1 cup chopped green pepper
- 2 cans (15 ounces each) tomato sauce
- 2 cans (6 ounces each) tomato paste
- ½ cup water
- 1 teaspoon dried basil
- 1 teaspoon dried oregano
- 1 teaspoon salt
- 1 teaspoon pepper
- ⅛ teaspoon garlic powder
- 2 cans (8¾ ounces each) whole kernel corn, drained
- 2 cans (2¼ ounces each) sliced ripe olives, drained
- 1 package (16 ounces) wide noodles, cooked and drained
- 8 ounces cheddar cheese, cut into strips

1. In a Dutch oven over medium heat, cook the sausage, beef, onion and green pepper until the meat is no longer pink; drain. Add the tomato sauce, tomato paste, water and seasonings; bring to a boil. Reduce heat; cover and simmer for 15 minutes. Add corn and olives. Cover and simmer for 5 minutes. Stir in the noodles.

2. Pour into two greased 13x9-in. baking dishes. Top with cheese. Cover and bake at 350° for 25-30 minutes or until heated through.

SPOON BREAD CORN CASSEROLE

To keep our wedding simple and fun, Joe and I asked our guests to bring their favorite covered dish and a copy of the recipe to donate to our wedding cookbook. We ended up with an outstanding buffet, including this delightful down-home casserole.

—LINDA FABIAN WHEATLAND, WY

PREP: 15 MIN. • **BAKE:** 55 MIN.
MAKES: 2 CASSEROLES (16 SERVINGS EACH)

- 2 cups sour cream
- 1 cup butter, melted and cooled
- 2 packages (8½ ounces each) corn bread/muffin mix
- 2 cans (15¼ ounces each) whole kernel corn, drained
- 2 cans (14¾ ounces each) cream-style corn
- ¼ cup diced pimientos
- ⅛ teaspoon salt
- ⅛ teaspoon pepper
- ⅛ teaspoon cayenne pepper

1. In a large bowl, combine the sour cream and butter; stir in muffin mixes. Fold in the remaining ingredients.

2. Transfer to two greased 8-in. square baking dishes. Bake, uncovered, at 350° for 55-60 minutes or until a knife inserted near the center comes out clean. Serve warm.

NOTE *You can make this dish ahead of time. Bake as directed, cool, cover and refrigerate. To use, reheat at 350°, uncovered, for 15 to 20 minutes.*

TEST KITCHEN TIP
If you're looking for a butter substitute, make sure you get margarine and not a vegetable oil spread. Margarine can generally be used in place of butter unless the flavor of butter is key, as with butter cookies. Both butter and margarine contain 80% fat—11g per tablespoon. Vegetable oil spreads swap out some of the fat for water. Check the nutrition label to be sure you have the right product.

TORTELLINI SPINACH CASSEROLE

Spinach gives this popular dish a fresh taste that will delight even those who say they don't like spinach. People often are surprised at just how good it is! Whenever I bring it to a gathering, it never sits around long.

—BARBARA KELLEN ANTIOCH, IL

PREP: 20 MIN. • **BAKE:** 20 MIN.
MAKES: 12 SERVINGS

- 1 package (19 ounces) frozen cheese tortellini
- 1 pound sliced fresh mushrooms
- 1 teaspoon garlic powder
- ¼ teaspoon onion powder
- ¼ teaspoon pepper
- ½ cup butter, divided
- 1 can (12 ounces) evaporated milk
- ½ pound brick cheese, cubed
- 3 packages (10 ounces each) frozen chopped spinach, thawed and squeezed dry
- 2 cups shredded part-skim mozzarella cheese

1. Preheat oven to 350°. Cook the tortellini according to the package directions.

2. Meanwhile, in a large skillet, saute mushrooms, garlic powder, onion powder and pepper in ¼ cup butter until mushrooms are tender. Remove and keep warm.

3. In the same skillet, combine milk and remaining butter. Bring to a gentle boil; stir in brick cheese until smooth. Drain tortellini; place in a large bowl. Stir in the mushroom mixture and spinach. Add the cheese sauce and toss to coat.

4. Transfer to a greased 13x9-in. baking dish; sprinkle with mozzarella cheese. Cover and bake for 15 minutes. Uncover; bake 5-10 minutes longer or until heated through and cheese is melted.

CREAMY TURKEY CASSEROLE

This satisfying supper puts Thanksgiving leftovers to terrific use. I sometimes make turkey just so I'll have ingredients for my creamy turkey casserole.

—MARY JO O'BRIEN HASTINGS, MN

PREP: 15 MIN. • **BAKE:** 40 MIN.
MAKES: 12 SERVINGS

- 1 can (10¾ ounces) condensed cream of celery soup, undiluted
- 1 can (10¾ ounces) condensed cream of mushroom soup, undiluted
- 1 can (10¾ ounces) condensed cream of onion soup, undiluted
- 5 ounces process cheese (Velveeta), cubed
- ⅓ cup mayonnaise
- 3½ to 4 cups shredded cooked turkey
- 1 package (16 ounces) frozen broccoli florets or cuts, thawed
- 1½ cups cooked white rice
- 1½ cups cooked wild rice
- 1 can (8 ounces) sliced water chestnuts, drained
- 1 jar (4 ounces) sliced mushrooms, drained
- 1½ to 2 cups salad croutons

1. Combine the soups, cheese and mayonnaise. Stir in the turkey, broccoli, rice, water chestnuts and mushrooms.

2. Transfer to a greased 13x9-in. baking dish. Bake, uncovered, at 350° for 30 minutes; stir. Sprinkle with croutons. Bake until bubbly, 8-12 minutes longer.

★ ★ ★ ★ ★ **READER REVIEW**

"This turkey casserole is so yummy! My mom has even asked for the recipe. It makes a lot, but freezes well. Great for a cold winter night!"

KAREN421 TASTEOFHOME.COM

CREAMY TURKEY
CASSEROLE

STRAWBERRY
MASCARPONE CAKE,
PAGE 178

IDEAL
DESSERTS

"How priceless is your unfailing love, O God!
People take refuge in the shadow of your wings.
They feast on the abundance of your house;
you give them drink from your river of delights."

PSALM 36:7-8

PUMPKIN PECAN BITES

Since this recipe makes a lot, these bite-size treats are ideal for potlucks. To easily frost them, try putting the frosting in a pastry bag and piping it on top of the cupcakes.

—CAROL BEYERL EAST WENATCHEE, WA

PREP: 20 MIN. • **BAKE:** 20 MIN. + COOLING
MAKES: ABOUT 6 DOZEN

- 1 package spice cake mix (regular size)
- 1 can (15 ounces) solid-pack pumpkin
- 3 large eggs
- ½ cup canola oil
- 1 tablespoon ground cinnamon
- 1 teaspoon baking soda
- ¼ teaspoon ground cloves
- 36 pecan halves, cut in half

CREAM CHEESE FROSTING

- ½ cup butter, softened
- 4 ounces cream cheese, softened
- 1 teaspoon vanilla extract
- 3¾ cups confectioners' sugar
- 2 to 3 whole tablespoons milk
  Ground cinnamon

1. In a large bowl, combine the cake mix, pumpkin, eggs, oil, cinnamon, baking soda and cloves; beat on low speed for 30 seconds. Beat on medium for 2 minutes.

2. Fill paper-lined miniature muffin cups two-thirds full. Press a pecan piece into each. Bake at 350° for 17-20 minutes or until a toothpick inserted in the center comes out clean. Cool for 5 minutes before removing cupcakes from the pans to wire racks to cool completely.

3. In a small bowl, cream the butter, cream cheese and vanilla until light and fluffy. Gradually add the confectioners' sugar and mix well. Add enough milk to achieve spreading consistency. Frost cupcakes. Sprinkle with cinnamon.

NOTE *This recipe can be prepared in 2 dozen regular-size muffin cups. Increase baking time to 22-26 minutes.*

FROSTED FUDGE BROWNIES

A neighbor brought over a pan of these rich brownies along with the recipe when I came home from the hospital with our baby daughter. I've made them ever since for family occasions and potlucks.

—SUE SODERLUND ELGIN, IL

PREP: 10 MIN. + COOLING • **BAKE:** 25 MIN. + COOLING
MAKES: 2 DOZEN

- 1 cup plus 3 tablespoons butter, cubed
- ¾ cup baking cocoa
- 4 large eggs
- 2 cups sugar
- 1½ cups all-purpose flour
- 1 teaspoon baking powder
- 1 teaspoon salt
- 1 teaspoon vanilla extract

FROSTING

- 6 tablespoons butter, softened
- 2⅔ cups confectioners' sugar
- ½ cup baking cocoa
- 1 teaspoon vanilla extract
- ¼ to ⅓ cup whole milk

1. In a saucepan, melt butter. Remove from the heat. Stir in cocoa; cool. In a large bowl, beat eggs and sugar until blended. Combine flour, baking powder and salt; gradually add to the egg mixture. Stir in vanilla and the cooled chocolate mixture until well blended.

2. Spread into a greased 13x9-in. baking pan. Bake at 350° for 25-28 minutes or until a toothpick inserted in the center comes out clean (do not overbake). Cool on a wire rack.

3. For frosting, in a large bowl, cream butter and confectioners' sugar until light and fluffy. Beat in cocoa and vanilla. Add enough milk until the frosting achieves spreading consistency. Spread over the brownies. Cut into bars.

FROSTED FUDGE BROWNIES

STRAWBERRY MASCARPONE CAKE

This recipe has a lot of steps, but it's so easy to assemble! The cake bakes up high and fluffy, and the berries add a fresh fruity flavor. Cream cheese is a good substitute if you don't have mascarpone cheese handy.

—CAROL WIT TINLEY PARK, IL

PREP: 1 HOUR + CHILLING • **BAKE:** 30 MIN. + COOLING
MAKES: 12 SERVINGS

- 6 cups fresh strawberries, halved (2 pounds)
- 2 tablespoons sugar
- 1 teaspoon grated orange peel
- 1 tablespoon orange juice
- ½ teaspoon almond extract

CAKE

- 6 large eggs, separated
- 2 cups cake flour
- 2 teaspoons baking powder
- ¼ teaspoon salt
- 1½ cups sugar, divided
- ½ cup canola oil
- ¼ cup water
- 1 tablespoon grated orange peel
- ½ teaspoon almond extract

WHIPPED CREAM

- 2 cups heavy whipping cream
- ⅓ cup confectioners' sugar
- 2 teaspoons vanilla extract

FILLING

- 1 cup mascarpone cheese
- ½ cup heavy whipping cream

1. In a large bowl, combine the first five ingredients. Refrigerate, covered, at least 30 minutes.

2. Place egg whites in a large bowl; let stand at room temperature 30 minutes. Meanwhile, preheat oven to 350°. Grease bottoms of two 8-in. round baking pans; line with parchment paper. Sift flour, baking powder and salt together twice; place in another large bowl.

3. In a small bowl, whisk the egg yolks, 1¼ cups sugar, oil, water, orange peel and almond extract until blended. Add to the flour mixture; beat until well blended.

4. With clean beaters, beat the egg whites on medium speed until soft peaks form. Gradually add the remaining sugar, 1 tablespoon at a time, beating on high after each addition until sugar is dissolved. Continue beating until soft glossy peaks form. Fold a fourth of the egg whites into batter, then fold in the remaining whites.

5. Gently transfer to prepared pans. Bake on lowest oven rack for 30-35 minutes or until the top springs back when lightly touched. Cool in pans 10 minutes before removing to wire racks; remove paper. Cool layers completely.

6. For whipped cream, in a large bowl, beat the cream until it begins to thicken. Add confectioners' sugar and vanilla; beat until soft peaks form. Refrigerate, covered, at least 1 hour. For filling, in a small bowl, beat mascarpone cheese and cream until stiff peaks form. Refrigerate until assembling.

7. Drain strawberries, reserving the juice mixture. Set aside a few strawberries for garnish. If the cake layers are domed, use a serrated knife to trim them. Place a cake layer on a serving plate. Brush with half the reserved juice mixture; spread with ¾ cup filling. Arrange strawberries over top in an even layer; spread with remaining filling. Brush second cake layer with the remaining juice mixture; place layer over filling, brushed side down.

8. Gently stir the whipped cream; spread over top and sides of cake. Just before serving, arrange the reserved strawberries over the cake.

BUTTERMILK CHOCOLATE CUPCAKES

Cupcakes make a great get-up-and-go treat any time of the year. These have been a frosted favorite with family and friends for at least 35 years. They're really popular at bake sales.

—ELLEN MOORE SPRINGFIELD, NH

PREP: 30 MIN. • **BAKE:** 15 MIN. + COOLING
MAKES: 2 DOZEN

- ½ cup butter, softened
- 1½ cups sugar
- 2 large eggs
- 1 teaspoon vanilla extract
- 1½ cups all-purpose flour
- ½ cup baking cocoa
- 1 teaspoon baking soda
- ¼ teaspoon salt
- ½ cup buttermilk
- ½ cup water

FROSTING
- ½ cup butter, softened
- 3¾ cups confectioners' sugar
- 2 ounces unsweetened chocolate, melted
- 2 tablespoons evaporated milk
- 1 teaspoon vanilla extract
- ¼ teaspoon salt
- Chocolate sprinkles

1. Preheat oven to 375°. In a large bowl, cream butter and sugar until light and fluffy. Add eggs, one at a time, beating well after each addition. Beat in vanilla. Combine flour, cocoa, baking soda and salt. Combine buttermilk and water. Add the dry ingredients to the creamed mixture alternately with the buttermilk and water, beating well after each addition.

2. Fill paper-lined muffin cups two-thirds full. Bake 15-20 minutes or until a toothpick inserted in the center comes out clean. Cool 10 minutes before removing cupcakes from the pans to wire racks to cool completely.

3. For frosting, in a small bowl, beat butter and confectioners' sugar until smooth. Beat in melted chocolate, milk, vanilla and salt. Frost cupcakes; garnish with chocolate sprinkles.

TOFFEE PECAN BARS

Curl up with a hot cup of coffee and one of these oh-so-sweet treats. The golden topping and flaky crust combine well with the heartwarming taste of old-fashioned pecan pie.

—DIANNA CROSKEY GIBSONIA, PA

PREP: 15 MIN. • **BAKE:** 40 MIN. + CHILLING
MAKES: 3 DOZEN

- 2 cups all-purpose flour
- ½ cup confectioners' sugar
- 1 cup cold butter, cubed
- 1 large egg
- 1 can (14 ounces) sweetened condensed milk
- 1 teaspoon vanilla extract
- 1 package English toffee bits (10 ounces) or almond brickle chips (7½ ounces)
- 1 cup chopped pecans

1. Preheat oven to 350°. In a large bowl, mix flour and confectioners' sugar; cut in butter until the mixture is crumbly.

2. Press into a greased 13x9-in. baking pan. Bake for 15 minutes. Meanwhile, in a small bowl, mix the egg, milk and vanilla. Fold in toffee bits and pecans. Spoon over crust. Bake 24-26 minutes or until golden brown. Refrigerate until firm. Cut into bars.

**SALTED CARAMEL
& NUT CUPS**
Roxanne Chan
Albany, CA

SALTED CARAMEL & NUT CUPS

Over the years, these indulgent cookie cups, with four kinds of nuts, have helped make many of my holiday get-togethers even more special.

—ROXANNE CHAN ALBANY, CA

PREP: 30 MIN. + CHILLING • **BAKE:** 20 MIN. + COOLING
MAKES: 1½ DOZEN

- ½ cup butter, softened
- 3 ounces cream cheese, softened
- 2 tablespoons sugar
- 1 cup all-purpose flour
- 1 large egg
- ¼ cup hot caramel ice cream topping
- ¼ to ½ teaspoon ground allspice
- ¼ cup chopped pecans
- ¼ cup chopped slivered almonds
- ¼ cup chopped macadamia nuts
- ¼ cup chopped pistachios
  - Coarse sea salt
  - Sweetened whipped cream, optional

1. In a small bowl, beat butter, cream cheese and sugar until blended. Gradually beat in flour. Refrigerate, covered, 30 minutes or until firm.

2. Preheat oven to 350°. Shape level tablespoons of dough into balls; press evenly onto bottoms and up the sides of greased mini-muffin cups.

3. In a small bowl, whisk egg, caramel topping and allspice until blended. Stir in nuts. Place about 2 teaspoons of mixture in each cup.

4. Bake for 20-22 minutes or until edges are golden and filling is set. Immediately sprinkle tops with salt. Cool in pans 10 minutes. Remove to wire racks to cool. If desired, serve with whipped cream.

TEST KITCHEN TIP
Here's a neat trick for slicing refrigerator cookies so that they keep their nice round shape—dental floss! Slide a piece of floss (about 1 foot long) under the roll of dough, crisscross the ends above the dough and pull until you've cut through the dough. We recommend that you use plain floss, not mint-flavored!

LEMON TEA COOKIES

My mother got this recipe for rich butter cookies from a French friend in the 1950s, and it's been popular in our family ever since. Mom always made them at Christmas, and now my sister and I do too.

—PHYLLIS DIETZ WESTLAND, MI

PREP: 25 MIN. + CHILLING • **BAKE:** 10 MIN./BATCH
MAKES: ABOUT 4½ DOZEN

- ¾ cup butter, softened
- ½ cup sugar
- 1 large egg yolk
- ½ teaspoon vanilla extract
- 2 cups all-purpose flour
- ¼ cup finely chopped walnuts

FILLING
- 3 tablespoons butter, softened
- 4½ teaspoons lemon juice
- ¾ teaspoon grated orange peel
- 1½ cups confectioners' sugar
- 2 drops yellow food coloring, optional

1. In a large bowl, cream butter and sugar until light and fluffy. Beat in the egg yolk and vanilla. Gradually add flour and mix well.

2. Shape into two 14-in. rolls; reshape each roll into a 14x1⅛x1⅛-in. block. Wrap each in plastic wrap. Refrigerate overnight.

3. Unwrap blocks and cut into ¼-in. slices. Place the slices 2 in. apart on ungreased baking sheets. Sprinkle half of the cookies with the nuts, gently pressing them into dough.

4. Bake at 400° for 8-10 minutes or until golden brown around the edges. Remove to wire racks to cool.

5. In a small bowl, cream the butter, lemon juice and orange peel until fluffy. Gradually add confectioners' sugar until smooth. If desired, tint yellow. Spread about 1 teaspoon of filling on bottoms of the plain cookies; place nut-topped cookies over the filling.

BANANA-PECAN SHEET CAKE

A dear friend of mine gave me this recipe, and I prepare it often, especially for potlucks. Sometimes I make the cake ahead and freeze it, frosting it right before the party.

—MERRILL POWERS SPEARVILLE, KS

PREP: 35 MIN. • **BAKE:** 20 MIN. + COOLING
MAKES: 24 SERVINGS

- ½ cup butter, softened
- 1⅔ cups sugar
- 2 large eggs
- 1½ cups mashed ripe bananas
- 2½ cups all-purpose flour
- 3 teaspoons baking powder
- 1 teaspoon salt
- ¼ teaspoon baking soda
- ⅔ cup buttermilk
- ½ cup chopped pecans

FROSTING
- ⅓ cup butter, softened
- 3 cups confectioners' sugar
- 1½ teaspoons vanilla extract
- 3 to 4 tablespoons fat-free milk
- ⅓ cup finely chopped pecans, toasted

1. Preheat oven to 350°. Coat a 15x10x1-in. baking pan with cooking spray.

2. In a large bowl, beat the butter and sugar until blended. Add eggs, one at a time, beating well after each addition. Add the bananas, mixing well (the mixture will appear curdled).

3. In another bowl, whisk the flour, baking powder, salt and baking soda; add to the butter mixture alternately with buttermilk, beating well after each addition. Fold in pecans.

4. Transfer to prepared pan. Bake 20-25 minutes or until a toothpick inserted in center comes out clean. Cool completely in the pan on a wire rack.

5. For frosting, in a large bowl, combine butter, confectioners' sugar and vanilla. Add enough milk to achieve the desired consistency. Frost cake. Sprinkle with the toasted pecans.

CRAN-ORANGE OATMEAL COOKIES

The combination of dried cranberries, coconut and orange makes this crisp, chewy oatmeal cookie a real standout from the others.

—ELLEN WOODHAM-JOHNSON MATTESON, IL

PREP: 20 MIN. • **BAKE:** 15 MIN./BATCH
MAKES: 4 DOZEN

- 1 cup butter, softened
- 1 cup packed brown sugar
- ½ cup sugar
- 1 large egg
- 1 tablespoon grated orange peel
- 1½ teaspoons orange extract
- 1¾ cups all-purpose flour
- 1 teaspoon baking powder
- ¼ teaspoon baking soda
- 2 cups old-fashioned oats
- 1 cup dried cranberries
- 1 cup flaked coconut

1. In a large bowl, cream butter and sugars until light and fluffy. Beat in egg, orange peel and extract.

2. Combine flour, baking powder and baking soda; gradually add to the creamed mixture and mix well. Stir in the oats, cranberries and coconut. Shape into 1-in. balls; place balls 2 in. apart on ungreased baking sheets.

3. Bake at 375° for 11-13 minutes or until the bottoms are browned. Remove to wire racks. Store in an airtight container.

STRAWBERRY PRETZEL DESSERT

STRAWBERRY PRETZEL DESSERT

Need to bring a dish to pass this weekend? This make-ahead layered salad will disappear quickly at any potluck.
—**ALDENE BELCH** FLINT, MI

PREP: 20 MIN. • **BAKE:** 10 MIN. + CHILLING
MAKES: 12-16 SERVINGS

- 2 cups crushed pretzels (about 8 ounces)
- ¾ cup butter, melted
- 3 tablespoons sugar

FILLING
- 2 cups whipped topping
- 1 package (8 ounces) cream cheese, softened
- 1 cup sugar

TOPPING
- 2 packages (3 ounces each) strawberry gelatin
- 2 cups boiling water
- 2 packages (16 ounces each) frozen sweetened sliced strawberries, thawed
  Additional whipped topping, optional

1. In a bowl, combine the pretzels, butter and sugar. Press into an ungreased 13x9-in. baking dish. Bake at 350° for 10 minutes. Cool on a wire rack.
2. For filling, in a small bowl, beat whipped topping, cream cheese and sugar until smooth. Spread over the pretzel crust. Refrigerate until chilled.
3. For topping, dissolve gelatin in boiling water in a large bowl. Stir in strawberries with syrup; chill until partially set. Carefully spoon over the filling. Chill for 4-6 hours or until firm. Cut into squares; if desired, serve with whipped topping.

★ ★ ★ ★ ★ **READER REVIEW**

"This is a family favorite. I find the saltiest pretzels to use because the sweet/salty is such a great combination."
MARYXMAS15 TASTEOFHOME.COM

MOCHA HAZELNUT TORTE

I make this pretty cake on birthdays and other special occasions because it looks and tastes so amazing. The combination of mild hazelnut and coffee flavors is impossible to resist.

—CHRISTINA POPE SPEEDWAY, IN

PREP: 35 MIN. • **BAKE:** 25 MIN. + COOLING
MAKES: 16 SERVINGS

- ¾ cup butter, softened
- 1¼ cups packed brown sugar
- 1 cup sugar
- 3 large eggs
- 3 ounces unsweetened chocolate, melted and cooled slightly
- 2 teaspoons vanilla extract
- 2¼ cups all-purpose flour
- 1 tablespoon instant espresso powder
- 1 teaspoon baking soda
- ½ teaspoon baking powder
- ¼ teaspoon salt
- 1½ cups 2% milk

FROSTING

- 1 cup butter, softened
- 1 cup Nutella
- 4 cups confectioners' sugar
- 1 teaspoon vanilla extract
- 3 to 4 tablespoons 2% milk
- ½ cup chopped hazelnuts, toasted

1. Preheat oven to 350°. Line bottoms of two greased 9-in. round baking pans with parchment paper; grease paper.

2. In a large bowl, cream butter and sugars until light and fluffy. Add eggs, one at a time, beating well after each addition. Beat in melted chocolate and vanilla. In another bowl, whisk flour, espresso powder, baking soda, baking powder and salt; add to the creamed mixture alternately with milk, beating well after each addition.

3. Transfer the batter to prepared pans. Bake 25-30 minutes or until a toothpick inserted in center comes out clean. Cool in pans 10 minutes before removing to wire racks; remove paper. Cool completely.

4. For frosting, in a large bowl, beat butter and Nutella until blended. Gradually beat in the confectioners' sugar, vanilla and enough milk to reach desired consistency.

5. Place one cake layer on a serving plate; spread with 1 cup frosting. Sprinkle with ¼ cup hazelnuts. Top with the remaining cake layer. Frost top and sides with the remaining frosting. Sprinkle with remaining hazelnuts.

NOTE *To toast nuts, bake in a shallow pan in a 350° oven for 5-10 minutes or cook in a skillet over low heat until lightly browned, stirring occasionally.*

APPLE KUCHEN BARS

This recipe is about family, comfort and simplicity. My mom made these bars, and now I bake them in my own kitchen. I make double batches to pass along the love!

—ELIZABETH MONFORT CELINA, OH

PREP: 35 MIN. • **BAKE:** 1 HOUR + COOLING
MAKES: 2 DOZEN

- 3 cups all-purpose flour, divided
- ¼ teaspoon salt
- 1½ cups cold butter, divided
- 4 to 5 tablespoons ice water
- 8 cups thinly sliced peeled tart apples (about 8 medium)
- 2 cups sugar, divided
- 2 teaspoons ground cinnamon

1. Preheat oven to 350°. Place 2 cups flour and salt in a food processor; pulse until blended. Add 1 cup butter; pulse until butter is the size of peas. While pulsing, add just enough ice water to form moist crumbs. Press the mixture onto the bottom of a greased 13x9-in. baking pan. Bake 20-25 minutes or until edges are lightly browned. Cool on a wire rack.

2. In a large bowl, combine apples, 1 cup sugar and cinnamon; toss to coat. Spoon over the crust. Place the remaining flour, butter and sugar in food processor; pulse until coarse crumbs form. Sprinkle over apples. Bake 60-70 minutes or until golden brown and apples are tender. Cool completely on a wire rack. Cut into bars.

MOCHA HAZELNUT
TORTE

BLUE-RIBBON BUTTER CAKE

I found this recipe in an old cookbook I bought at a garage sale and couldn't wait to try it. The well-worn page told me this buttery cake had been someone's favorite.

—**JOAN GERTZ** PALMETTO, FL

PREP: 20 MIN. • **BAKE:** 65 MIN. + COOLING
MAKES: 16 SERVINGS

- 1 cup butter, softened
- 2 cups sugar
- 4 large eggs
- 2 teaspoons vanilla extract
- 3 cups all-purpose flour
- 1 teaspoon baking powder
- ½ teaspoon baking soda
- ½ teaspoon salt
- 1 cup buttermilk

BUTTER SAUCE
- 1 cup sugar
- ½ cup butter, cubed
- ¼ cup water
- 1½ teaspoons almond extract
- 1½ teaspoons vanilla extract

1. In a large bowl, cream butter and sugar until light and fluffy. Add eggs, one at a time, beating well after each addition. Beat in vanilla. Combine the flour, baking powder, baking soda and salt; add to the creamed mixture alternately with the buttermilk, beating well after each addition.

2. Pour batter into a greased and floured 10-in. tube pan. Bake at 350° for 65-70 minutes or until a toothpick inserted in center comes out clean. Cool 10 minutes. Run a knife around the edges and center tube of pan. Invert cake onto a wire rack over waxed paper.

3. For sauce, combine the sugar, butter and water in a small saucepan. Cook over medium heat just until butter is melted and sugar is dissolved. Remove from the heat; stir in extracts.

4. Poke holes in the top of the warm cake; spoon ¼ cup sauce over cake. Let stand until sauce is absorbed. Repeat twice. Poke holes into sides of cake; brush remaining sauce over sides. Cool the cake completely.

UPSIDE-DOWN BERRY CAKE

Here's a summery cake that's delicious warm or cold and served with whipped topping or ice cream. It soaks up loads of flavor from the berries.

—**CANDICE SCHOLL** WEST SUNBURY, PA

PREP: 20 MIN. • **BAKE:** 30 MIN. + COOLING
MAKES: 15 SERVINGS

- ½ cup chopped walnuts
- 1 cup fresh or frozen blueberries
- 1 cup fresh or frozen raspberries, halved
- 1 cup sliced fresh strawberries
- ¼ cup sugar
- 1 package (3 ounces) raspberry gelatin
- 1 package yellow cake mix (regular size)
- 2 large eggs
- 1¼ cups water
- 2 tablespoons canola oil
- 1½ cups miniature marshmallows

1. In a well-greased 13x9-in. baking pan, layer the walnuts and berries; sprinkle with sugar and gelatin. In a large bowl, combine the cake mix, eggs, water and oil; beat on low speed for 30 seconds. Beat on medium for 2 minutes. Fold in marshmallows. Pour over top of berry mixture.

2. Bake at 350° for 35-40 minutes or until a toothpick inserted in the center comes out clean. Cool for 5 minutes before inverting onto a serving platter. Refrigerate leftovers.

DOUBLE CHOCOLATE COOKIES

When I make these yummy treats with my young grandson, Ben, I use an extra-big mixing bowl to prevent the flour and other ingredients from flying all over. He seems to enjoy making the cookies almost as much as eating them.

—**CHANTAL CORNWALL** PRINCE RUPERT, BC

PREP: 15 MIN. • **BAKE:** 10 MIN./BATCH
MAKES: ABOUT 9 DOZEN

- 1¼ cups butter, softened
- 2 cups sugar
- 2 large eggs
- 2 teaspoons vanilla extract
- 2 cups all-purpose flour
- ¾ cup baking cocoa
- 1 teaspoon baking soda
- ½ teaspoon salt
- 2 cups (12 ounces) semisweet chocolate chips

1. In a large bowl, cream butter and sugar until light and fluffy. Beat in the eggs and vanilla. Combine the flour, cocoa, baking soda and salt; gradually add to the creamed mixture and mix well. Stir in the chocolate chips.

2. Drop by rounded teaspoonfuls 2 in. apart onto greased baking sheets. Bake at 350° for 8-10 minutes or until set. Cool for 2 minutes before removing from pans to wire racks.

★ ★ ★ ★ ★ **READER REVIEW**

"Absolutely delicious! The best chocolate cookie I have tasted in a long time!"

COUNTESSCOOKIE TASTEOFHOME.COM

ALMOND BLONDIES

Here's a sweet change from the typical chocolate brownie. When I bake up a batch, they never last long at my house.

—**CINDY PRUITT** GROVE, OK

PREP: 15 MIN. • **BAKE:** 25 MIN. + COOLING
MAKES: 16 SERVINGS

- 2 large eggs
- ½ cup sugar
- ½ cup packed brown sugar
- ⅓ cup butter, melted
- 1 teaspoon vanilla extract
- ¼ teaspoon almond extract
- 1⅓ cups all-purpose flour
- ½ teaspoon baking powder
- ¼ teaspoon salt
- ¼ cup chopped almonds

1. In a large bowl, beat the eggs, sugar and brown sugar for 3 minutes. Add butter and extracts; mix well. Combine the flour, baking powder and salt. Gradually add to the creamed mixture, beating just until blended. Fold in the almonds.

2. Pour into an 8-in. square baking pan coated with cooking spray. Bake at 350° for 25-30 minutes or until a toothpick inserted in the center comes out clean. Cool on a wire rack. Cut into squares.

**BUTTERY ORANGE
SUGAR COOKIES**
Heather McKillip
Aurora, IL

BUTTERY ORANGE SUGAR COOKIES

My husband's grandmother made a variety of cookies every year at Christmastime. She would box them up and give each grandchild his or her own box. This crisp, orange-flavored cookie is one of my favorites from her collection.

—HEATHER MCKILLIP AURORA, IL

PREP: 25 MIN. • **BAKE:** 10 MIN./BATCH
MAKES: 4 DOZEN

- 1 cup butter, softened
- 1 cup sugar
- 4 teaspoons grated orange peel
- 2 teaspoons vanilla extract
- 1¼ cups all-purpose flour
- ¾ cup rye flour
- 1 teaspoon baking soda
- ¾ teaspoon salt

1. Preheat oven to 350°. In a large bowl, cream the butter and sugar until light and fluffy. Beat in orange peel and vanilla. In another bowl, whisk remaining ingredients; gradually beat into creamed mixture.

2. Shape level tablespoons of dough into balls; place 2 in. apart on ungreased baking sheets. Bake 10-12 minutes or until edges are light brown. Cool on pans for 2 minutes. Remove to wire racks to cool. Store in airtight containers.

COME-HOME-TO-MAMA CHOCOLATE CAKE

It will take you less than a half hour to whip up this cure-all cake. Sour cream and chocolate pudding make it rich and moist, and chocolate, chocolate and more chocolate make it the finest in gratifying comfort food.

—*TASTE OF HOME* TEST KITCHEN

PREP: 25 MIN. • **BAKE:** 40 MIN. + COOLING
MAKES: 12 SERVINGS

- 1 package devil's food cake mix (regular size)
- 1 cup (8 ounces) sour cream
- 1 package (3.9 ounces) instant chocolate fudge pudding mix

- 4 large eggs
- ⅓ cup canola oil
- ¼ cup water
- ¼ cup buttermilk
- 2 tablespoons chocolate syrup
- 2 teaspoons vanilla extract

FROSTING

- 1 pound semisweet chocolate, chopped
- 6 tablespoons Dutch-process cocoa powder
- 6 tablespoons boiling water
- 1½ cups butter, softened
- ½ cup confectioners' sugar

1. In a large bowl, combine first nine ingredients; beat on low speed for 30 seconds. Beat on medium for 2 minutes. Pour into two greased and floured 8-in. baking pans.

2. Bake at 350° for 38-43 minutes or until a toothpick inserted in the center comes out clean. Cool for 10 minutes before removing from pans to wire racks to cool completely.

3. For frosting, in a microwave, melt chocolate; stir until smooth. Let cool to room temperature, about 20-30 minutes. Meanwhile, dissolve cocoa in boiling water; cool.

4. In a large bowl, beat butter and confectioners' sugar until fluffy. Add melted chocolate; beat on low speed until combined, scraping sides of the bowl as needed. Beat in cocoa mixture.

5. Place one cake layer on a serving plate; spread with 1½ cups frosting. Top with remaining cake layer. Spread remaining frosting over top and sides of cake.

★ ★ ★ ★ ★ **READER REVIEW**

"When I am asked to make a birthday cake for a chocolate lover, this is the cake I always go to!"

ALYSSASPRING TASTEOFHOME.COM

RHUBARB CUSTARD BARS

Once I tried these rich, gooey bars, I just had to have the recipe so I could make them for my family and friends. The shortbread-like crust and the rhubarb and custard layers inspire people to track down rhubarb so they can fix a batch for themselves.

—**SHARI ROACH** SOUTH MILWAUKEE, WI

PREP: 25 MIN. + CHILLING • **BAKE:** 50 MIN.
MAKES: 3 DOZEN

- 2 cups all-purpose flour
- ¼ cup sugar
- 1 cup cold butter

FILLING

- 2 cups sugar
- 7 tablespoons all-purpose flour
- 1 cup heavy whipping cream
- 3 large eggs, beaten
- 5 cups finely chopped fresh rhubarb or frozen rhubarb, thawed and drained

TOPPING

- 6 ounces cream cheese, softened
- ½ cup sugar
- ½ teaspoon vanilla extract
- 1 cup heavy whipping cream, whipped

1. In a bowl, combine the flour and sugar; cut in butter until the mixture resembles coarse crumbs. Press into a greased 13x9-in. baking pan. Bake at 350° for 10 minutes.

2. Meanwhile, for filling, combine sugar and flour in a bowl. Whisk in cream and eggs. Stir in the rhubarb. Pour over crust. Bake at 350° for 40-45 minutes or until the custard is set. Cool.

3. For topping, beat the cream cheese, sugar and vanilla until smooth; fold in the whipped cream. Spread over top of the filling. Cover and chill. Cut into bars. Store in the refrigerator.

BROWN SUGAR DATE SQUARES

A delightful filling and crumbly topping have made these bars a longtime favorite. Even people who say they don't like dates enjoy these treats.

—**SUZANNE CAITHAMER** WALTON, KY

PREP: 25 MIN. • **BAKE:** 25 MIN. + COOLING
MAKES: 2 DOZEN

- 1 pound pitted whole dates
- ⅔ cup packed brown sugar
- ⅔ cup orange juice
- 3 teaspoons vanilla extract

CRUST

- 1½ cups all-purpose flour
- 1½ cups old-fashioned oats
- 1 cup packed brown sugar
- 1 teaspoon ground cinnamon
- ½ teaspoon baking soda
  - Dash salt
- 1 cup cold butter, cubed
- ¾ cup coarsely chopped walnuts
  - Vanilla ice cream, optional

1. In a small saucepan, combine the dates, brown sugar and orange juice. Bring to a boil. Reduce heat; simmer, uncovered, 3-4 minutes or until thickened and dates are tender, stirring constantly. Remove from the heat; stir in vanilla.

2. In a large bowl, combine the flour, oats, brown sugar, cinnamon, baking soda and salt. Cut in butter until crumbly. Press half into a greased 13x9-in. baking dish. Carefully spread with date mixture.

3. Stir walnuts into the remaining crumb mixture. Sprinkle over the filling; press down gently. Bake at 350° for 25-30 minutes or until lightly browned. Cool on a wire rack. Cut into squares. Serve with ice cream if desired.

**CONTEST-WINNING
MOIST CHOCOLATE CAKE**

CONTEST-WINNING MOIST CHOCOLATE CAKE

You don't have to spend a lot of time to serve an elegant and delicious dessert. You can quickly mix up the batter in one bowl, bake your cake and serve a crowd.

—**CHRISTA HAGEMAN** TELFORD, PA

PREP: 15 MIN. • **BAKE:** 45 MIN. + COOLING
MAKES: 12 SERVINGS

- 2 cups sugar
- 1¾ cups all-purpose flour
- ¾ cup baking cocoa
- 2 teaspoons baking soda
- 1 teaspoon baking powder
- 1 teaspoon salt
- 2 large eggs
- 1 cup strong brewed coffee
- 1 cup buttermilk
- ½ cup canola oil
- 1 teaspoon vanilla extract
- 1 tablespoon confectioners' sugar

1. In a large bowl, combine the first six ingredients. Add the eggs, coffee, buttermilk, oil and vanilla; beat on medium speed for 2 minutes (the batter will be thin). Pour into a greased and floured 10-in. fluted tube pan.

2. Bake at 350° for 45-50 minutes or until a toothpick inserted in the center comes out clean. Cool for 10 minutes before removing the cake from the pan to a wire rack to cool completely. Dust with confectioners' sugar.

SOUR CREAM COFFEE CAKE

With a lovely, tender interior and a slightly crunchy crust, this coffee cake has a texture not unlike pound cake. But it's the lemon and almond flavors plus the full cup of walnuts that really take it over the top on taste.

—**JANICE KUHLMANN** STAFFORD SPRINGS, CT

PREP: 30 MIN. • **BAKE:** 50 MIN. + COOLING
MAKES: 16 SERVINGS

- 1 cup butter, softened
- 2 cups sugar
- 6 large eggs
- 2 teaspoons lemon juice
- 1 teaspoon grated lemon peel
- ½ teaspoon almond extract
- 3 cups all-purpose flour
- 1 teaspoon baking soda
- ¾ teaspoon salt
- 1 cup sour cream
- 1 cup chopped walnuts
- 2 teaspoons confectioners' sugar

1. In a large bowl, cream the butter and sugar until light and fluffy. Add the eggs, one at a time, beating well after each addition. Stir in the lemon juice, lemon peel and extract. Combine flour, baking soda and salt; add to the creamed mixture alternately with sour cream, beating well after each addition.
2. Transfer to a greased and floured 10-in. fluted tube pan. Bake at 350° for 50-60 minutes or until a toothpick inserted in the center comes out clean. Cool for 10 minutes before removing from the pan to a wire rack to cool completely. Dust with the confectioners' sugar.

PEANUT BUTTER SHEET CAKE

I received the recipe for this simple, classic sheet cake from a minister's wife, and my family loves it. Buttermilk makes it rich, and the peanut butter gives it crunch!

—**BRENDA JACKSON** GARDEN CITY, KS

PREP: 15 MIN. • **BAKE:** 20 MIN. + COOLING
MAKES: 24 SERVINGS

- 2 cups all-purpose flour
- 2 cups sugar
- 1 teaspoon baking soda
- ½ teaspoon salt
- 1 cup water
- ¾ cup butter, cubed
- ½ cup chunky peanut butter
- ¼ cup canola oil
- 2 large eggs
- ½ cup buttermilk
- 1 teaspoon vanilla extract

GLAZE
- ⅔ cup sugar
- ⅓ cup evaporated milk
- 1 tablespoon butter
- ⅓ cup chunky peanut butter
- ⅓ cup miniature marshmallows
- ½ teaspoon vanilla extract

1. Preheat oven to 350°. Grease a 15x10x1-in. baking pan.
2. In a large bowl, whisk the flour, sugar, baking soda and salt. In a small saucepan, combine water and butter; bring just to a boil. Stir in the peanut butter and oil until blended. Stir into the flour mixture. In a small bowl, whisk eggs, buttermilk and vanilla until blended; add to flour mixture, whisking constantly.
3. Transfer to prepared pan. Bake for 20-25 minutes or until a toothpick inserted in the center comes out clean.
4. For the glaze, combine sugar, milk and butter in a saucepan. Bring to a boil, stirring constantly; cook and stir 2 minutes. Remove from heat; stir in peanut butter, marshmallows and vanilla until blended. Spoon over warm cake, spreading evenly. Cool on a wire rack.

**PEANUT BUTTER
SHEET CAKE**

TOFFEE ALMOND SANDIES

These crispy classics are loaded with crunchy chopped toffee and almonds, so there's no doubt as to why they're my husband's favorite cookie. I used to bake them in large batches when our four sons still lived at home. Now I whip them up for the grandchildren!

—**ALICE KAHNK** KENNARD, NE

PREP: 35 MIN. • **BAKE:** 15 MIN./BATCH
MAKES: ABOUT 12 DOZEN

- 1 cup butter, softened
- 1 cup sugar
- 1 cup confectioners' sugar
- 1 cup canola oil
- 2 large eggs
- 1 teaspoon almond extract
- 3½ cups all-purpose flour
- 1 cup whole wheat flour
- 1 teaspoon baking soda
- 1 teaspoon cream of tartar
- 1 teaspoon salt
- 2 cups chopped almonds
- 1 package (8 ounces) milk chocolate English toffee bits
  Additional sugar

1. In a large bowl, cream butter and sugars until light and fluffy. Beat in the oil, eggs and extract.

Combine the flours, baking soda, cream of tartar and salt; gradually add to the creamed mixture and mix well. Stir in the almonds and toffee bits.
2. Shape into 1-in. balls; roll in sugar. Place balls on ungreased baking sheets and flatten them with a fork. Bake at 350° for 12-14 minutes or until lightly browned.

APPLE BAVARIAN TORTE

Layer a cream cheese filling, apples and almonds on a cookie-like crust for a picture-perfect torte that's ideal for autumn.

—**SHEILA SWIFT** DOBSON, NC

PREP: 20 MIN. • **BAKE:** 45 MIN. + COOLING
MAKES: 16 SERVINGS

- ½ cup butter, softened
- ⅓ cup sugar
- 1 cup all-purpose flour
- ¼ teaspoon vanilla extract

FILLING
- 1 package (8 ounces) cream cheese, softened
- ¼ cup plus ⅓ cup sugar, divided
- 1 large egg, lightly beaten
- ½ teaspoon vanilla extract
- 5½ cups thinly sliced peeled tart apples (about 6 medium)
- ½ teaspoon ground cinnamon
- ¼ cup sliced almonds

1. Preheat oven to 450°. In a small bowl, cream butter and sugar. Beat in flour and vanilla until blended. Press onto the bottom of a greased 9-in. springform pan.
2. In a large bowl, beat cream cheese and ¼ cup sugar until fluffy. Beat in egg and vanilla. Pour mixture over crust. In another large bowl, toss apples with cinnamon and the remaining sugar. Spoon over the cream cheese layer.
3. Bake for 10 minutes. Reduce oven setting to 400°; bake 25 minutes longer. Sprinkle almonds over the top; bake 10-15 minutes longer or until lightly browned and a toothpick inserted in the center comes out clean. Cool on a wire rack. Remove the sides of the pan before slicing. Store in the refrigerator.

MINT BROWNIE CHEESECAKE CUPS

These brownie cheesecake bites are bursting with mint chocolate—at holidays or any time of year, they'll be the talk of the party.

—JANET PAYNE LAWRENCEVILLE, GA

PREP: 20 MIN. • **BAKE:** 25 MIN. + COOLING
MAKES: 2½ DOZEN

- ½ cup crushed chocolate cream-filled chocolate sandwich cookies (about 7 cookies)
- 1 package (4.67 ounces) Andes mint candies or 1 cup Andes creme de menthe baking chips
- 1 package (8 ounces) cream cheese, softened
- ¼ cup sugar
- 1 large egg
- ½ teaspoon vanilla extract
  Additional Andes mint candies or Andes creme de menthe baking chips, melted

1. Grease or paper-line miniature muffin cups. Press 1 teaspoon cookie crumbs onto the bottom of each muffin cup; set aside.

2. Heat candies on high in a microwave-safe bowl for 30-60 seconds or until melted, stirring every 15 seconds. Cool to room temperature.

3. Beat cream cheese and sugar in a small bowl until smooth. Beat in egg and vanilla. Stir in the melted candies.

4. Spoon 1 tablespoon chocolate-mint mixture into each cup. Bake at 350° for 25-30 minutes or until tops appear dry and begin to crack. Cool for 1 minute before removing to wire racks to cool completely. Drizzle with additional melted candies. Store in the refrigerator.

TEST KITCHEN TIP
When choosing fresh blueberries, look for berries that are firm, dry, plump, smooth-skinned and relatively free from leaves and stems. Berries should be deep purple-blue to blue-black; reddish berries aren't ripe, but may be used in cooking.

BLUEBERRY LEMON TRIFLE

A refreshing lemon filling and fresh blueberries give this sunny dessert sensation plenty of color. Don't worry about heating up the oven—this doesn't require baking.

—ELLEN PEDEN HOUSTON, TX

PREP: 15 MIN. + CHILLING
MAKES: 12-14 SERVINGS

- 3 cups fresh blueberries, divided
- 2 cans (15¾ ounces each) lemon pie filling
- 2 cups (8 ounces) lemon yogurt
- 1 prepared angel food cake (8 to 10 ounces), cut into 1-inch cubes
- 1 carton (8 ounces) frozen whipped topping, thawed
  Lemon slices and fresh mint, optional

1. Set aside ¼ cup blueberries for garnish. In a large bowl, combine pie filling and yogurt.

2. In a 3½-qt. serving or trifle bowl, layer a third of the cake cubes, lemon mixture and blueberries. Repeat the layers twice. Top with whipped topping. Cover and refrigerate for at least 2 hours. Garnish with the reserved blueberries, and, if desired, lemon slices and mint.

RICOTTA
CHEESECAKE

MAKE AHEAD
RICOTTA CHEESECAKE

When I was a nurse, my coworkers and I regularly swapped recipes during lunch breaks. This creamy cheesecake was one of the best I ever received.

—GEORGIANN FRANKLIN CANFIELD, OH

PREP: 30 MIN. • **BAKE:** 50 MIN. + CHILLING
MAKES: 12 SERVINGS

- 1¼ cups graham cracker crumbs
- 3 tablespoons sugar
- ⅓ cup butter, melted

FILLING
- 2 cartons (15 ounces each) ricotta cheese
- 1 cup sugar
- 3 large eggs, lightly beaten
- 2 tablespoons all-purpose flour
- 1 teaspoon vanilla extract
  Cherry pie filling, optional

1. In a bowl, combine the graham cracker crumbs and sugar; stir in butter. Press onto the bottom and 1 in. up the sides of a greased 9-in. springform pan.
2. Place on a baking sheet. Bake at 400° for 6-8 minutes or until the crust is lightly browned around the edges. Cool on a wire rack.
3. In a large bowl, beat ricotta cheese on medium speed for 1 minute. Add sugar; beat for 1 minute. Add eggs; beat just until combined. Beat in flour and vanilla. Pour into crust.
4. Place pan on a baking sheet. Bake at 350° for 50-60 minutes or until the center is almost set. Cool on a wire rack for 10 minutes. Carefully run a knife around the edge of the pan to loosen; cool 1 hour longer. Refrigerate overnight. Remove sides of pan. If desired, serve with cherry pie filling. Refrigerate any leftovers.

ALMOND PEAR TORTE

Pears and nutmeg complement each other in this creamy torte. Sprinkling slivered almonds on top adds a nice crunch.

—TRISHA KRUSE EAGLE, ID

PREP: 30 MIN. • **BAKE:** 55 MIN. + COOLING
MAKES: 14 SERVINGS

- 1⅓ cups all-purpose flour
- ¾ cup butter, softened
- ½ cup sugar
- ½ cup ground almonds, toasted
- ¼ teaspoon ground nutmeg

FILLING
- 2 packages (8 ounces each) cream cheese, softened
- ¼ cup packed brown sugar
- ¼ teaspoon almond extract
- 2 large eggs

TOPPING
- ½ cup packed brown sugar
- ¼ teaspoon ground nutmeg
- 3 cups thinly sliced peeled fresh pears
- ½ cup slivered almonds

1. In a small bowl, combine the flour, butter, sugar, almonds and nutmeg. Press onto the bottom of a greased 9-in. springform pan; set aside.
2. In a large bowl, beat the cream cheese, brown sugar and extract until smooth. Add eggs; beat on low speed just until combined. Pour over crust.
3. For topping, combine brown sugar and nutmeg. Add pears; toss to coat. Arrange over top. Sprinkle with almonds.
4. Bake at 350° for 50-60 minutes or until center is almost set. Cool on a wire rack for 10 minutes. Carefully run a knife around the edge of the pan to loosen; cool 1 hour longer. Refrigerate leftovers.

GRAN'S APPLE CAKE

My grandmother occasionally brought over this wonderful cake warm from the oven. The spicy apple flavor combined with the sweet cream cheese frosting made this dessert a treasured recipe. I've lightened it up a bit, and it's still a family favorite.
—**LAURIS CONRAD** TURLOCK, CA

PREP: 20 MIN. • **BAKE:** 35 MIN. + COOLING
MAKES: 18 SERVINGS

- 1⅔ cups sugar
- 2 large eggs
- ½ cup unsweetened applesauce
- 2 tablespoons canola oil
- 2 teaspoons vanilla extract
- 2 cups all-purpose flour
- 2 teaspoons baking soda
- 2 teaspoons ground cinnamon
- ¾ teaspoon salt
- 6 cups chopped peeled tart apples
- ½ cup chopped pecans

FROSTING

- 4 ounces reduced-fat cream cheese
- 2 tablespoons butter, softened
- 1 teaspoon vanilla extract
- 1 cup confectioners' sugar

1. Preheat oven to 350°. Coat a 13x9-in. baking pan with cooking spray.

2. In a large bowl, beat sugar, eggs, applesauce, oil and vanilla until well blended. In another bowl, whisk flour, baking soda, cinnamon and salt; gradually beat into the sugar mixture. Fold in apples and pecans.

3. Transfer to prepared pan. Bake 35-40 minutes or until the top is golden brown and a toothpick inserted in the center comes out clean. Cool completely in pan on a wire rack.

4. In a small bowl, beat cream cheese, butter and vanilla until smooth. Gradually beat in confectioners' sugar (mixture will be soft). Spread over the cake. Refrigerate leftovers.

ULTIMATE DOUBLE CHOCOLATE BROWNIES

We live in the city—but within just a block of our house, we can see cattle grazing in a grassy green pasture. It's a sight that I never tire of. As someone who grew up in the country, I love nature—and I love homestyle recipes like this one.
—**CAROL PREWETT** CHEYENNE, WY

PREP: 15 MIN. • **BAKE:** 35 MIN.
MAKES: 3 DOZEN

- ¾ cup baking cocoa
- ½ teaspoon baking soda
- ⅔ cup butter, melted, divided
- ½ cup boiling water
- 2 cups sugar
- 2 large eggs
- 1⅓ cups all-purpose flour
- 1 teaspoon vanilla extract
- ¼ teaspoon salt
- ½ cup coarsely chopped pecans
- 2 cups (12 ounces) semisweet chocolate chunks

1. Preheat oven to 350°. In a large bowl, combine cocoa and baking soda; blend in ⅓ cup melted butter. Add boiling water; stir until well blended. Stir in sugar, eggs and the remaining butter. Add flour, vanilla and salt. Stir in pecans and chocolate chunks.

2. Pour into a greased 13x9-in. baking pan. Bake 35-40 minutes or until the brownies begin to pull away from the sides of the pan. Cool.

RAINBOW
LAYERED COOKIES

RAINBOW LAYERED COOKIES

*Balanced beautifully in the sweet spot between
cake and cookie, these sensational slices will be
the centerpiece of your cookie tray.*

—SHERRY THOMPSON SENECA, SC

PREP: 45 MIN. • **BAKE:** 10 MIN./BATCH + CHILLING
MAKES: 12 DOZEN

- ⅔ **cup blanched hazelnuts or macadamia nuts**
- ⅔ **cup confectioners' sugar**
- 1 **large egg white**
- 4 **large eggs**
- 1 **cup sugar**
- 1 **cup butter, melted and cooled**
- 1½ **teaspoons rum extract**
- 1 **cup all-purpose flour**
- ½ **teaspoon salt**
- 6 **to 8 drops red food coloring**
- 6 **to 8 drops green food coloring**
- 2 **tablespoons seedless strawberry jam**
- 2 **tablespoons apricot preserves**
- 1 **cup dark chocolate chips**
- 1 **teaspoon shortening**

1. Place the hazelnuts in a food processor; cover
and process until ground. Add the confectioners'
sugar and egg white; cover and process until
blended.

2. In a large bowl, beat the eggs and sugar on high
speed for 2-3 minutes or until thick and lemon-
colored. Gradually beat in the hazelnut mixture,
then butter. Beat in rum extract. Combine flour
and salt; add to the egg mixture.

3. Divide the batter into thirds. Stir red food
coloring into one portion of the batter; stir green
food coloring into another portion. Leave the
remaining batter plain. Spread one portion into
each of three well-greased 11x7-in. baking dishes.

4. Bake at 375° for 10-12 minutes or until a
toothpick inserted in the center comes out
clean and the edges begin to brown. Cool for
10 minutes before removing from pans to wire
racks to cool completely.

5. Place the red layer on a waxed paper-lined
baking sheet; spread with strawberry jam. Top
with plain layer; spread with apricot preserves.
Add the green layer; press down gently.

6. In a microwave, melt the chocolate chips
and shortening; stir until smooth. Spread half
over the green layer. Refrigerate for 20 minutes
or until set. Turn over; spread remaining chocolate
over the red layer. Refrigerate for 20 minutes or
until set.

7. With a sharp knife, trim the edges. Cut
lengthwise into fourths. Cut each portion into
¼-in. slices.

BAKE-SALE LEMON BARS

The recipe for these tangy lemon bars comes from my cousin Bernice, a farmer's wife famous for cooking up feasts.

—**MILDRED KELLER** ROCKFORD, IL

PREP: 25 MIN. • **BAKE:** 20 MIN. + COOLING
MAKES: 4 DOZEN

- ¾ cup butter, softened
- ⅔ cup confectioners' sugar
- 1½ cups plus 3 tablespoons all-purpose flour, divided
- 3 large eggs
- 1½ cups sugar
- ¼ cup lemon juice
  Additional confectioners' sugar

1. Preheat oven to 350°. In a large bowl, beat the butter and confectioners' sugar until blended. Gradually beat in 1½ cups flour. Press onto the bottom of a greased 13x9-in. baking pan. Bake 18-20 minutes or until golden brown.

2. Meanwhile, in a small bowl, whisk the eggs, sugar, lemon juice and the remaining flour until frothy; pour over the hot crust.

3. Bake 20-25 minutes or until the lemon mixture is set and lightly browned. Cool completely on a wire rack. Dust with additional confectioners' sugar. Cut into bars. Refrigerate leftovers.

MARVELOUS MARBLE CAKE

Pound cake and chocolate go together to make the best marble cake.

—**ELLEN RILEY** MURFREESBORO, TN

PREP: 45 MIN. • **BAKE:** 20 MIN. + COOLING
MAKES: 16 SERVINGS

- 4 ounces bittersweet chocolate, chopped
- 3 tablespoons plus 1¼ cups butter, softened, divided
- 2 cups sugar
- 5 large eggs
- 3 teaspoons vanilla extract
- 2¼ cups all-purpose flour
- 2 teaspoons baking powder
- ½ teaspoon salt
- ½ cup sour cream
- ½ cup miniature semisweet chocolate chips, optional

FROSTING
- ¾ cup butter, softened
- 6¾ cups confectioners' sugar
- 2 teaspoons vanilla extract
- ½ to ⅔ cup 2% milk
- 2 tablespoons miniature semisweet chocolate chips

1. In the top of a double boiler or a metal bowl over barely simmering water, melt chocolate and 3 tablespoons butter; stir until smooth. Cool to room temperature.

2. Preheat oven to 375°. Line bottoms of three greased 8-in. round baking pans with parchment paper; grease paper.

3. In a large bowl, cream the remaining butter and sugar until light and fluffy. Add eggs, one at a time, beating well after each addition. Beat in vanilla. Whisk flour, baking powder and salt; add to the creamed mixture alternately with sour cream, beating well after each addition.

4. Remove 2 cups batter to a small bowl; stir in cooled chocolate mixture and, if desired, chocolate chips until blended. Drop plain and chocolate batters by tablespoonfuls into prepared pans, dividing batters evenly among pans. To make batter level in pans, bang cake pans several times on counter.

5. Bake 20-25 minutes or until a toothpick inserted in center comes out clean. Cool in pans 10 minutes before removing to wire racks. Cool completely.

6. For frosting, in a large bowl, beat the butter until smooth. Gradually beat in the confectioners' sugar, vanilla and enough milk to reach the desired consistency.

7. If the cake layers have rounded tops, trim with a serrated knife to level them. In a microwave, melt chocolate chips; stir until smooth. Cool slightly.

8. Place one cake layer on a serving plate; spread with ½ cup frosting. Repeat. Top with remaining cake layer. Frost top and sides of cake.

9. Drop cooled chocolate by ½ teaspoonfuls over frosting. Using a large offset spatula, smear chocolate to create a marble design in the frosting.

MARVELOUS
MARBLE CAKE

**ELEGANT SMOKED
SALMON STRATA, PAGE 207**

SEASONAL DELIGHTS

||||||||||||||||||||||||||||||||||||||||||||||||||||||||||||||||||||||||||||||||||||||||||||||||||

"...Go and enjoy choice food and sweet drinks, and send some to those who have nothing prepared."

NEHEMIAH 8:10

BAKED PARMESAN BROCCOLI

I began making this creamy side dish years ago as a way to get my kids to eat broccoli. They've since grown up but still request this satisfying casserole. It's truly a family favorite.

—BARBARA UHL WESLEY CHAPEL, FL

PREP: 30 MIN. • **BAKE:** 15 MIN.
MAKES: 12 SERVINGS

- 4 bunches broccoli, cut into florets
- 6 tablespoons butter, divided
- 1 small onion, finely chopped
- 1 garlic clove, minced
- ¼ cup all-purpose flour
- 2 cups 2% milk
- 1 large egg yolk, beaten
- 1 cup grated Parmesan cheese
- ½ teaspoon salt
- ⅛ teaspoon pepper
- ½ cup seasoned bread crumbs

1. Preheat oven to 400°. Place half of broccoli in a steamer basket; place in a large saucepan over 1 in. of water. Bring to a boil; cover and steam for 3-4 minutes or until crisp-tender. Place in a greased 13x9-in. baking dish; repeat with remaining broccoli.
2. Meanwhile, in a small saucepan over medium heat, melt 4 tablespoons butter. Add the onion; cook and stir until tender. Add the garlic; cook 1 minute longer.
3. Stir in flour until blended; gradually add milk. Bring to a boil; cook and stir for 2 minutes or until thickened. Stir a small amount of the hot mixture into the egg yolk; return all to the pan, stirring constantly. Cook and stir mixture 1 minute longer. Remove from heat; stir in cheese, salt and pepper.
4. Pour over the broccoli. In a small skillet, cook bread crumbs in the remaining butter until golden brown; sprinkle over the top.
5. Bake, uncovered, for 15-18 minutes or until casserole is heated through.

CHOCOLATE-COVERED EGGS

These chocolaty eggs beat store-bought varieties hands down! The smiles you'll see when you serve these pretty candies make them worth the effort.

—LOUISE OBERFOELL BOWMAN, ND

PREP: 1 HOUR + CHILLING
MAKES: 2 DOZEN

- ¼ cup butter, softened
- 1 jar (7 ounces) marshmallow creme
- 1 teaspoon vanilla extract
- 3 cups plus 1 tablespoon confectioners' sugar, divided
- 3 to 4 drops yellow food coloring
- 2 cups white baking chips or semisweet chocolate chips
- 2 tablespoons shortening
  Icing of your choice
  Assorted decorating candies

1. In a large bowl, beat the butter, marshmallow creme and vanilla until smooth. Gradually beat in 3 cups of the confectioners' sugar. Place ¼ cup of the butter mixture in a bowl; add yellow food coloring and mix well. Shape into 24 small balls; cover and chill for 30 minutes. Wrap plain mixture in plastic wrap; chill for 30 minutes.
2. Dust work surface with remaining confectioners' sugar. Divide the plain dough into 24 pieces. Wrap one piece of plain dough around each yellow ball and form into an egg shape. Place on a waxed paper-lined baking sheet; cover with plastic wrap. Freeze for 15 minutes or until firm.
3. In a microwave, melt chips and shortening; stir until smooth. Dip eggs in mixture; allow excess to drip off. Return the eggs to waxed paper. Refrigerate for 30 minutes or until set. Decorate with icing and decorating candies as desired. Store in an airtight container in the refrigerator.

CHOCOLATE-
COVERED EGGS

EASTER BASKET CUPCAKES

My mother and I would make these when I was growing up, and I had just as much fun sharing the experience with my own children when they were young.

—**KATHY KITTELL** LENEXA, KS

PREP: 35 MIN. • **BAKE:** 20 MIN. + COOLING
MAKES: 2½ DOZEN

- 4 large eggs
- 1 cup sugar
- 1 cup packed brown sugar
- 1 cup canola oil
- 3 teaspoons vanilla extract
- 3 cups all-purpose flour
- 2 teaspoons baking powder
- 2 teaspoons ground cinnamon
- 1 teaspoon salt
- 1 teaspoon baking soda
- ½ teaspoon ground ginger
- ¼ teaspoon ground nutmeg
- ¾ cup buttermilk
- 1 pound carrots, grated
- 2 cups chopped walnuts, toasted
- 1 can (8 ounces) crushed pineapple, drained
- 1 cup flaked coconut

FROSTING/DECORATIONS

- 1 package (8 ounces) cream cheese, softened
- ½ cup butter, softened
- 1 teaspoon grated orange peel
- 1 teaspoon vanilla extract
- 4 cups confectioners' sugar
- 1 teaspoon water
- 6 drops green food coloring
- 3 cups flaked coconut
  Optional candies: jelly beans, bunny Peeps candy and Sour Punch straws

1. Preheat oven to 350°. Line 30 muffin cups with paper liners. In a large bowl, beat eggs, sugar, brown sugar, oil and vanilla until well blended. In another bowl, whisk flour, baking powder, cinnamon, salt, baking soda, ginger and nutmeg; add to the egg mixture alternately with buttermilk, beating well after each addition. Stir in the carrots, walnuts, pineapple and coconut.

2. Fill the prepared cups three-fourths full. Bake 20-25 minutes or until a toothpick inserted in the center comes out clean. Cool in pans 10 minutes before removing to wire racks to cool completely.

3. In a large bowl, beat cream cheese and butter until blended. Beat in orange peel and vanilla. Gradually beat in confectioners' sugar until smooth. Frost the cupcakes.

4. In a large resealable plastic bag, mix water and food coloring; add coconut. Seal bag and shake until the coconut is evenly tinted. Sprinkle coconut over the cupcakes. Decorate with candies as desired. Refrigerate until serving.

NOTE *To toast nuts, bake in a shallow pan in a 350° oven for 5-10 minutes or cook in a skillet over low heat until lightly browned, stirring occasionally.*

ELEGANT SMOKED SALMON STRATA

This fancy overnight egg bake is ideal for guests. In the morning, you can simply let it come to room temperature and whip up side dishes as it bakes. Then get ready for compliments!

—**LISA SPEER** PALM BEACH, FL

PREP: 30 MIN. + CHILLING • **BAKE:** 55 MIN. + STANDING
MAKES: 12 SERVINGS

  4 cups cubed ciabatta bread
  2 tablespoons butter, melted
  2 tablespoons olive oil
  2 cups shredded Gruyere or Swiss cheese
  2 cups shredded white cheddar cheese
10 green onions, sliced
 ½ pound smoked salmon or lox, coarsely chopped
  8 large eggs
  4 cups 2% milk
  4 teaspoons Dijon mustard
 ¼ teaspoon salt
 ¼ teaspoon pepper
    Creme fraiche or sour cream and minced chives

1. In a large bowl, toss bread cubes with butter and oil; transfer to a greased 13x9-in. baking dish. Sprinkle with the cheeses, onions and salmon. In another bowl, whisk the eggs, milk, mustard, salt and pepper; pour over top. Cover and refrigerate strata overnight.

2. Remove from the refrigerator 30 minutes before baking. Cover and bake at 350° for 30 minutes. Uncover; bake 25-30 minutes longer or until a knife inserted near the center comes out clean. Let stand for 10 minutes before serving. Serve with creme fraiche and chives.

JELLY BEAN BARK

Homemade Easter candy really doesn't get any easier than this. It's so simple—all you need are three ingredients, a microwave and a pan!

—**MAVIS DEMENT** MARCUS, IA

PREP: 15 MIN. + STANDING
MAKES: 2 POUNDS

  1 tablespoon butter
1¼ pounds white candy coating, coarsely chopped
  2 cups small jelly beans

1. Line a 15x10x1-in. pan with foil; grease foil with butter. In a microwave, melt candy coating; stir until smooth. Spread into the prepared pan. Top with jelly beans, pressing to adhere. Let stand until set.

2. Cut or break the bark into pieces. Store in an airtight container.

ORANGE-GLAZED
PORK LOIN

ORANGE-GLAZED PORK LOIN

This crazy-good tenderloin sprinkled with thyme and ginger is one of the best pork recipes I've ever tried. Guests always ask for the recipe. Try it this spring!

—LYNNETTE MIETE ALNA, ME

PREP: 10 MIN. • **BAKE:** 1 HOUR 20 MIN. + STANDING
MAKES: 16 SERVINGS

- 1 **teaspoon salt**
- 1 **garlic clove, minced**
- ¼ **teaspoon dried thyme**
- ¼ **teaspoon ground ginger**
- ¼ **teaspoon pepper**
- 1 **boneless pork loin roast (5 pounds)**

GLAZE

- 1 **cup orange juice**
- ¼ **cup packed brown sugar**
- 1 **tablespoon Dijon mustard**
- ⅓ **cup water**
- 1 **tablespoon cornstarch**

1. Preheat oven to 350°. Combine the first five ingredients; rub over the roast. Place the roast fat side up on a rack in a shallow roasting pan. Bake, uncovered, for 1 hour.
2. Meanwhile, in a saucepan over medium heat, combine the orange juice, brown sugar and mustard. In a small bowl, mix water and cornstarch until smooth. Add to orange juice mixture. Bring to a boil; cook and stir 2 minutes. Reserve 1 cup glaze for serving; brush half of remaining glaze over roast.
3. Bake until a thermometer reads 145°, about 20-40 minutes longer, brushing occasionally with remaining glaze. Let stand 10 minutes before slicing. Reheat the reserved glaze; serve with the roast.

AU GRATIN POTATOES 'N' LEEKS

I love making casseroles during the holidays. This one made me a fan of Gruyere cheese for au gratin dishes.

—ROSALIE HUGHES BOISE, ID

PREP: 45 MIN. • **BAKE:** 55 MIN.
MAKES: 12 SERVINGS

- 8 **cups sliced peeled potatoes (¼-inch slices)**
- 3 **medium leeks (white portion only), cut into ½-inch slices**
- 2 **tablespoons butter**
- 3 **tablespoons all-purpose flour**
- ½ **teaspoon salt**
- ⅛ **teaspoon pepper**
- 1⅓ **cups 2% milk**
- 4 **ounces Gruyere or Swiss cheese, shredded**
- ⅛ **teaspoon ground nutmeg**

CRUMB TOPPING

- ⅓ **cup dry bread crumbs**
- 2 **tablespoons butter, melted**
- ¼ **cup shredded cheddar cheese**

1. Place potatoes in a Dutch oven and cover with water. Bring to a boil. Add leeks; return to a boil. Cover and cook for 5 minutes. Drain and pat dry. Place in a greased 13x9-in. baking dish.
2. In a large saucepan, melt butter. Stir in the flour, salt and pepper until smooth; gradually add milk. Bring to a boil; cook and stir for 2 minutes or until thickened. Stir in the cheese and nutmeg until the cheese is melted. Pour over potato mixture. Toss bread crumbs and butter; sprinkle over the top.
3. Cover and bake at 325° for 40 minutes. Uncover; sprinkle with cheddar cheese. Bake for 15-20 minutes longer or until the potatoes are tender.

TEST KITCHEN TIP
When buying leeks, look for crisp, brightly colored leaves and an unblemished white stalk. Leeks that are larger than 1½ inches in diameter will be less tender. Refrigerate leeks in a plastic bag for up to 5 days. To use, cut off the roots and trim the tough leaf ends. Slit the leek from end to end and wash thoroughly under cold water to remove dirt trapped between the leaf layers.

PEEPS SUNFLOWER CAKE

The yellow Peeps make the petals of a sunflower, and chocolate chips resemble the seeds. It's a fun addition to the end of any meal.
—**BETHANY ELEDGE** CLEVELAND, TN

PREP: 15 MIN. • **BAKE:** 30 MIN. + COOLING
MAKES: 12 SERVINGS

- 1 package yellow cake mix (regular size)
- 2 cans (16 ounces each) chocolate frosting
- 19 to 20 yellow chick Peeps candies
- 1½ cups semisweet chocolate chips (assorted sizes)

1. Prepare and bake cake mix according to package directions, using two parchment paper-lined and greased 9-in. round baking pans. Cool cake layers in the pans 10 minutes before removing to wire racks; remove paper. Cool completely.
2. If cake layers have rounded tops, trim with a long serrated knife to make level. Spread frosting between layers and over top and sides of cake.
3. For petals, arrange Peeps around the edge of the cake, curving slightly and being careful not to separate the chicks. For the sunflower seeds, arrange chocolate chips in center of cake.

CLOVERLEAF POTATO ROLLS

I found this recipe in a magazine 40 years ago. They're the lightest and tastiest rolls I make, as popular at fellowship dinners as at home.
—**BEATRICE MCGRATH** NORRIDGEWOCK, ME

PREP: 25 MIN. + RISING • **BAKE:** 15 MIN.
MAKES: 2 DOZEN

- 1 package (¼ ounce) active dry yeast
- ¼ cup warm water (110° to 115°)
- 1 cup warm 2% milk (110° to 115°)
- ¼ cup shortening
- ½ cup warm mashed potatoes
- 1 large egg
- ¼ cup sugar
- 1¼ teaspoons salt
- 4 cups all-purpose flour, divided

1. In a large bowl, dissolve the yeast in water. Add the milk, shortening, potatoes, egg, sugar, salt and 2 cups of the flour. Beat until smooth. Add enough remaining flour to form a soft dough.
2. Turn dough onto a floured surface; knead until smooth and elastic, about 6-8 minutes. Place in a greased bowl, turning once to grease top. Cover and let rise in a warm place until doubled, about 1 hour.
3. Punch dough down and divide in half. Divide each half into 36 pieces; shape into balls. Place the dough balls into greased muffin cups—three in each cup. Cover and let rise in a warm place until doubled, about 30 minutes.
4. Bake at 400° for 12-15 minutes or until golden. Remove to wire racks. Serve warm.

★ ★ ★ ★ ★ **READER REVIEW**

"My grandkids loved helping me make this sunflower cake— but then they didn't want to cut it! Thanks for the fun!"
CHICTHIA1 TASTEOFHOME.COM

ASPARAGUS PASTRY PUFFS

ASPARAGUS PASTRY PUFFS

When the first asparagus of the season appears, we serve it rolled inside puff pastry with a yummy cheese filling. Our guests always compliment us on these lovely treats.

—**CINDY JAMIESON** TONAWANDA, NY

PREP: 30 MIN. • **BAKE:** 25 MIN.
MAKES: 16 SERVINGS

- 1 **pound fresh asparagus, trimmed**
- 4 **ounces cream cheese, softened**
- ¼ **cup grated Parmesan cheese**
- 1 **tablespoon stone-ground mustard**
- 2 **teaspoons lemon juice**
- ¼ **teaspoon salt**
- ¼ **teaspoon pepper**
- 1 **package (17.3 ounces) frozen puff pastry, thawed**
- 1 **large egg**
- 2 **tablespoons water**

1. Preheat oven to 400°. In a large skillet, bring 1½ in. of water to a boil. Add the asparagus; cook, uncovered, 1-3 minutes or until crisp-tender. Remove asparagus and immediately drop into ice water. Drain and pat dry.

2. In a small bowl, mix the cream cheese, Parmesan cheese, mustard, lemon juice, salt and pepper until blended. Unfold the puff pastry sheets; cut each sheet in half to make a total of four rectangles. Spread each rectangle with a fourth of the cream cheese mixture to within ¼ in. of the edges. Arrange the asparagus over top, allowing tips to show at each end; roll up jelly-roll style. Using a serrated knife, cut each roll crosswise into four sections.

3. Place on a parchment paper-lined baking sheet, seam side down. In a small bowl, whisk egg with water until blended; brush lightly over tops.

4. Bake 25-30 minutes or until golden brown. Remove from pan to a wire rack; serve warm.

HONEY
CHIPOTLE
RIBS

HONEY CHIPOTLE RIBS

Nothing's better than having a sauce with the perfect consistency to stick to the ribs. Here's one that's a great taste sensation, too. Go ahead and make the sauce up to a week ahead for an easier grilling experience.

—**CAITLIN HAWES** WESTWOOD, MA

PREP: 5 MIN. • **COOK:** 1½ HOURS
MAKES: 12 SERVINGS

- 6 pounds pork baby back ribs

BARBECUE SAUCE

- 3 cups ketchup
- 2 bottles (11.2 ounces each) Guinness beer
- 2 cups barbecue sauce
- ⅔ cup honey
- 1 small onion, chopped
- ¼ cup Worcestershire sauce
- 2 tablespoons Dijon mustard
- 2 tablespoons chopped chipotle peppers in adobo sauce
- 4 teaspoons ground chipotle pepper
- 1 teaspoon salt
- 1 teaspoon garlic powder
- ½ teaspoon pepper

1. Wrap the ribs in large pieces of heavy-duty foil; seal the edges of foil. Grill, covered, over indirect medium heat for 1 to 1½ hours or until tender.
2. In a large saucepan, combine the sauce ingredients; bring to a boil. Reduce heat; simmer, uncovered, for about 45 minutes or until sauce is thickened, stirring occasionally.
3. Carefully remove the ribs from the foil. Place over direct heat; baste with some of the sauce. Grill, covered, over medium heat for about 30 minutes or until browned, turning once and basting occasionally with additional sauce. Serve with the remaining sauce.

INSIDE-OUT BACON CHEESEBURGERS

During grilling season, I often put these tender, garlicky burgers on my menus. With cheese and bacon stuffed inside and caramelized onions on top, they are anything but ordinary.

—**MARY BILYEU** ANN ARBOR, MI

PREP: 70 MIN. • **GRILL:** 10 MIN.
MAKES: 12 SERVINGS

- 12 bacon strips, chopped
- 2 whole garlic bulbs
- 2 tablespoons Worcestershire sauce
- 2 teaspoons pepper
- 1 teaspoon salt
- 5 pounds ground beef
- 12 slices Swiss cheese, quartered
- 2 large onions, halved and thinly sliced
- 12 kaiser rolls, split

1. In a large skillet, cook bacon over medium heat until crisp. Remove to paper towels with a slotted spoon; drain, reserving ½ cup of the drippings.
2. Remove the papery outer skin from the garlic (do not peel or separate the cloves). Cut tops off of the garlic bulbs. Brush with 1 tablespoon of the bacon drippings. Wrap each bulb in heavy-duty foil. Bake at 425° for 30-35 minutes or until softened. Cool for 10-15 minutes.
3. Squeeze the softened garlic into a large bowl; add the Worcestershire sauce, pepper and salt. Crumble the beef over the mixture and mix well. Shape into 24 patties. Layer 2 pieces of cheese, bacon and then the remaining cheese onto the center of each of 12 patties. Top with the remaining patties; press edges firmly to seal.
4. In a large skillet, cook onions in the remaining reserved drippings over medium heat for 15-20 minutes or until golden brown, stirring occasionally.
5. Meanwhile, grill the burgers, covered, over medium heat for 5-7 minutes on each side or until a meat thermometer reads 160° and juices run clear. Grill the rolls, uncovered, for 1-2 minutes or until toasted. Serve burgers on rolls with onions.

BLUEBERRY ZUCCHINI SQUARES

I saw a bar recipe using apple and lemon peel on a muffin mix box. I tried it from scratch with shredded zucchini and fresh blueberries instead. It's a nifty combo.

—**SHELLY BEVINGTON** HERMISTON, OR

PREP: 30 MIN. • **BAKE:** 30 MIN. + COOLING
MAKES: 2 DOZEN

- 2 cups shredded zucchini (do not pack)
- ½ cup buttermilk
- 1 tablespoon grated lemon peel
- 3 tablespoons lemon juice
- 1 cup butter, softened
- 2½ cups sugar
- 2 large eggs
- 3¼ cups plus 2 tablespoons all-purpose flour, divided
- 1 teaspoon baking soda
- ½ teaspoon salt
- 2 cups fresh or frozen blueberries

GLAZE

- 2 cups confectioners' sugar
- ¼ cup buttermilk
- 1 tablespoon grated lemon peel
- 2 teaspoons lemon juice
- ⅛ teaspoon salt

1. Preheat oven to 350°. Grease a 15x10x1-in. baking pan.

2. In a small bowl, combine zucchini, buttermilk, lemon peel and lemon juice; toss to combine. In a large bowl, cream butter and sugar until light and fluffy. Beat in eggs, one at a time. In another bowl, whisk 3¼ cups flour, baking soda and salt; gradually add to the creamed mixture alternately with the zucchini mixture, mixing well after each addition. Toss blueberries with the remaining flour; fold into the batter.

3. Transfer the batter to the prepared pan, spreading evenly (pan will be full). Bake 30-35 minutes or until light golden brown and a toothpick inserted in the center comes out clean. Cool completely in the pan on a wire rack.

4. In a small bowl, mix the glaze ingredients until smooth; spread over top. Let stand until set.

NOTE *If using frozen blueberries, use without thawing to avoid discoloring the batter.*

FAST FIX

COLORFUL SPIRAL PASTA SALAD

Tricolor spiral pasta, broccoli, tomatoes and olives make a beautiful and colorful combo. Better yet, you can set this salad out on the buffet and forget it—it will stay fresh for the duration of your party.

—**AMANDA CABLE** BOXFORD, MA

START TO FINISH: 20 MIN.
MAKES: 14 SERVINGS

- 1 package (12 ounces) tricolor spiral pasta
- 4 cups fresh broccoli florets
- 1 pint grape tomatoes
- 1 can (6 ounces) pitted ripe olives, drained
- ⅛ teaspoon salt
- ⅛ teaspoon pepper
- 1½ cups Italian salad dressing with roasted red pepper and Parmesan

1. In a Dutch oven, cook pasta according to package directions, adding the broccoli during the last 2 minutes of cooking. Drain and rinse in cold water.

2. Transfer pasta and broccoli to a large bowl. Add the tomatoes, olives, salt and pepper. Drizzle with salad dressing; toss to coat. Chill until serving.

FOURTH OF JULY BEAN CASSEROLE

The outstanding barbecue taste of these beans makes them a favorite for cookouts all summer and into the fall. It's a popular dish that even kids like. Bacon and beef take this side a couple steps beyond plain pork and beans.

—DONNA FANCHER LAWRENCE, IN

PREP: 20 MIN. • **BAKE:** 1 HOUR
MAKES: 12 SERVINGS

- ½ pound bacon strips, diced
- ½ pound ground beef
- 1 cup chopped onion
- 1 can (28 ounces) pork and beans
- 1 can (16 ounces) kidney beans, rinsed and drained
- 1 can (15¼ ounces) lima beans
- ½ cup barbecue sauce
- ½ cup ketchup
- ½ cup sugar
- ½ cup packed brown sugar
- 2 tablespoons prepared mustard
- 2 tablespoons molasses
- 1 teaspoon salt
- ½ teaspoon chili powder

1. In a large skillet over medium heat, cook bacon, beef and onion until beef is no longer pink; drain.
2. Transfer to a greased 2½-qt. baking dish; add all of the beans and mix well. In a small bowl, combine the remaining ingredients; stir into the beef and bean mixture.
3. Cover and bake at 350° for 45 minutes. Uncover; bake 15 minutes longer.

★ ★ ★ ★ ★ **READER REVIEW**

"I'd never been much of a baked bean fan, but I was asked to make some for a church get-together. This recipe has made me a fan!"

ANNOLIVERI TASTEOFHOME.COM

FAST FIX ▶
HEIRLOOM TOMATO & ZUCCHINI SALAD

Tomato wedges give this salad a juicy bite. It's a great use of fresh herbs and veggies from your own garden or the farmers market.

—MATTHEW HASS FRANKLIN, WI

START TO FINISH: 25 MIN.
MAKES: 12 SERVINGS

- 7 large heirloom tomatoes (about 2½ pounds), cut into wedges
- 3 medium zucchini, halved lengthwise and thinly sliced
- 2 medium sweet yellow peppers, thinly sliced
- ⅓ cup cider vinegar
- 3 tablespoons olive oil
- 1 tablespoon sugar
- 1½ teaspoons salt
- 1 tablespoon each minced fresh basil, parsley and tarragon

1. In a large bowl, combine the tomatoes, zucchini and peppers. In a small bowl, whisk the vinegar, oil, sugar and salt until blended. Stir in the herbs.
2. Just before serving, drizzle the dressing over the salad; toss gently to coat.

ROASTED SWEET AND GOLD POTATO SALAD

I added Mexicorn and black beans to a potato salad for an extra-festive look and taste. The zesty dressing is easy to throw together.

—JEANNIE TRUDELL DEL NORTE, CO

PREP: 1½ HOURS
MAKES: 16 SERVINGS

- 2½ pounds Yukon Gold potatoes (about 8 medium)
- 1½ pounds sweet potatoes (about 2 large)
- 2 tablespoons olive oil
- 1 tablespoon ground cumin
- 2 teaspoons chili powder
- 2 teaspoons garlic powder
- 4 thick-sliced bacon strips, chopped
- 4 green onions, sliced
- 1 medium sweet red pepper, finely chopped
- ½ cup minced fresh cilantro
- 2 hard-cooked large eggs, chopped
- ¾ cup mayonnaise
- 1 tablespoon chopped chipotle pepper in adobo sauce
- 2 teaspoons sugar
- 1 large ripe avocado, peeled and finely chopped
- 2 tablespoons lime juice

1. Peel and cut potatoes and sweet potatoes into ¾-in. cubes. Place in a large bowl; drizzle with oil and sprinkle with seasonings. Toss to coat. Transfer to two greased 15x10x1-in. baking pans. Bake at 450° for 45-55 minutes or until tender, stirring occasionally. Cool slightly.

2. In a small skillet, cook the bacon over medium heat until crisp. Remove to paper towels with a slotted spoon; drain.

3. In a large bowl, combine the potatoes, bacon, onions, red pepper, cilantro and eggs. Combine the mayonnaise, chipotle and sugar; pour over the potato mixture and toss to coat. In a small bowl, toss the avocado with lime juice; gently stir into the salad. Serve warm or cold.

MAKE AHEAD

TRES LECHES CUPCAKES

A sweet, silky mixture using a trio of milks makes these little cakes three times as good. Because they soak overnight, they're a great make-ahead dessert for a potluck.

—*TASTE OF HOME* TEST KITCHEN

PREP: 45 MIN. + CHILLING • **BAKE:** 15 MIN. + COOLING
MAKES: 4 DOZEN

- 1 package yellow cake mix (regular size)
- 1¼ cups water
- 4 large eggs
- 1 can (14 ounces) sweetened condensed milk
- 1 cup coconut milk
- 1 can (5 ounces) evaporated milk
  Dash salt

WHIPPED CREAM

- 3 cups heavy whipping cream
- ⅓ cup confectioners' sugar
  Assorted fresh berries

1. Preheat oven to 350°. Line 48 muffin cups with paper liners.

2. In a large bowl, combine cake mix, water and eggs; beat on low speed 30 seconds. Beat on medium 2 minutes.

3. Fill the prepared cups halfway, allowing room in liners for the milk mixture. Bake 11-13 minutes or until a toothpick inserted in center comes out clean. Cool cupcakes for 5 minutes before removing from pans to wire racks.

4. Transfer cupcakes to baking sheets. Poke holes in cupcakes with a skewer. In a small bowl, mix milks and salt; spoon about 1 tablespoon of the milk mixture over each cupcake. Cover and refrigerate overnight.

5. In a large bowl, beat cream until it begins to thicken. Add confectioners' sugar; beat until soft peaks form. Spread over cupcakes; top with berries. Refrigerate leftovers.

TRES LECHES CUPCAKES

SPICY CHICKEN WINGS

These fall-off-the-bone-tender wings have just the right amount of heat, and cool blue cheese dressing creates the perfect flavor combination for dipping.

—KEVALYN HENDERSON HAYWARD, WI

PREP: 25 MIN. + MARINATING • **BAKE:** 2 HOURS
MAKES: 2 DOZEN (1¾ CUPS DIP)

- 1 cup reduced-sodium soy sauce
- ⅔ cup sugar
- 2 teaspoons salt
- 2 teaspoons grated orange peel
- 2 garlic cloves, minced
- ½ teaspoon pepper
- 3 pounds chicken wingettes and drumettes
- 3 teaspoons chili powder
- ¾ teaspoon cayenne pepper
- ¾ teaspoon hot pepper sauce

BLUE CHEESE DIP
- 1 cup mayonnaise
- ½ cup blue cheese salad dressing
- ⅓ cup buttermilk
- 2 teaspoons Italian salad dressing mix

1. In a small bowl, combine the soy sauce, sugar, salt, orange peel, garlic and pepper. Pour half of the marinade into a large resealable plastic bag. Add the chicken; seal bag and turn to coat. Refrigerate for 1 hour. Cover and refrigerate remaining marinade.
2. Drain and discard marinade. Transfer the chicken to a greased 13x9-in. baking dish. Cover and bake at 325° for 1½ hours or until chicken juices run clear.
3. Using tongs, transfer the chicken to a greased 15x10x1-in. baking pan. In a small bowl, combine the chili powder, cayenne, pepper sauce and the reserved marinade. Drizzle over the chicken.
4. Bake, uncovered, for 30 minutes, turning once. In a small bowl, whisk the dip ingredients. Serve with wings.

SWEET RASPBERRY TEA

You only need a handful of ingredients to stir together this bright and refreshing sipper as the weather heats up.

—TASTE OF HOME TEST KITCHEN

PREP: 10 MIN. • **COOK:** 15 MIN. + CHILLING
MAKES: 15 SERVINGS

- 4 quarts water, divided
- 10 individual tea bags
- 1 package (12 ounces) frozen unsweetened raspberries, thawed and undrained
- 1 cup sugar
- 3 tablespoons lime juice

1. In a saucepan, bring 2 quarts water to a boil; remove from heat. Add tea bags; steep, covered, 5-8 minutes according to taste. Discard tea bags.
2. Place the raspberries, sugar and the remaining water in a large saucepan; bring to a boil, stirring to dissolve the sugar. Reduce heat; simmer syrup, uncovered, 3 minutes. Press the mixture through a fine-mesh strainer into a bowl; discard the pulp and seeds.
3. In a large pitcher, combine tea, raspberry syrup and lime juice. Refrigerate, covered, until cold.

STRAWBERRY CORN SALSA

STRAWBERRY CORN SALSA

All the colors of summer are captured right here! The salsa has a fresh, light flavor; it can be served with chips, alone as a side dish or over grilled meat.

—**CATHERINE GOZA** LELAND, NC

PREP: 15 MIN. + CHILLING
MAKES: 5½ CUPS

- 2 cups fresh strawberries, chopped
- 2 cups grape tomatoes, chopped
- 1 package (10 ounces) frozen corn, thawed
- 2 green onions, chopped
- 3 tablespoons minced fresh cilantro
- ⅓ cup olive oil
- 2 tablespoons raspberry vinegar
- 2 tablespoons lime juice
- ½ teaspoon salt
  Baked tortilla chips

In a large bowl, combine the first five ingredients. In a small bowl, whisk the oil, vinegar, lime juice and salt. Drizzle over strawberry mixture; toss to coat. Refrigerate for 1 hour. Serve with chips.

FRESH HERB-BRINED TURKEY

To brine or not to brine? If you want a tender, juicy bird with lots of flavor, the choice is easy. We flavor our brine with parsley, rosemary and a touch of thyme.

—FELICIA SAATHOFF VASHON, WA

PREP: 40 MIN. + BRINING
BAKE: 2½ HOURS + STANDING • **MAKES:** 16 SERVINGS

- 4 **quarts water**
- 2 **cups sugar**
- 1½ **cups salt**
- 10 **fresh parsley sprigs**
- 10 **fresh thyme sprigs**
- 5 **fresh rosemary sprigs**
- 7 **bay leaves**
- 4 **teaspoons crushed red pepper flakes**
- 4 **teaspoons whole peppercorns**
- 4½ **quarts cold water**
- 2 **turkey-size oven roasting bags**
- 1 **turkey (14 to 16 pounds)**

TURKEY

- 2 **tablespoons olive oil**
- ½ **teaspoon pepper**
- ½ **teaspoon salt, optional**

1. In a large stockpot, combine the first nine ingredients; bring to a boil. Cook and stir until the sugar and salt are dissolved. Remove from heat. Add cold water to cool the brine to room temperature.

2. Place one oven roasting bag inside the other. Place turkey inside both bags; pour in cooled brine. Seal bags, pressing out as much air as possible; turn to coat the turkey. Place in a shallow roasting pan. Refrigerate 18-24 hours, turning occasionally.

3. Preheat oven to 350°. Remove the turkey from the brine; rinse and pat dry. Discard brine. Place the turkey on a rack in a shallow roasting pan, breast side up. Tuck wings under turkey; tie the drumsticks together. Rub oil over the outside of the turkey; sprinkle with pepper and, if desired, salt.

4. Roast, uncovered, 2½ to 3 hours or until a thermometer inserted in the thickest part of the thigh reads 170°-175°. (Cover loosely with foil if the turkey browns too quickly.)

5. Remove the turkey from oven; tent with foil. Let stand 20 minutes before carving.

NOTE *If using a prebasted turkey, omit the salt sprinkled on the outside of the turkey.*

★ ★ ★ ★ ★ **READER REVIEW**

"This was the first time I've used brine on a turkey. It certainly kept the bird moist. The herbs and spices looked beautiful. They smelled wonderful."

HAVINGFUNWITHMYFAMILY TASTEOFHOME.COM

DRIED CHERRY & SAUSAGE DRESSING

Apples and dried cherries add a sweet-tart flavor to my homemade stuffing. It makes a holiday dinner to remember.

—CONNIE BOLL CHILTON, WI

PREP: 40 MIN. • **BAKE:** 45 MIN.
MAKES: 20 SERVINGS (¾ CUP EACH)

- 1 loaf (1 pound) unsliced Italian bread
- ¼ cup cherry juice blend or unsweetened apple juice
- 1 cup dried cherries
- 1 pound bulk Italian sausage
- 2 celery ribs, chopped
- 1 medium onion, chopped
- 2 medium Granny Smith apples, chopped
- ½ cup chopped fresh parsley
- ½ cup butter, melted
- 1 teaspoon Italian seasoning
- 1 teaspoon fennel seed
- 1 teaspoon rubbed sage
- ½ teaspoon salt
- ¼ teaspoon pepper
- 2 large eggs
- 2 cups chicken stock

1. Preheat oven to 375°. Cut the bread into 1-in. cubes; transfer to two 15x10x1-in. baking pans. Bake 10-15 minutes or until toasted. Cool slightly. In a small saucepan, bring the juice to a boil. Stir in the cherries. Remove from heat; let stand for 10 minutes. Drain.

2. Meanwhile, in a large skillet, cook sausage, celery and onion over medium heat for 8-10 minutes or until the sausage is no longer pink and vegetables are tender, breaking up the sausage into crumbles; drain. Transfer to a large bowl; stir in the apples, parsley, butter, seasonings, bread cubes and drained cherries. In a small bowl, whisk eggs and stock; pour over the bread mixture and toss to coat.

3. Transfer to a greased 13x9-in. baking dish (the dish will be full). Bake, covered, 30 minutes. Bake, uncovered, 15-20 minutes or until golden brown.

MAKE-AHEAD BUTTERHORNS

Mom loved to make these lightly sweet, golden rolls. They're beautiful and impressive to serve, and they have a wonderful taste that carries with it the best memories of home.

—BERNICE MORRIS MARSHFIELD, MO

PREP: 30 MIN. + RISING • **BAKE:** 15 MIN. + FREEZING
MAKES: 32 ROLLS

- 2 packages (¼ ounce each) active dry yeast
- ⅓ cup warm water (110° to 115°)
- 2 cups warm 2% milk (110° to 115°)
- 1 cup shortening
- 1 cup sugar
- 6 large eggs
- 2 teaspoon salt
- 9 cups all-purpose flour, divided
- 3 to 4 tablespoons butter, melted

1. Preheat oven to 375°. In a large bowl, dissolve yeast in water. Add milk, shortening, sugar, eggs, salt and 4 cups flour; beat for 3 minutes or until smooth. Add enough of the remaining flour to form a soft dough.

2. Turn dough onto a floured surface; knead lightly. Place in a greased bowl, turning once to grease top. Cover and let rise in a warm place until doubled, about 2 hours.

3. Punch dough down; divide into four equal parts. Roll each into a 9-in. circle; brush with butter. Cut each circle into eight pie-shaped wedges; roll up each wedge from wide edge to tip of dough and pinch to seal.

4. Place rolls with tip down on baking sheets; freeze. When frozen, place in freezer bags and seal. Store in freezer for up to 4 weeks.

5. Place on greased baking sheets; thaw 5 hours or until doubled in size. Bake 12-15 minutes or until lightly browned. Remove from baking sheets; serve warm, or cool on wire rack.

**MAPLE BUTTER
TWISTS**

MAPLE BUTTER TWISTS

My stepmother passed along the recipe for this delicious yeast coffee cake that's shaped into pretty rings. When I make it for friends, they always ask for seconds.

—JUNE GILLILAND HOPE, IN

PREP: 35 MIN. + RISING • **BAKE:** 25 MIN. + COOLING
MAKES: 2 COFFEE CAKES

- 3¼ to 3½ cups all-purpose flour, divided
- 3 tablespoons sugar
- 1½ teaspoons salt
- 1 package (¼ ounce) active dry yeast
- ¾ cup milk
- ¼ cup butter
- 2 large eggs

FILLING
- ⅓ cup packed brown sugar
- ¼ cup sugar
- 3 tablespoons butter, softened
- 3 tablespoons maple syrup
- 4½ teaspoons all-purpose flour
- ¾ teaspoon ground cinnamon
- ¾ teaspoon maple flavoring
- ⅓ cup chopped walnuts

GLAZE
- ½ cup confectioners' sugar
- ¼ teaspoon maple flavoring
- 2 to 3 teaspoons milk

1. In a large bowl, combine 1½ cups flour, sugar, salt and yeast. In a saucepan, heat milk and butter to 120°-130°. Add to the dry ingredients; beat just until moistened. Add the eggs; beat on medium for 2 minutes. Stir in enough of the remaining flour to form a firm dough. Turn onto a floured surface; knead until smooth and elastic, about 5-7 minutes. Place in a greased bowl, turning once to grease top. Cover and let rise in a warm place until doubled, about 70 minutes.

2. In a small bowl, combine the first seven filling ingredients; beat for 2 minutes. Punch dough down; turn onto a lightly floured surface. Divide in half; roll each into a 16x8-in. rectangle. Spread filling to within ½ in. of the edges. Sprinkle with nuts. Roll up jelly-roll style, starting with a long side.

3. With a sharp knife, cut each roll in half lengthwise. Open the halves so the cut sides are up; gently twist the ropes together. Transfer to two greased 9-in. round baking pans, coiling into a circle. Tuck ends under; pinch to seal. Cover and let rise in a warm place until doubled, about 45 minutes.

4. Bake at 350° for 25-30 minutes or until golden brown. Cool for 10 minutes; remove from pans to wire racks. Combine the confectioners' sugar, maple flavoring and enough milk to achieve the desired consistency; drizzle over warm cakes.

FAST FIX
CASHEW-PEAR TOSSED SALAD

A friend who does a lot of catering fixed this salad for our staff Christmas party several years ago, and we all asked for the recipe. The unexpected sweet-salty mix and lovely dressing make it a standout.

—ARLENE MULLER KINGWOOD, TX

START TO FINISH: 15 MIN.
MAKES: 15 SERVINGS

- 1 bunch romaine, torn
- 1 cup (4 ounces) shredded Swiss cheese
- 1 cup salted cashews
- 1 medium pear, thinly sliced
- ½ cup dried cranberries

POPPY SEED VINAIGRETTE
- ⅔ cup olive oil
- ½ cup sugar
- ⅓ cup lemon juice
- 2 to 3 teaspoons poppy seeds
- 2 teaspoons finely chopped red onion
- 1 teaspoon prepared mustard
- ½ teaspoon salt

In a large salad bowl, combine the romaine, cheese, cashews, pear and cranberries. In a small bowl, whisk the vinaigrette ingredients. Drizzle over the salad and toss to coat.

1. Line a greased 15x10x1-in. baking pan with waxed paper. Grease the paper; set aside. In a bowl, beat eggs for 3 minutes. Gradually add sugar; beat for 2 minutes or until the mixture becomes thick and lemon-colored. Stir in pumpkin and lemon juice. Combine the dry ingredients; fold into the pumpkin mixture. Spread batter evenly in prepared pan. Sprinkle with walnuts.

2. Bake at 375° for 12-14 minutes or until the cake springs back when lightly touched in center. Cool for 5 minutes. Turn the cake out of pan onto a clean kitchen towel dusted with confectioners' sugar. Gently peel off waxed paper. Roll up cake in the towel jelly-roll style, starting with a long side. Cool completely on a wire rack.

3. In a bowl, combine the filling ingredients; beat until smooth. Unroll the cake; spread evenly with filling to within ½ in. of the edges. Roll up again. Cover and refrigerate for 1 hour before cutting. Refrigerate leftovers.

WALNUT PUMPKIN CAKE ROLL

This is one of my family's favorite dessert recipes, especially for holiday gatherings.

—**MARY GECHA** CENTER RUTLAND, VT

PREP: 20 MIN. + CHILLING • **BAKE:** 15 MIN. + COOLING
MAKES: 12 SERVINGS

- 3 large eggs
- 1 cup sugar
- ⅔ cup canned pumpkin
- 1 teaspoon lemon juice
- ¾ cup all-purpose flour
- 2 teaspoons ground cinnamon
- 1 teaspoon baking powder
- 1 teaspoon ground ginger
- ½ teaspoon salt
- ½ teaspoon ground nutmeg
- 1 cup finely chopped walnuts
  Confectioners' sugar

FILLING

- 6 ounces cream cheese, softened
- 1 cup confectioners' sugar
- ¼ cup butter, softened
- ½ teaspoon vanilla extract

SLOW COOKER

PEAR CIDER

A wonderful alternative to traditional apple cider, our perfectly spiced, pear-flavored beverage will warm you from head to toe.

—*TASTE OF HOME* TEST KITCHEN

PREP: 5 MIN. • **COOK:** 3 HOURS
MAKES: 20 SERVINGS (¾ CUP EACH)

- 12 cups unsweetened apple juice
- 4 cups pear nectar
- 8 cinnamon sticks (3 inches)
- 1 tablespoon whole allspice
- 1 tablespoon whole cloves

1. In a 6-qt. slow cooker, combine juice and nectar. Place the cinnamon sticks, allspice and cloves on a double thickness of cheesecloth; bring up corners of cloth and tie with string to form a bag. Place in the slow cooker.

2. Cover and cook on low for 3-4 hours or until heated through. Discard the spice bag. Serve warm cider in mugs.

CRANBERRY-BRIE
TARTLETS

CRANBERRY-BRIE TARTLETS

*My family hosts a holiday open house each year, and
that's where these can't-resist tartlets made their
first appearance. They're easy to make, but they look
like a gourmet treat.*

—**CINDY DAVIS** BONITA SPRINGS, FL

PREP: 30 MIN. • **BAKE:** 10 MIN.
MAKES: 4 DOZEN

- 2 tubes (8 ounces each) refrigerated
  crescent rolls
- 6 ounces Brie cheese, rind removed
- 1 cup whole-berry cranberry sauce
- ½ cup chopped pecans

1. Preheat oven to 375°. Unroll one tube of
crescent dough into one long rectangle; press
the perforations to seal. Cut dough into 24 pieces;
lightly press each piece onto the bottom and up
sides of an ungreased mini-muffin cup. Repeat with
the remaining crescent dough.

2. Place about 1 rounded teaspoon cheese in each
muffin cup; top with cranberry sauce and sprinkle
with pecans. Bake for 10-15 minutes or until golden
brown. Serve warm.

BRIE CHERRY PASTRY CUPS *Substitute ⅔ cup
cherry preserves for the cranberry sauce. After
baking sprinkle the appetizers with 2 tablespoons
minced chives.*

BRANDIED CRANBERRY BRIE CUPS *Decrease
cranberry sauce to ½ cup. Heat in a saucepan
with 2 tablespoons each of honey and orange
marmalade, 1 tablespoon brandy and ¼ teaspoon
each ground ginger and apple pie spice. Proceed
as directed.*

TEST KITCHEN TIP
For best results when trimming the
rind from a soft cheese like brie, use
a sharp clean knife and cut the cheese
while it's cold.

CRAB CRESCENT TRIANGLES

When some friends who love crab were planning a party, I created this recipe for them. The comforting baked bundles wrap up a cheesy seafood filling in convenient crescent roll dough.

—**NOELLE MYERS** GRAND FORKS, ND

PREP: 30 MIN. • **BAKE:** 10 MIN.
MAKES: 40 APPETIZERS

- 1 package (8 ounces) cream cheese, softened
- 2 teaspoons mayonnaise
- 1½ teaspoons Dijon mustard
- 1½ cups shredded Colby-Monterey Jack cheese
- ¾ cup shredded carrot (about 1 medium)
- ¼ cup finely chopped celery
- 2 green onions, chopped
- 1 garlic clove, minced
- 1 can (6 ounces) lump crabmeat, drained
- 2 tubes (8 ounces each) refrigerated seamless crescent dough sheet

1. Preheat oven to 375°. In a large bowl, beat the cream cheese, mayonnaise and mustard until blended. Stir in cheese, carrot, celery, green onions and garlic. Gently fold in crab.

2. Unroll the crescent dough and roll each tube of dough into a 12½x10-in. rectangle. Cut each sheet into twenty 2½-in. squares.

3. Spoon a heaping teaspoonful of cream cheese mixture diagonally over half of each square to within ½ in. of edges. Fold one corner of the dough over the filling to the opposite corner, forming a triangle. Pinch seams to seal; press the edges with a fork. Place on ungreased baking sheets. Bake for 8-10 minutes or until golden brown.

LATTICE-TOPPED PEAR SLAB PIE

A lattice top makes a charming frame for this dessert of pears and candied fruit—perfect for the fall and winter. Dollop the slices with whipped cream if you like.

—**JOHNNA JOHNSON** SCOTTSDALE, AZ

PREP: 30 MIN. + CHILLING • **BAKE:** 40 MIN. + COOLING
MAKES: 24 SERVINGS

- 1 cup butter, softened
- 1 package (8 ounces) cream cheese, softened
- 2 tablespoons sugar
- ½ teaspoon salt
- 2¼ cups all-purpose flour

FILLING
- ¾ cup sugar
- 3 tablespoons all-purpose flour
- 2 teaspoons grated lemon peel
- 8 cups thinly sliced peeled fresh pears (about 7 medium)
- 1 cup chopped mixed candied fruit
- 1 tablespoon 2% milk
- 3 tablespoons coarse sugar

1. In a small bowl, beat butter, cream cheese, sugar and salt until blended. Gradually beat in flour. Divide dough in two portions so that one portion is slightly larger than the other. Shape each into a rectangle; wrap in plastic wrap. Refrigerate 1 hour or overnight.

2. Preheat oven to 350°. For the filling, in a large bowl, combine sugar, flour and lemon peel. Add pears and candied fruit; toss to coat.

3. On a lightly floured surface, roll out the larger portion of dough into an 18x13-in. rectangle. Transfer to a greased 15x10x1-in. baking pan. Press onto the bottom and up the sides of pan; add filling.

4. Roll out the remaining dough to a ⅛-in.-thick rectangle; cut into ½-in.-wide strips. Arrange strips over the filling in a lattice pattern. Trim and seal the strips to the edge of the bottom pastry. Brush pastry with milk; sprinkle with coarse sugar.

5. Bake for 40-45 minutes or until crust is golden brown and filling is bubbly. Cool on a wire rack.

**LATTICE-TOPPED
PEAR SLAB PIE**
Johnna Johnson
Scottsdale, AZ

**ROASTED BEEF
TENDERLOIN**

MAKE AHEAD

ROASTED BEEF TENDERLOIN

An overnight marinade provides a savory seasoning for this tenderloin. I've served this simple but elegant roast on may special occasions.

—SCHELBY THOMPSON CAMDEN WYOMING, DE

PREP: 10 MIN. + MARINATING
BAKE: 40 MIN. + STANDING
MAKES: 12 SERVINGS

- ½ cup port wine or ½ cup beef broth and 1 tablespoon balsamic vinegar
- ½ cup reduced-sodium soy sauce
- 2 tablespoons olive oil
- 4 to 5 garlic cloves, minced
- 1 teaspoon dried thyme
- 1 teaspoon pepper
- ½ teaspoon hot pepper sauce
- 1 beef tenderloin roast (3 pounds)
- 1 bay leaf

1. In a small bowl, whisk the first seven ingredients until blended. Pour ¾ cup of the marinade into a large resealable plastic bag. Add roast and bay leaf; seal bag and turn to coat. Refrigerate the roast for 8 hours or overnight. Cover and refrigerate the remaining marinade.

2. Preheat oven to 425°. Drain beef, discarding marinade and bay leaf in the bag. Place roast on a rack in a shallow roasting pan. Roast 40-50 minutes or until the meat reaches desired doneness (for medium-rare, a thermometer should read 145°; medium, 160°; well-done, 170°); baste meat with reserved marinade. Remove roast from oven; tent with foil. Let stand 10 minutes before slicing.

TEST KITCHEN TIP
Bottles simply labeled olive oil or light olive oil (as opposed to virgin or extra virgin) contain oil with up to 3% acidity. It has a light color and mild flavor. The word "light" refers to the color and flavor of the oil, not its calorie content. Light olive oil has gone through a fine filtration process, giving it a very mild flavor and light color. This oil is perfect for cooking and baking.

WINTER SQUASH, SAUSAGE & FETA BAKE

I can't resist butternut squash with its bright color and full flavor. I make this casserole for potlucks—it's a guaranteed hit.

—CRAIG SIMPSON SAVANNAH, GA

PREP: 30 MIN. • **BAKE:** 45 MIN.
MAKES: 20 SERVINGS (¾ CUP EACH)

- 1 pound bulk Italian sausage
- 2 large onions, chopped
- ½ teaspoon crushed red pepper flakes, divided
- ¼ cup olive oil
- 2 teaspoons minced fresh rosemary
- 1½ teaspoons salt
- 1 teaspoon Worcestershire sauce
- 1 teaspoon pepper
- 1 medium butternut squash (about 4 pounds), peeled and cut into 1-inch cubes
- 1 medium acorn squash, peeled and cut into 1-inch cubes
- 2 cups crumbled feta cheese
- 2 small sweet red peppers, chopped

1. Preheat oven to 375°. In a large skillet, cook the sausage, onions and ¼ teaspoon pepper flakes over medium heat 8-10 minutes or until the sausage is no longer pink and the onions are tender, breaking up the sausage into crumbles; drain.

2. In a large bowl, combine oil, rosemary, salt, Worcestershire sauce, pepper and the remaining pepper flakes. Add butternut and acorn squash, cheese, red peppers and the sausage mixture; toss to coat.

3. Transfer to an ungreased shallow roasting pan. Cover and bake for 35 minutes. Uncover; bake 10-15 minutes longer or until the squash is tender.

FAST FIX

BRUSSELS SPROUTS WITH BACON & GARLIC

When we have company, these sprouts are my go-to side dish because they look and taste fantastic. If you want to fancy them up a notch, use pancetta instead of bacon.

—**MANDY RIVERS** LEXINGTON, SC

START TO FINISH: 30 MIN.
MAKES: 12 SERVINGS

- 2 pounds fresh Brussels sprouts (about 10 cups)
- 8 bacon strips, coarsely chopped
- 3 garlic cloves, minced
- ¾ cup chicken broth
- ½ teaspoon salt
- ¼ teaspoon pepper

1. Trim Brussels sprouts. Cut sprouts lengthwise in half; cut crosswise into thin slices. In a 6-qt. stockpot, cook bacon over medium heat until crisp, stirring occasionally. Add garlic; cook 30 seconds longer. Remove with a slotted spoon; drain on paper towels.

2. Add Brussels sprouts to the bacon drippings; cook and stir for 4-6 minutes or until the sprouts begin to brown lightly. Stir in broth, salt and pepper; cook, covered, 4-6 minutes longer or until the Brussels sprouts are tender. Stir in bacon mixture.

RED VELVET PANCAKES

The recipe makes mix for five batches of pancakes, so you can make one or more batches at a time, depending on how large your crowd is. We make a Christmastime tradition of having a lazy pancake breakfast and reading J.R.R. Tolkien's Letters from Father Christmas, *fables he wrote for his children.*

—**SUE BROWN** WEST BEND, WI

PREP: 30 MIN. • **COOK:** 15 MIN./BATCH
MAKES: 16 PANCAKES PER BATCH

- 10 cups all-purpose flour
- 1¼ cups sugar
- ⅔ cup baking cocoa
- 6 teaspoons baking soda
- 4 teaspoons baking powder
- 5 teaspoons salt

ADDITIONAL INGREDIENTS (FOR EACH BATCH)

- 2 cups buttermilk
- 2 large eggs
- 2 tablespoons red food coloring
  Butter and maple syrup

1. In a large bowl, combine the first six ingredients. Place 2 cups of mix in each of five resealable plastic bags or containers. Store in a cool dry place for up to 6 months.

2. To prepare pancakes, pour mix into a large bowl. In a small bowl, whisk the buttermilk, eggs and food coloring. Stir into the dry ingredients just until they are moistened.

3. Pour batter by ¼ cupfuls onto a greased hot griddle; turn when bubbles form on top. Cook until the second side is golden brown. Serve with butter and syrup.

FAST FIX ▶

HOT BUTTERED CIDER MIX

Put the butter base for this beverage in a decorative jar and attach a copy of the recipe for a great gift from your kitchen.

—*TASTE OF HOME* TEST KITCHEN

START TO FINISH: 10 MIN.
MAKES: 64 SERVINGS (2 CUPS BUTTERED CIDER MIX)

- 1 cup butter, softened
- 1 cup packed brown sugar
- ½ cup honey
- 1 teaspoon ground cinnamon
- ½ teaspoon ground cardamom
- ¼ teaspoon ground cloves

EACH SERVING

- ¾ cup hot apple cider or juice

1. Beat butter and brown sugar until blended; beat in honey and spices. Transfer to an airtight container; store in refrigerator for up to 2 weeks.
2. To prepare hot cider, place 1½ teaspoons buttered cider mix in a mug. Stir in hot cider.

PEPPERMINT STICK COOKIES

With cool mint flavor and a festive look, these whimsical creations will make you feel like you're at the North Pole. The chilled dough is easy to shape, too.

—NANCY KNAPKE FORT RECOVERY, OH

PREP: 1 HOUR + CHILLING
BAKE: 10 MIN./BATCH + COOLING
MAKES: 4 DOZEN

- 1 cup unsalted butter, softened
- 1 cup sugar
- 1 large egg
- 2 teaspoons mint extract
- ½ teaspoon vanilla extract
- 2¾ cups all-purpose flour
- ½ teaspoon salt
- 12 drops red food coloring
- 12 drops green food coloring
- 1½ cups white baking chips
  Crushed mint candies

1. In a large bowl, cream butter and sugar until light and fluffy. Beat in egg and extracts. Combine flour and salt; gradually add to the creamed mixture and mix well.
2. Set aside half the dough. Divide the remaining dough in half; add green food coloring to one portion and red food coloring to the other. Wrap dough separately in plastic wrap. Refrigerate 1-2 hours or until easy to handle.
3. Preheat oven to 350°. Divide the green and red dough into 24 portions each. Divide the plain dough into 48 portions. Roll each into a 4-in. rope. Place each green rope next to a white rope; press together gently and twist. Repeat with the red ropes and the remaining white ropes. Place 2 in. apart on ungreased baking sheets.
4. Bake 10-12 minutes or until set. Cool 2 minutes before carefully removing from pans to wire racks to cool completely.
5. In a microwave, melt white chips; stir until smooth. Dip cookie ends into the melted chips; allow excess to drip off. Sprinkle with crushed candies and place on waxed paper. Let stand until set. Store in an airtight container.

CANDY CANE CHOCOLATE LOAVES

Having a bunch of leftover candy canes after the holidays inspired me to use them up by adding them to a chocolate bread. Coffee and cocoa intensify the flavor.

—**SHELLY PLATTEN** AMHERST, WI

PREP: 25 MIN. • **BAKE:** 50 MIN. + COOLING
MAKES: 3 LOAVES (12 SLICES EACH)

- ¼ cup butter, softened
- 1⅔ cups packed brown sugar
- 4 large egg whites
- 2 large eggs
- ¾ cup strong brewed coffee
- ½ cup vanilla yogurt
- ¼ cup canola oil
- 1 tablespoon vanilla extract
- ¼ teaspoon peppermint extract
- 3½ cups all-purpose flour
- ¾ cup baking cocoa
- 1½ teaspoons baking soda
- ½ teaspoon salt
- 1½ cups buttermilk
- 1 cup (6 ounces) miniature semisweet chocolate chips

TOPPING

- 2 ounces white baking chocolate, melted
- 3 tablespoons crushed candy canes

1. Preheat oven to 350°. Coat three 8x4-in. loaf pans with cooking spray. In a large bowl, beat butter and brown sugar until crumbly, about 2 minutes. Add egg whites, eggs, coffee, yogurt, oil and extracts until blended.

2. In another bowl, whisk flour, cocoa, baking soda and salt; add to the brown sugar mixture alternately with buttermilk, beating well after each addition. Fold in chocolate chips.

3. Transfer to prepared pans. Bake 50-55 minutes or until a toothpick inserted in the center comes out clean. Cool for 10 minutes before removing from pans to wire racks to cool completely.

4. Drizzle melted white baking chocolate over the loaves. Sprinkle with crushed candies.

SPINACH-CORN BREAD BITES

Although this recipe makes a big batch, I never have any leftovers. These appetizers are just that popular!

—**LAURA MAHAFFEY** ANNAPOLIS, MD

PREP: 25 MIN. • **BAKE:** 15 MIN./BATCH
MAKES: 4 DOZEN

- 1 package (8½ ounces) corn bread/muffin mix
- ½ cup grated Parmesan cheese
- ⅛ teaspoon garlic powder
- 2 large eggs
- ½ cup blue cheese salad dressing
- ¼ cup butter, melted
- 1 package (10 ounces) frozen chopped spinach, thawed and squeezed dry
- ½ cup shredded cheddar cheese
- ½ cup finely chopped onion

1. In a large bowl, combine muffin mix, Parmesan cheese and garlic powder. In another bowl, whisk the eggs, salad dressing and butter; stir into the dry ingredients just until moistened. Fold in the spinach, cheddar cheese and onion.

2. Fill greased miniature muffin cups two-thirds full. Bake at 350° for 12-14 minutes or until a toothpick inserted in the center comes out clean. Cool for 5 minutes before removing from pans to wire racks. Serve warm. Refrigerate leftovers.

GARLIC KNOTS

FAST FIX ▶
GARLIC KNOTS

Here's a handy bread that can be made in no time flat. Refrigerated biscuits make preparation simple. The classic Italian flavors complement a variety of meals.

—**JANE PASCHKE** UNIVERSITY PARK, FL

START TO FINISH: 30 MIN.
MAKES: 2½ DOZEN

- 1 tube (12 ounces) refrigerated buttermilk biscuits
- ¼ cup canola oil
- 3 tablespoons grated Parmesan cheese
- 1 teaspoon garlic powder
- 1 teaspoon dried oregano
- 1 teaspoon dried parsley flakes

1. Preheat oven to 400°. Cut each biscuit into thirds. Roll each piece into a 3-in. rope and tie into a knot; tuck ends under. Place 2 in. apart on a greased baking sheet. Bake 8-10 minutes or until golden brown.
2. In a large bowl, combine the remaining ingredients; add the warm knots and gently toss to coat.

CHRISTMAS CRANBERRY SALAD

My family has requested this delicious holiday salad every year since the first time I served it. The not-too-sweet flavor is a perfect pairing with just about any meat.

—**JENNIFER MASTNICK-COOK** HARTVILLE, OH

PREP: 30 MIN. + CHILLING
MAKES: 12 SERVINGS

- 2 packages (3 ounces each) raspberry gelatin
- 2 cups boiling water, divided
- 1 can (14 ounces) whole-berry cranberry sauce
- 2 tablespoons lemon juice
- 1 cup heavy whipping cream
- 1 package (8 ounces) cream cheese, softened
- ½ cup chopped pecans

1. In a small bowl, dissolve gelatin in 1 cup boiling water. In another bowl, combine cranberry sauce and remaining water; add the gelatin mixture and lemon juice. Pour into a 13x9-in. dish coated with cooking spray; refrigerate until firm, about 1 hour.
2. In a large bowl, beat cream until stiff peaks form. In another bowl, beat cream cheese until smooth. Stir in ½ cup whipped cream; fold in the remaining whipped cream. Spread over the gelatin mixture; sprinkle with pecans. Refrigerate mixure for at least 2 hours.

BEST LEG OF LAMB

When Julia Child visited my cousin's winery over 20 years ago for a TV segment, she prepared leg of lamb using these ingredients. She didn't give the amounts, but I've experimented and come pretty close to duplicating her recipe.

—KAREN MCASHAN KERRVILLE, TX

PREP: 15 MIN. + MARINATING
BAKE: 2½ HOURS + STANDING
MAKES: 12 SERVINGS

- ⅓ cup minced fresh rosemary
- 2 tablespoons Dijon mustard
- 2 tablespoons olive oil
- 8 garlic cloves, minced
- 1 teaspoon reduced-sodium soy sauce
- ½ teaspoon salt
- ½ teaspoon pepper
- 1 bone-in leg of lamb (7 to 9 pounds), trimmed
- 1 cup chicken broth

1. In a small bowl, combine the first seven ingredients; rub over leg of lamb. Cover and refrigerate overnight.

2. Place the lamb, fat side up, on a rack in a shallow roasting pan. Bake, uncovered, at 325° for 1½ hours.

3. Add broth to pan; cover loosely with foil. Bake 1 to 1½ hours longer or until meat reaches desired doneness (for medium-rare, a thermometer should read 145°; medium, 160°; well-done, 170°). Let stand for 10-15 minutes before slicing.

★ ★ ★ ★ ★ **READER REVIEW**

"This was a fabulous recipe. I served it with an amazing pilaf and braised French green beans."

ALLUPINTHEKITCHEN TASTEOFHOME.COM

RASPBERRY RED BAKEWELL TART

I fell for this British dessert while stationed in Dubai. Jam with almond filling is traditional, but red velvet makes it a holiday dazzler. The recipe makes enough icing to cover the top; you can use less, as shown.

—CRYSTAL SCHLUETER NORTHGLENN, CO

PREP: 30 MIN. + FREEZING • **BAKE:** 30 MIN. + COOLING
MAKES: 12 SERVINGS

- 1 sheet refrigerated pie pastry
- 1 large egg white, lightly beaten

FILLING

- ¼ cup seedless raspberry jam
- ⅔ cup butter, softened
- ¾ cup sugar
- 3 large eggs
- 1 large egg yolk
- 1 tablespoon baking cocoa
- 2 teaspoons red paste food coloring
- 1 cup ground almonds

ICING

- 2½ cups confectioners' sugar
- 3 tablespoons water
- ¼ teaspoon almond extract

1. Preheat oven to 350°. Unroll pastry sheet into a 9-in. fluted tart pan with removable bottom; trim even with rim. Freeze for 10 minutes.

2. Line unpricked pastry with a double thickness of foil. Fill with pie weights, dried beans or uncooked rice. Bake 12-15 minutes or until the edges are golden brown.

3. Remove foil and weights; brush bottom of crust with egg white. Bake 6-8 minutes longer or until golden brown. Cool on a wire rack.

4. Spread jam over the bottom of the crust. In a bowl, cream butter and sugar until light and fluffy. Gradually beat in eggs, egg yolk, cocoa and food coloring. Fold in ground almonds. Spread over jam.

5. Bake 30-35 minutes or until the filling is set. Cool completely on a wire rack.

6. In a small bowl, mix confectioners' sugar, water and extract until smooth; drizzle or pipe over tart. Refrigerate leftovers.

NOTE *Let pie weights cool, then store. Do not use beans and rice used for pie weights for cooking.*

**RASPBERRY RED
BAKEWELL TART**

BAKED SWEET CORN
CROQUETTES, PAGE 240

FEEDING A CROWD

"Taking the five loaves and the two fish and looking up to heaven, he gave thanks and broke the loaves. Then he gave them to his disciples to distribute to the people. He also divided the two fish among them all. They all ate and were satisfied."

MARK 6:41-42

RICH FRUIT KUCHENS

This German classic is such a part of our reunions, we designate a special place to serve it. Five generations flock to the Kuchen Room for this coffee cake.

—**STEPHANIE SCHENTZEL** NORTHVILLE, SD

PREP: 40 MIN. + CHILLING • **BAKE:** 35 MIN.
MAKES: 4 COFFEE CAKES (8 SERVINGS EACH)

- 1 ⅛ teaspoons active dry yeast
- ½ cup warm water (110° to 115°)
- ½ cup warm milk (110° to 115°)
- ½ cup sugar
- ½ teaspoon salt
- ½ cup canola oil
- 1 large egg, lightly beaten
- 3½ cups all-purpose flour, divided

CUSTARD

- 4 large eggs, lightly beaten
- 2 cups heavy whipping cream
- 1½ cups sugar
- 8 to 10 cups sliced peeled tart apples or canned sliced peaches, drained, or combination of fruits

TOPPING

- ½ cup sugar
- ½ cup all-purpose flour
- 1 teaspoon ground cinnamon
- ¼ cup cold butter

1. In a large bowl, dissolve yeast in warm water. Add the milk, sugar, salt, oil, egg and 2½ cups flour; beat until smooth. Stir in enough remaining flour to form a soft dough. Place in a greased bowl, turning once to grease top. Do not knead. Cover and refrigerate overnight.

2. The next day, for custard, whisk the eggs, cream and sugar in a large bowl until combined; set aside. Divide dough into four portions.

3. On a lightly floured surface, roll each portion into a 10-in. circle. Press each circle onto the bottom and up the sides of an ungreased 9-in. pie plate. Arrange 2 to 2½ cups of fruit in each crust. Pour 1 cup custard over fruit.

4. For the topping, combine the sugar, flour and cinnamon in a small bowl. Cut in butter until mixture

resembles coarse crumbs. Sprinkle ⅓ cup over each coffee cake. Cover edges of dough with foil. Bake at 350° for 35-40 minutes or until golden brown and custard reaches 160°.

MAKE AHEAD
CHICKEN WILD RICE DISH

This special dish will be sure to delight guests. You can assemble it the night before and bake it the day of the event.

—*TASTE OF HOME* TEST KITCHEN

PREP: 35 MIN. • **BAKE:** 1½ HOURS
MAKES: 4 CASSEROLES (50 SERVINGS)

- 2 pounds sliced fresh mushrooms
- 4 cups chopped celery
- 4 cups chopped sweet red pepper
- 2⅔ cups chopped green onions
- 8 garlic cloves, minced
- 1⅓ cups butter, cubed
- 4 cans (14½ ounces each) chicken broth
- 24 cups cubed cooked chicken
- 16 cups cooked wild rice
- 16 cups cooked long grain rice
- 8 cups shredded cheddar cheese
- 3 tablespoons salt
- 3 tablespoons dried basil
- 2 teaspoons pepper

In a stockpot, saute the first five ingredients in butter until tender. Add remaining ingredients and mix well. Spoon into four greased 13x9-in. baking dishes. Cover and bake at 350° for 75 minutes. Uncover and bake for 15 minutes longer or until heated through.

NOTE *This dish may be assembled and refrigerated overnight. Remove from the refrigerator 1 hour before baking.*

TEST KITCHEN TIP
When bulk chicken is on sale, buy several packages. Bake the chicken pieces, skin side up, on foil-lined pans. When cool, remove skin and bones, cube the meat and freeze it in measured portions to make it easy to use in recipes.

RICH FRUIT KUCHENS

BAKED SWEET CORN CROQUETTES

My delicious corn croquettes are baked like muffins instead of fried. They can be served with butter, but my family prefers salsa as an accompaniment.
—**KAREN KUEBLER** DALLAS, TX

PREP: 30 MIN. • **BAKE:** 10 MIN./BATCH
MAKES: 5½ DOZEN

- 3 cups fresh corn, divided
- 1 cup cornmeal
- 1 cup 2% milk
- 1 teaspoon sugar
- ¼ teaspoon ground cinnamon, optional
- 4 ounces cream cheese, softened
- ¼ cup butter, softened
- 2 large eggs
- 3 cups shredded cheddar cheese
  Sour cream and minced chives

1. Preheat oven to 350°. Place 2 cups corn kernels in a food processor; process until pureed. Transfer pureed corn to a large bowl; whisk in cornmeal, milk, sugar, the remaining corn and, if desired, cinnamon until blended. In another bowl, beat cream cheese, butter and eggs until pale yellow and slightly thickened, about 10 minutes. Fold in cheddar cheese. Stir in the corn mixture.
2. Fill greased mini-muffin cups three-fourths full.

Bake 8-10 minutes or until a toothpick inserted in the center comes out clean. Serve warm; top with sour cream and chives.

MAKE AHEAD
SWISS & CARAWAY FLATBREADS

My mom came across this rustic-looking flatbread recipe many years ago and always made it on Christmas Eve. Now I make it for my own family throughout the year. It's easy to double or cut in half depending on how many you're serving.
—**DIANE BERGER** SEQUIM, WA

PREP: 20 MIN. + RISING • **BAKE:** 10 MIN.
MAKES: 2 LOAVES (16 PIECES EACH)

- 2 loaves (1 pound each) frozen bread dough, thawed
- ¼ cup butter, melted
- ¼ cup canola oil
- 1 tablespoon dried minced onion
- 1 tablespoon Dijon mustard
- 2 teaspoons caraway seeds
- 1 teaspoon Worcestershire sauce
- 1 tablespoon dry sherry, optional
- 2 cups shredded Swiss cheese

1. On a lightly floured surface, roll each portion of dough into a 15x10-in. rectangle. Transfer to two greased 15x10x1-in. baking pans. Cover with kitchen towels; let rise in a warm place until doubled, about 45 minutes.
2. Preheat oven to 425°. Using your fingertips, press several dimples into the dough. In a small bowl, whisk melted butter, oil, onion, mustard, caraway seeds, Worcestershire sauce and, if desired, sherry until blended; brush over the dough. Sprinkle with cheese. Bake 10-15 minutes or until golden brown. Serve warm.
FREEZE OPTION *Cut the cooled flatbreads into pieces. Freeze in resealable plastic freezer bags. To use, reheat flatbreads on an ungreased baking sheet in a preheated 425° oven until they are heated through.*

CROWD-PLEASING RAVIOLI NACHOS

Take lightly breaded and deep-fried ravioli to a new level in a nacho-like appetizer that's easy to make and sure to please. Kids and grown-ups can't get enough of these crispy, cheesy, flavorful bites.
—ROBERT DOORNBOS JENISON, MI

PREP: 1 HOUR • **BAKE:** 5 MIN.
MAKES: 6½ DOZEN

- 1 package (25 ounces) frozen cheese ravioli
- 1 package (25 ounces) frozen sausage ravioli
- 3 large eggs, lightly beaten
- 2 cups seasoned bread crumbs
- 2 tablespoons grated Parmesan cheese
- ¼ teaspoon crushed red pepper flakes
- ¼ teaspoon pepper
- ⅛ teaspoon garlic salt
  Oil for deep-fat frying
- ¾ cup Alfredo sauce
- ¾ cup spaghetti sauce
- 2 cups shredded cheddar cheese
- 5 green onions, sliced
- 1 can (3.8 ounces) sliced ripe olives, drained
  Additional spaghetti sauce, optional

1. Cook ravioli according to package directions. Drain and pat dry. Place eggs in a shallow bowl. In another shallow bowl, combine bread crumbs, Parmesan cheese, pepper flakes, pepper and garlic salt. Dip the ravioli in the eggs, then in the bread crumb mixture.
2. In an electric skillet or deep-fat fryer, heat oil to 375°. Fry the ravioli, a few at a time, for 1-2 minutes on each side or until golden brown. Drain ravioli on paper towels.
3. Arrange the ravioli in an ungreased 15x10x1-in. baking pan. Spoon sauces over the ravioli; sprinkle with cheddar cheese.
4. Bake at 350° for 3-5 minutes or until the cheese is melted. Sprinkle with onions and olives. Serve immediately with the additional spaghetti sauce if desired.

EASY MACARONI SALAD

This hearty pasta salad is sure to please appetites of all ages—and it serves a lot of folks!
—LAVERNA M JONES MOORHEAD, MN

PREP: 15 MIN. + CHILLING
MAKES: 34 SERVINGS

- 2 pounds uncooked elbow macaroni
- 12 hard-cooked large eggs, chopped
- 2½ pounds fully cooked ham, cubed
- 1 package (16 ounces) frozen peas, thawed
- 3 cups sliced celery
- 1 large green pepper, chopped
- ½ cup chopped onion
- 1 jar (4 ounces) diced pimientos, drained
- 4 cups mayonnaise

1. Cook macaroni according to package directions. Rinse in cold water; drain and cool completely.
2. Place macaroni in a large bowl; stir in the remaining ingredients. Cover and refrigerate for at least 3 hours.

**SMOKED GOUDA
& ROAST BEEF
PINWHEELS**
Pamela Shank
Parkersburg, WV

SMOKED GOUDA & ROAST BEEF PINWHEELS

Our local deli makes terrific roast beef sandwiches; I made this pinwheel appetizer to re-create that taste. So many flavors for such a little treat!

—PAMELA SHANK PARKERSBURG, WV

PREP: 20 MIN. • **BAKE:** 15 MIN./BATCH
MAKES: 4 DOZEN

- ¾ pound sliced deli roast beef, finely chopped
- 1 package (10 ounces) frozen chopped spinach, thawed and squeezed dry
- 1 package (6½ ounces) garlic-herb spreadable cheese
- 1 cup shredded smoked Gouda cheese
- ¼ cup finely chopped red onion
- 2 tubes (8 ounces each) refrigerated crescent rolls

1. Preheat oven to 375°. In a small bowl, mix the first five ingredients until blended. On a lightly floured surface, unroll one tube of crescent dough into one long rectangle; press perforations to seal.

2. Spread half of the roast beef mixture over the dough. Roll up jelly-roll style, starting with a long side; pinch seam to seal. Using a serrated knife, cut the roll crosswise into twenty-four ½-inch slices. Place on parchment paper-lined baking sheets, cut side down. Repeat with the remaining crescent dough and roast beef mixture.

3. Bake 12-14 minutes or until golden brown. Refrigerate leftovers.

★ ★ ★ ★ ★ **READER REVIEW**

"These pinwheels were a huge hit at my sister's baby shower. They look so fancy and really aren't hard to make at all!"

CURLYLISS85 TASTEOFHOME.COM

DILLED MUSHROOM TURNOVERS

My bite-size mushroom pastries are hard to resist. For parties, I prep and freeze them, then pop them in the oven when guests are on the way.

—ISABELLA MICHEL-CLARK SPARKS, NV

PREP: 1 HOUR + CHILLING • **BAKE:** 15 MIN./BATCH
MAKES: ABOUT 5 DOZEN

- 1 cup butter, softened
- 2 packages (8 ounces each) cream cheese, softened
- 3 cups all-purpose flour

FILLING

- 3 tablespoons butter
- ½ pound fresh mushrooms, finely chopped
- 1 large onion, finely chopped
- ¼ cup sour cream
- 2 tablespoons all-purpose flour
- 1 teaspoon salt
- 1 teaspoon snipped fresh dill
- 1 large egg, beaten

1. In a large bowl, cream butter and cream cheese until smooth. Gradually beat in flour. Divide dough in half. Shape each half into a disk; wrap in plastic. Refrigerate 1 hour or until firm enough to handle.

2. For the filling, in a large skillet, heat butter over medium heat. Add mushrooms and onion; cook and stir 6-8 minutes or until the vegetables are tender. Remove from heat; stir in sour cream, flour, salt and dill. Cool to room temperature.

3. Preheat oven to 400°. On a lightly floured surface, roll the dough to ⅛-in. thickness. Cut circles with a floured 2½-in. round cookie cutter. Place about 1 teaspoon filling on one side of each circle. Brush edges with egg; fold the dough over the filling. Press the edges with a fork to seal.

4. Place on ungreased baking sheets; brush egg over tops. Bake 12-14 minutes or until the edges are golden brown.

FREEZE OPTION: *Cover and freeze unbaked turnovers on waxed paper-lined baking sheets until firm. Transfer to resealable plastic freezer bags; return to freezer. To use, bake the turnovers as directed, increasing time by 2-3 minutes.*

DELICIOUS POTATO DOUGHNUTS

I first tried these treats at my sister's house and thought they were the best I'd ever had. They're easy to make, and the fudge frosting tops them off well.

—PAT DAVIS BEULAH, MI

PREP: 20 MIN. • **COOK:** 40 MIN.
MAKES: 4 DOZEN

- 2 cups hot mashed potatoes (with added milk and butter)
- 2½ cups sugar
- 2 cups buttermilk
- 2 large eggs, lightly beaten
- 2 tablespoons butter, melted
- 2 teaspoons baking soda
- 2 teaspoons baking powder
- 1 teaspoon salt
- 1 teaspoon ground nutmeg
- 6½ to 7 cups all-purpose flour
  Oil for deep-fat frying

FAST FUDGE FROSTING
- 3¾ cups confectioners' sugar
- ½ cup baking cocoa
- ¼ teaspoon salt
- ⅓ cup boiling water
- ⅓ cup butter, melted
- 1 teaspoon vanilla extract

1. In a large bowl, combine the potatoes, sugar, buttermilk and eggs. Stir in the butter, baking soda, baking powder, salt, nutmeg and enough of the flour to form a soft dough. Turn onto a lightly floured surface; pat out to ¾-in. thickness. Cut with a 2½-in. floured doughnut cutter.

2. In an electric skillet, heat 1 in. of oil to 375°. Fry the doughnuts for 2 minutes on each side or until browned. Place on paper towels.

3. For the frosting, combine the confectioners' sugar, cocoa and salt in a large bowl. Stir in the water, butter and vanilla. Dip tops of the warm doughnuts in frosting.

PANCAKES FOR A CROWD

The next time you're in charge of fixing a breakfast for 70 people or more, pull out this tried-and-true recipe. The batter for these buttermilk pancakes comes together easily, and the flapjacks couldn't be more delightful.

—PENELOPE HAMILTON RIVERSIDE, CA

PREP: 25 MIN. • **COOK:** 35 MIN.
MAKES: 70-80 SERVINGS (5 GALLONS OF BATTER)

- 40 cups all-purpose flour
- 3 cups sugar
- 1½ cups baking powder
- 1½ cups baking soda
- ¾ cup salt
- 28 large eggs
- 2 gallons milk
- 1 gallon buttermilk
- 64 ounces canola oil

1. In several large bowls, combine flour, sugar, baking powder, baking soda and salt. Combine eggs, milk, buttermilk and oil; stir into the dry ingredients just until blended.

2. Pour batter by ⅓ cupfuls onto a greased hot griddle. Turn when bubbles form on top; cook until the second side is golden brown.

CHORIZO BEAN DIP

With zesty flavors and tempting toppings, this Mexican dip is always a hit. I serve it with extra-thick tortilla chips for some serious scooping!

—**ELAINE SWEET** DALLAS, TX

PREP: 25 MIN. • **BAKE:** 20 MIN.
MAKES: 48 SERVINGS

- 1 pound ground sirloin
- ⅓ pound uncooked chorizo or bulk spicy pork sausage
- 1 medium onion, chopped
- 1 envelope taco seasoning
- 2 cans (16 ounces each) refried black beans
- 1 cup shredded Monterey Jack cheese
- 1⅓ cups salsa
- 2 cans (2¼ ounces each) sliced ripe olives, drained
- 2 cups guacamole
- 6 green onions, thinly sliced
- 1 cup sour cream
- ½ cup minced fresh cilantro
- ¾ cup jalapeno-stuffed olives, sliced Tortilla chips

1. Crumble beef and chorizo into a large skillet; add onion and taco seasoning. Cook over medium heat until the meat is no longer pink; drain.

2. Spread the beans into a greased 13x9-in. baking dish. Layer with the meat mixture, cheese, salsa and ripe olives. Cover and bake at 350° for 20-25 minutes or until heated through.

3. Spread guacamole over the top. Combine the green onions, sour cream and cilantro; spread over the guacamole. Sprinkle with stuffed olives. Serve immediately with tortilla chips. Refrigerate leftovers.

TEST KITCHEN TIP
Chorizo is a coarsely ground pork sausage that has Mexican, Spanish and Portuguese origins. Chorizo comes in three forms—fresh, uncooked ground sausage (which may be sold in a casing); a smoked link that resembles a kielbasa; and a cured, air-dried link. Make sure you know what kind your recipe calls for!

MAKE AHEAD
REFRIGERATOR GARDEN PICKLES

Canning isn't necessary for these crisp-tender, tangy pickles—they'll keep in the fridge for up to a month.

—**LINDA CHAIPMAN** MERIDEN, IA

PREP: 20 MIN. • **COOK:** 15 MIN. + CHILLING
MAKES: 7 PINTS

- 6 cups sugar
- 6 cups white vinegar
- ¼ cup celery seed
- ¼ cup mustard seed
- 2 tablespoons canning salt
- 10 medium carrots, halved lengthwise and cut into 2-inch pieces
- 3 medium cucumbers, sliced
- 3 medium sweet red peppers, cut into 1-inch pieces
- 2 large onions, halved and sliced
- 1 bunch green onions, cut into 2-inch pieces

1. In a Dutch oven, combine the first five ingredients; bring to a boil, stirring to dissolve sugar. Meanwhile, place the remaining ingredients in a large bowl.

2. Pour the hot liquid over the vegetables; cool. Transfer to jars; cover tightly. Refrigerate for 6-8 hours before serving. Store in the refrigerator for up to 1 month.

BARBECUE GLAZED MEATBALLS

Stock your freezer with these meatballs and you'll always have a tasty snack available for unexpected guests. We like to eat them as a main dish with rice or noodles on busy weeknights.

—**ANNA FINLEY** COLUMBIA, MO

PREP: 30 MIN. • **BAKE:** 15 MIN./BATCH
MAKES: 8 DOZEN

- 2 cups quick-cooking oats
- 1 can (12 ounces) fat-free evaporated milk
- 1 small onion, finely chopped
- 2 teaspoons garlic powder
- 2 teaspoons chili powder
- 3 pounds lean ground beef (90% lean)

SAUCE
- 2½ cups ketchup
- 1 small onion, finely chopped
- ⅓ cup packed brown sugar
- 2 teaspoons liquid smoke, optional
- 1¼ teaspoons chili powder
- ¾ teaspoon garlic powder

1. Preheat oven to 400°. In a large bowl, combine the first five ingredients. Add beef; mix lightly but thoroughly. Shape into 1-in. balls.

2. Place meatballs on greased racks in shallow baking pans. Bake 15-20 minutes or until cooked through. Drain on paper towels.

3. In a Dutch oven, combine the sauce ingredients. Bring to a boil over medium heat, stirring constantly. Reduce heat; simmer, uncovered, 2-3 minutes or until slightly thickened. Add the meatballs; heat through, stirring gently.

FREEZE OPTION *Freeze cooled meatballs (in sauce) in freezer containers. To use, partially thaw in refrigerator overnight. Microwave, covered, on high in a microwave-safe dish until heated through, gently stirring and adding a little water if necessary.*

HONEY WHOLE WHEAT PAN ROLLS

With their pleasant wheat flavor and a honey of a glaze, these rolls impress my guests. When I take them to potlucks, I come home with an empty pan.

—**NANCYE THOMPSON** PADUCAH, KY

PREP: 35 MIN. + CHILLING • **BAKE:** 20 MIN.
MAKES: 5 DOZEN (1¼ CUPS HONEY BUTTER)

- 4 to 5 cups bread flour, divided
- ¼ cup sugar
- 2 packages (¼ ounce each) active dry yeast
- 1 teaspoon salt
- 1 cup 2% milk
- 1 cup butter, cubed
- ½ cup water
- 2 large eggs
- 2 cups whole wheat flour

HONEY BUTTER
- 1 cup butter, softened
- 7 tablespoons honey

HONEY GLAZE
- 2 tablespoons honey
- 1 tablespoon butter, melted

1. In a large bowl, combine 2 cups bread flour, sugar, yeast and salt. In a small saucepan, heat milk, butter and water to 120°-130°. Add to the dry ingredients; beat just until moistened. Beat in eggs. Stir in the whole wheat flour and enough of the remaining bread flour to form a soft dough.

2. Turn dough onto a floured surface; knead until smooth and elastic, about 10 minutes. Cover and let rest 15 minutes.

3. Divide the dough into thirds. Roll each portion into a 20-in. rope. Cut each into 20 pieces; shape each into a ball. Grease three 9-in. round baking pans; arrange 20 balls in each pan. Cover and refrigerate overnight.

4. Let rise in a warm place until doubled, about 1¼ hours. Bake at 350° for 18-22 minutes or until golden brown. In a small bowl, cream butter. Add honey; beat until light and fluffy. Remove rolls from pans to wire racks. Combine glaze ingredients; brush over warm rolls. Serve with honey butter.

HONEY WHOLE WHEAT PAN ROLLS

HEARTY RICE DRESSING

This satisfying dressing has always been received well at church socials and family reunions. I cut back on the recipe if I'm serving a smaller group.

—**RUTH HAYWARD** LAKE CHARLES, LA

PREP: 25 MIN. • **BAKE:** 1 HOUR
MAKES: 3 CASSEROLES (50 SERVINGS)

- 3 pounds ground beef
- 2 pounds ground pork
- 2 large onions, chopped
- 3 celery ribs, chopped
- 1 large green pepper, chopped
- 1 jar (4 ounces) diced pimientos, drained
- 5 cups water
- 2 cans (10¾ ounces each) condensed cream of chicken soup, undiluted
- 2 cans (10½ ounces each) condensed French onion soup
- 1 can (10¾ ounces) condensed cream of mushroom soup, undiluted
- 2 tablespoons Creole seasoning
- 1 teaspoon salt
- 1 teaspoon pepper
- ½ teaspoon cayenne pepper
- 4 cups uncooked long grain rice

1. Combine beef, pork and onions. Divide the mixture evenly among several large Dutch ovens or stockpots; cook, crumbling the meat, over medium heat until no longer pink. Drain.

2. In a large bowl, combine celery, green pepper and pimientos. Add water, soups and seasonings. Stir into the Dutch ovens or stockpots, dividing the vegetable-soup mixture evenly among them. Bring to a boil; stir in rice.

3. Carefully transfer mixture to three greased 13x9-in. baking dishes. Cover and bake at 350° for 30 minutes; stir. Cover and bake 30-40 minutes longer or until the rice is tender.

NOTE *The following spice mix may be substituted for 2 tablespoons Creole seasoning: 1½ teaspoon each salt, garlic powder and paprika; and ½ teaspoon each of dried thyme, ground cumin and cayenne pepper.*

MAKE AHEAD

FROZEN FRUIT CUPS

Add some sparkle to your next gathering with these sunny citrus treats. The petite cups burst with color and fresh flavor, and they look so cute served in shiny foil containers.

—**SUE ROSS** CASA GRANDE, AZ

PREP: 30 MIN. + FREEZING
MAKES: 9½ DOZEN

- 5 packages (3 ounces each) lemon gelatin
- 10 cups boiling water
- 5 cans (20 ounces each) unsweetened pineapple tidbits, undrained
- 5 cans (11 ounces each) mandarin oranges, drained
- 5 cans (6 ounces each) frozen orange juice concentrate, partially thawed
- 5 large firm bananas, sliced

1. In a very large bowl, dissolve gelatin in boiling water; cool for 10 minutes. Stir in the remaining ingredients.

2. Spoon into foil cups. Freeze until firm. Remove from the freezer 30 minutes before serving.

FUDGE-TOPPED BROWNIES

FUDGE-TOPPED BROWNIES

Why have only brownies or fudge when you can combine them? These exquisite brownies are the ultimate chocolate dessert.

—**JUDY OLSON** WHITECOURT, AB

PREP: 25 MIN. • **BAKE:** 25 MIN. + FREEZING
MAKES: ABOUT 10 DOZEN

- 1 cup butter
- 4 ounces unsweetened chocolate, chopped
- 2 cups sugar
- 2 teaspoons vanilla extract
- 4 large eggs
- 1½ cups all-purpose flour
- 1 teaspoon baking powder
- ½ teaspoon salt
- 1 cup chopped walnuts

TOPPING

- 4½ cups sugar
- 1 can (12 ounces) evaporated milk
- ½ cup butter, cubed
- 1 package (12 ounces) semisweet chocolate chips
- 1 package (11½ ounces) milk chocolate chips
- 1 jar (7 ounces) marshmallow creme
- 2 teaspoons vanilla extract
- 2 cups chopped walnuts

1. In a heavy saucepan or microwave, melt butter and chocolate; stir until smooth. Remove from the heat; blend in sugar and vanilla. Add eggs; mix well. Combine the flour, baking powder and salt; add to the chocolate mixture. Stir in walnuts. Pour into a greased 13x9-in. baking pan. Bake at 350° for 25-30 minutes or until the top springs back when lightly touched. Cool on a wire rack.

2. To make the topping, combine sugar, milk and butter in a large, heavy saucepan; bring to a boil over medium heat. Reduce the heat; simmer, uncovered, for 5 minutes, stirring constantly. Remove from the heat. Stir in chocolate chips, marshmallow creme and vanilla until smooth. Add walnuts. Spread over the warm (not hot) brownies. Freeze for 3 hours or until firm. Cut into 1-in. squares. Store in the refrigerator.

GENERAL RECIPE INDEX

Find every recipe by food category and major ingredient.

ALPHABETICAL RECIPE INDEX